Judith Butler's Precarious

This volume provides the first forum where political theorists engage in a series of critical encounters with Judith Butler's wide-ranging body of work. It brings together essays by 13 distinguished contributors, who address Butler's writing on topics ranging from feminism and phenomenology, to capitalism and culture, to law, rights and the livable life. Butler's work from the start has been profoundly philosophical, and therefore in principle multidisciplinary. Rather than claim her as a political theorist, this book instead exhibits the diversity of responses that political theorists have had to her work. The theorists in this collection are not merely surveying or synthesising Butler's writings. Instead, they use Butler's thought, putting it to work in diverse ways. These include philosophical issues of great abstraction; cross-cultural and interdisciplinary issues in comparative social thought; macro-issues in public policy and international politics; and contemporary politics as reflected and pursued in TV and cinematic drama. While not underrating Butler's achievements in reorienting the study of sex, gender and sexuality, this book situates that work, as Butler does, in relation to further issues, further controversies, further interventions in 'precarious politics'.

This book, along with its companion volume *Judith Butler and Political Theory: Troubling Politics* (by Samuel A. Chambers and Terrell Carver), makes a primary and fundamental contribution to political theory, just as it should have widespread implications for numerous fields: from women's studies, gender studies, and lesbian and gay studies, to queer theory, feminist theory and cultural studies.

Terrell Carver is Professor of Political Theory at the University of Bristol, UK. He has published extensively on issues relevant to sex, gender and sexuality in political theory and international relations.

Samuel A. Chambers is Senior Lecturer in Politics at Swansea University, where he teaches political theory and cultural politics. He writes broadly in contemporary thought, including work on language, culture, and the politics of gender and sexuality.

Judith Butler's Precarious Politics

Critical encounters

Edited by Terrell Carver and Samuel A. Chambers

LONDON AND NEW YORK

305.4201 JUD 12/08

First published 2008
by Routledge
2 Park Square, Milton Park, Abingdon, Oxon OX14 4RN

Simultaneously published in the USA and Canada
by Routledge
270 Madison Avenue, New York, NY 10016

Routledge is an imprint of the Taylor & Francis Group, an informa business

Typeset in Times New Roman by
Taylor & Francis Books
Printed and bound in Great Britain by
TJ International Ltd, Padstow, Cornwall

British Library Cataloguing in Publication Data
A catalogue record for this book is available from the British Library

Library of Congress Cataloging in Publication Data
Judith Butler's precarious politics : critical encounters / edited by Terrell
Carver and Samuel A. Chambers.
    1. Butler, Judith, 1956—Philosophy. 2. Feminist theory. 3.
Phenomenology. 4. Social ethics. I. Carver, Terrell. II. Chambers, Samuel
Allen, 1972-
    HQ1190.J83 2008
    305.4201–dc22
                            2007022684

ISBN13: 978-0-415-38442-1 (hbk)
ISBN13: 978-0-415-38443-8 (pbk)
ISBN13: 978-0-203-93745-7 (ebk)

Contents

Acknowledgements

We would like to thank Craig Fowlie at Routledge for his continued support and for helping to bring this volume into existence. Most of all we extend our heartfelt gratitude to all the contributors to the volume whose fine work has formed the book you have before you.

A number of the chapters in this volume were published previously and in different form, and we thank the authors and publishers for permission to use copyright material.

Ferguson, Kathy. 'This Species Which Is Not One: Identity Practices in *Star Trek: Deep Space Nine*'. *Strategies* 15.2 (2002): 181–95.

Kaufman-Osborn, Timothy. 'Gender Trouble at Abu Ghraib?' *Politics & Gender* 1.4 (2005): 597–619. Reprinted with Permission.

Seery, John E. 'Acclaim for *Antigone's Claim* Reclaimed (or, Steiner contra Butler)'. *Theory & Event* 9.1 (2006) © The Johns Hopkins University Press. Reprinted with permission of The Johns Hopkins University Press.

Smith, Anna Marie. 'Missing Poststructuralism, Missing Foucault: Butler and Fraser on Capitalism and the Regulation of Sexuality'. *Social Text 67* 19.2 (2001) © 2001 Duke University Press.

Zerilli, Linda M.G. Chapter 1 of *Feminism and the Abyss of Freedom*. Chicago: University of Chicago Press, 2006: 32–65. © Linda M.G. Zerilli.

Terrell Carver and
Samuel A. Chambers

Contributors

Terrell Carver is Professor of Political Theory at the University of Bristol. He has published extensively on sex, gender, and sexuality, including *Gender is Not A Synonym for Women* (Lynne Rienner, 1996), *Politics of Sexuality* (ed. with Veronique Mottier, Routledge, 1998, repr. 2006), and *Men in Political Theory* (Manchester University Press and St. Martin's Press, 2004). With Samuel A. Chambers he is co-author of a companion volume to this one, *Troubling Politics: The Political Theory of Judith Butler* (Routledge, 2008).

Samuel A. Chambers is Senior Lecturer in Politics at Swansea University, where he teaches political theory and cultural politics. He is the author of *Untimely Politics* (Edinburgh University Press, 2003) and *The Queer Politics of Television* (IB Tauris, 2008). With Terrell Carver he is co-editor of *William E. Connolly, Democracy, Pluralism and Political Theory* (Routledge, 2008), as well as co-author of a companion volume, *Troubling Politics: The Political Theory of Judith Butler* (Routledge, 2008).

Diana Coole is Professor of Political and Social Theory at Birkbeck College, University of London. She has written extensively on existential phenomenology and critical theory. Her publications include *Negativity and Politics: Dionysus and Dialectics from Kant to Poststructuralism* (Routledge, 2000) and *Merleau-Ponty and Modern Politics after Anti-Humanism* (Rowman & Littlefield, 2007). She is currently co-editing a volume on the New Materialism with Samantha Frost, for Duke University Press.

Jodi Dean teaches political theory at Hobart and William Smith Colleges in Geneva, New York. She has authored or edited eight books, including *Publicity's Secret* (Cornell University Press, 2002), *Žižek's Politics* (Routledge, 2006), and (co-edited with Paul A. Passavant) *Empire's New Clothes: Reading Hardt and Negri* (Routledge, 2004).

Lisa Jane Disch teaches contemporary political theory at the University of Minnesota – Twin Cities. She has published two books, *The Tyranny of* *the Two-Party System* (Columbia University Press, 2002) and *Hannah Arendt and the Limits of Philosophy* (Cornell University Press, 1996), along with numerous articles on feminist and democratic political theory.

Kathy E. Ferguson is Professor of Political Science and Women's Studies at the University of Hawai'i. Her books include *Gender and Globalization in Asia and the Pacific* (co-edited with Monique Mironesco, forthcoming from University of Hawai'i Press) and *Oh, Say, Can You See? The Semiotics of the Military in Hawai'i* (with Phyllis Turnbull, University of Minnesota Press, 1999). She is writing a book on Emma Goldman, continuing work with Phyllis Turnbull on the military in Hawai'i, and researching home schooling.

David S. Gutterman is Assistant Professor of Politics at Willamette University where he teaches courses on political theory, religion and politics in the United States, and political dissent. He has published work on the conversion of George W. Bush, narrative theory, religious social movements in the United States, and gender and politics. He is the author of *Prophetic Politics: Christian Social Movements and American Democracy* (Cornell University Press, 2005).

Timothy Kaufman-Osborn received his Ph.D. from Princeton University in 1982, and is currently the Baker Ferguson Professor of Politics and Leadership at Whitman College. His publications include *From Noose to Needle* (University of Michigan Press, 2002), *Creatures of Prometheus* (Rowman & Littlefield, 1997), and *Politics/Sense/Experience* (Cornell University Press, 1991). He has also published numerous scholarly articles on topics ranging from American pragmatism to feminist theory. From 2001 to 2003 he served as president of the Western Political Science Association, and he is currently a member of the executive council of the American Political Science Association.

Moya Lloyd is Senior Lecturer in Politics at Loughborough University. She has written widely on feminist theory, and, in particular, the work of Judith Butler. Her most recent books include *Beyond Identity Politics* (Sage, 2005) and *Judith Butler: from norms to politics* (Polity Press, 2007).

Elena Loizidou is a Senior Lecturer at the School of Law at Birkbeck College, University of London. She is the author of *Judith Butler: Ethics, Law, Politics* (Routledge-Cavendish, 2007). Her research focuses on gender, sexuality, and legal and political theory. Her current research project is focusing on anarchist practices/theory past and present.

Sara L. Rushing is Assistant Professor of Political Science at Montana State University. She is the editor, with Mark Bevir and Jill Hargis, of *Histories of*

Postmodernism (Routledge, 2007). She is currently at work on an article about Judith Butler's ethics and utopianism.

John E. Seery is Professor of Politics at Pomona College, where he teaches political theory. Currently he is editing an anthology on Walt Whitman for the University Press of Kentucky.

Anna Marie Smith is Professor of Government, Cornell University. Her research interests include theoretical approaches to the regulation of sexuality; feminist legal theory; critical race theory; and social theories of identity and power relations. She is the author of *Welfare Reform and Sexual Regulation* (Cambridge University Press, 2007), *Laclau and Mouffe: The Radical Democratic Imaginary* (Routledge, 1998), and *New Right Discourse on Race and Sexuality: Britain, 1968–1990* (Cambridge University Press, 1994). She has published articles in the *Michigan Journal of Gender and Law, Citizenship Studies, Constellations, Social Text, Radical Philosophy, Diacritics, Feminist Review*, and *New Formations*, as well as in numerous anthologies.

Robert E. Watkins is Assistant Professor of Political Science in the Liberal Education Department at Columbia College Chicago, where he teaches political theory, international relations, and cultural studies. He is working on a book about the constitutive role of culture, norms, and power that draws on the political theory of Hume and Burke.

Linda M.G. Zerilli is Professor of Political Science at Northwestern University. She has published widely in the area of feminist theory, democratic theory, and continental philosophy. Her books include *Signifying Woman: Culture and Chaos in Rousseau, Burke, and Mill* (Cornell University Press, 1994) and *Feminism and the Abyss of Freedom* (Chicago University Press, 2005). She is currently working on a new book, *Toward a Democratic Theory of Judgment*.

Karen Zivi is an Assistant Professor in the Jepson School of Leadership Studies at the University of Richmond. A political theorist with interests in democratic theory, feminist thought and politics, and rights, her research has appeared in a variety of journals including *American Journal of Political Science, Politics & Gender, Feminist Studies, Polity*, and *Law and Society Review*. She is currently working on a manuscript entitled *Making Rights Claims* exploring the relationship between the politics of rights and the practice of democracy.

1 Introduction

Terrell Carver and Samuel A. Chambers

This volume represents the first collective critical encounter between scholars of political theory and the works of Judith Butler. The terrain on which this encounter takes place is in part traditional to political theory (e.g. sovereignty, rights, capitalism, culture), and in part germane to the philosophical enquiries with which political theory necessarily engages (e.g. epistemology, feminism, ethics, phenomenology). The work of Butler herself also sets the terms for this encounter and includes concepts such as vulnerability, grieving, performativity, 'trouble', and the liveable life. The terms of political theory have thus been markedly supplemented by Butler's writings over the past twenty years – testimony not only to the power of Butler's intellect but also to the intensity with which her works engaged with the realm of the political.

Butler's most notable impact in the intellectual world continues to be her now famous reversal of the sex–gender conceptual relationship, and the implications of this deconstructive but decisive analysis for the theory and politics of feminism. However, in constructing this volume we refused to restrict its focus to that aspect alone of Butler's thought; we resisted the tendency in political theory to fix on a small selection of her early texts. Instead we take a much broader and more inclusive view: this volume draws on a wide range of Butler's work, tracking her thought from her pre-*Gender Trouble* writings in the 1980s to as close to our date of publication as possible. Above all, we have encouraged the contributors to *use* Butler's thought in a very broad array of contexts, thereby mirroring Butler's own eclectic engagements. While not underrating Butler's achievements in reorienting the philosophical, sociological, and political study of sex, gender, and sexuality, this volume situates that work, as Butler does, in relation to further topics, further issues, further controversies, further interventions in 'precarious politics'.

In this spirit, the contributors to this volume have been given extensive freedom with respect to choosing the issues and questions to which they find Butler's works variously relevant, and absolute freedom in their critical assessments. This volume is not a guide to Butler's work; it offers no chronological or thematic overviews of Butler's oeuvre. Nor is it, in any sense, a *Festschrift*. Rather, we based the selection of contributors on enquiries across the field of political theory in an effort to elicit engagements with Butler's writings across an extremely broad spectrum of issues and approaches – in order to explore the full range of critical views. We find the centrality of such critical engagements to be a defining strength of political theory as a discipline, and in assembling the volume we were guided by this ideal of staging and enacting a set of critical encounters with Butler's work.

The further benefit of this approach reveals itself in the variety of materials through which these scholarly encounters are pursued. The contributors put Butler's thought to work so as to explore philosophical issues of great weight and abstraction. Collectively, they contribute to the burgeoning project of working out Butler's political theory. And they consistently work on cross-cultural and interdisciplinary issues in comparative social thought: this includes the exploration of macro-issues in public policy and international politics and the elucidation of contemporary politics as reflected and pursued in TV and cinematic drama.

From the start, Butler's work has been profoundly philosophical, and therefore in principle multi-disciplinary; Butler herself emphasises this point. This volume therefore does not presume to *claim* her as in some proprietary sense exclusively a political theorist. For us, such categorical contentions are not helpful moves to make. Rather this collection exhibits the diversity of responses that political theorists have had to Butler, the array of issues and ideas to which her works have been made relevant, and most of all, the impact that her more recent books and articles have had over and above the famous inaugurating controversies about 'performativity', 'the body', and 'agency'.

This collection is thus not *about Butler* but rather about how political theorists *use* her work to *do things* with her concepts, her claims, her theories. Both in their writing and in their interpretation, the major texts of political theory can all be helpfully described as 'interventions' – interventions into both politics and broader fields of knowledge as they are constituted at a particular spatio-temporal nexus. Rather than merely describing Butler's interventions, these chapters make their own by calling on the diverse resources of Butler's work.

Given Butler's own grounding in philosophy, and her repeated returns to it, we open the volume on this native philosophical terrain. In 'Butler's Phenomenological Existentialism' Diana Coole situates Butler's work in relation to an ostensible break between the phenomenological/existentialist and post-structuralist/constructivist schools of thought. Coole suggests that Butler herself wrongly situates her own thought, particularly in *Gender Trouble* (1990, 2nd edn 1999), in an uncompromisingly anti-humanist setting. Further, Coole seeks to demonstrate that much of Butler's more recent work is self-evidently indebted to these disavowed approaches. This matters, Coole argues, because Butler's later thought, and indeed her political interventions, thus risk eclecticism and incoherence in relation to the experiential issues of corporeality, materiality, agency, intersubjectivity, politics, and society. Coole's critical *tour de force* resituates Butler's *Gender Trouble* by linking her earliest philosophical works with her much more recent, and more overtly political ones.

In 'Feminists Know Not What They Do', Linda M.G. Zerilli distances Butler (along with Foucault and Derrida) from the epistemological tradition in Western philosophy. Zerilli describes this tradition as having a 'craving for generality'; it presumes that knowledge must be universal if it is to survive an encounter with philosophical scepticism. Zerilli relates this to the 'trouble' that Butler caused within feminism, when Butler appeared either to invoke supposedly sceptical challenges to the category of 'woman' or to concede to them. Relating Butler's account of 'gender' as a practice to Wittgenstein's notion of following a rule – and his concomitant attack on the doubt that drives philosophical scepticism – Zerilli calls for a profound rethinking of feminist critique and hence of feminist politics. Drawing on Castoriadis's account of radical imagination, Zerilli advocates a freedom-centred feminism that challenges feminists to leave behind the false security of epistemology, and venture out into the world of action – where the very insecurities of contingency can be much more productively confronted.

Butler's impact on feminist philosophy and philosophising has of course been profound and dramatic, and above all, controversial. Lisa Jane Disch explores one relatively neglected aspect of this controversy in '"French Theory" goes to France'. Disch shows that 'French Theory' proves to be a rather bizarre construction, within an even stranger history: first it was a term applied by the North American academy to a select-yet-disparate group of French feminists, and now, with the recent translation of *Gender Trouble* into French, it becomes a term that French thinkers themselves use (in English) to designate what they deem a peculiarly American phenomenon. Disch offers a helpful and productive genealogy of French 'materialist' feminism, showing that French materialists were making a powerful set of critiques of standpoint feminism long before Butler and the influx of post-structuralist thinking came to the fore in the US and the UK. Disch opens with the question whether Butler's work really adds anything significant to that of the French materialist Wittig and concludes with an affirmative answer, delineating precisely how Butler produces a thoroughgoing critique of the naturalised conceptions of agency – the very conceptions through which democratic politics currently takes place.

John Seery takes issue with Butler's reading of Hegel in her published Wellek Library Lectures *Antigone's Claim* (2000). In 'Acclaim for *Antigone's Claim* Reclaimed' Seery recounts his initial advocacy of Butler's reading of Sophocles' play, in which she links incest with heteronormativity and thus adumbrates a manifesto for queer politics. Using Steiner's work *Antigones* (1984), Seery argues that Butler misreads Hegel and others on the question and import of incest both in the play and in past and present politics. In particular Butler links the character Antigone – an incest-born person with possible incestuous desires – with the issue of liveable and grieveable lives as they arise within current structures of intelligibility, in particular that of kinship. For Seery, Butler's queer politics is founded on a binary that recalls structuralist philosophy and analysis rather than the post-structuralism with which she is usually identified, and with which she herself has been in dialogue. Seery doubts whether 'statically oppositional' and 'schematic' language can offer a promising vehicle for the progressive politics that Butler advocates. And he questions the salience of a politics that derives from the 'exclusion and horror' of tragedy.

The nature of this progressive politics in its relation to the putative culture–economy dichotomy occupies the attention of two contributors who draw together Butler's early work with her more recent 'post-9/11' interventions in contemporary political controversy. In 'Missing Poststructuralism, Missing Foucault' Anna Marie Smith takes Butler's exchange with Nancy Fraser as indicative of current struggles over the central concepts of political theory. Agreeing with Butler's challenge to a logic that draws a strict boundary between the economic and the 'merely' cultural, Smith traces out the weaknesses of Fraser's position on the politics of sexuality. She notes, however, that Butler's reading sometimes proves totalistic in character and thus vulnerable to the critiques levelled at structuralist thought. Smith finds Butler's presumption that 'the cultural' is the condition of existence for 'the economic' suspect in empirical terms as well, especially in relation to institutional analysis. For Smith, Butler's social theory, perhaps surprisingly, turns out to be insufficiently post-structuralist, and thus not as well suited to contemporary queer politics as it might be. The claim resonates in particular given the possibilities – i.e. potential for close historical analysis of the ways that bio-power emerges through the regulation of sexualities – inherent in her theory of subjectivation.

In her chapter 'Towards a Cultural Politics of Vulnerability' Moya Lloyd explores Butler's recent writings and traces her continuing interest in grief and mourning vis-à-vis the development of a global political ethics. Lloyd finds Butler's account of the human subject deeply rooted in the puzzle of the subject's subjection, but Lloyd shows that Butler herself seeks to make sense of this dilemma in a rather puzzling way. That is, Butler resolves the problem of a subject that seeks its own subjection by resorting to an unexamined ontological claim about desire. Thus, Butler makes an implicit appeal to a pre-discursive, a move for which she has consistently criticised others. Is her ethics then pre-political at the outset, even though it becomes political within contexts of power? To answer this question Butler would need to work with a more historicised conception of the social, such that the emergence of discourses of desire can be understood politically, rather than merely posited philosophically. Like Smith, Lloyd finds that Butler's work needs more Foucauldian flesh on Derridean bones.

The next pair of contributions sharpens the focus on Butler's 'ethical turn' in the post-'9/11' works that themselves look back to *Excitable Speech*

(1997). In 'Change of Address' Jodi Dean argues that Butler's ethics presents openness and critique as preferable to condemnation and conviction, but does so at the expense of politics. According to Dean, Butler's argument that current practices of governmentality are founded on the fantasy of a sovereign speaker is simply misplaced; Butler misses the extent to which American law is itself a contested site, with multiple, de-centred points of access and judgement. Dean also resists Butler's argument that current American policies towards potential terrorists rest upon a prior exclusion of those individuals from the realm of the human. Condemnation, Dean advises, is not necessarily a statement of closure from a sovereign speaker, as Butler seems to suggest; rather it involves citationality and may help connect those who are focusing on political action. Butler's ethics demands a politics that is not itself haunted by fantasies of sovereignty.

David. S. Gutterman and Sara L. Rushing continue this exploration of Butler's current work in 'Sovereignty and Suffering', but from a very different perspective. Taking as their context the cycle of violence in American domestic as well as foreign policies in recent history, Gutterman and Rushing align Butler with Socrates. That is, they paint a picture of Butler as a moral philosopher who shares his concerns and engagements. Both suggest that our ethical grounds for judgement and action in politics should come from an acknowledgement of shared human fragility. The two diverge on the issue of self-knowledge: Socrates proposes a *quest* for self-knowledge and self-mastery, while Butler grounds her ethics in the *unknowability* of the self. Similarly, rather than appealing to a presumed commonality of rationality, discipline, and self-restraint, Butler's account of ethical obligations takes failures of recognition and limits to knowability as its conditions of possibility. A responsible politics thus cannot presume an ethics that requires a full account of oneself – a self transparent to the other. Butler appeals to humility, generosity, and restraint, arising out of grief, figured as an ethical and political resource.

Grieving, of course, is mourning for a life. In 'Butler and Life' Elena Loizidou addresses Butler's concern with creating better conditions for 'livable lives'. This entails an agonistic relationship between the various spheres of life, and therefore it also centrally concerns the law. In the current political situation Butler argues that the law becomes an instrument of power to be deployed by the state. Law is no longer that which creates the state, nor that which constrains it; rather, it is one more tool for the state to use. Nonetheless, the law could have a meaningful and important role in negotiating what it is to be human, and therefore to have a liveable and grieveable life. Disciplinary power, exercised through the development of norms, can be resisted and re-interpreted; when norms and the law are collapsed together, as the current George W. Bush administration in the US attempts to do, then trials and legal interventions are an important site for securing precarious lives. Butler's politics is thus rooted in agonism, rather than in any position or predilection that is 'for or against' the law.

In 'Rights and the Politics of Performativity' Karen Zivi continues the theme of explicating and analysing Butler's philosophically reasoned interventions into current political controversies. The theory of performativity earned Butler very heavy public criticism; this arose from charges that her thinking undermined political action, in particular action aimed at liberatory political change. Arguing to the contrary, Zivi explains how Butler's work on rights constitutes a progressive intervention in democratic politics. Moreover, Zivi shows that the practice of rights-claiming, far from proving impossible under Butler's conceptualisation, actually *illustrates* Butler's theory of performativity in an empowering way. While Butler argues that rights-claiming (specifically with regard to hate-speech) is problematic in licensing government regulation, and while her 'politics of the performative' has come to be associated with drag, parody, and similarly non-standard political tactics, Zivi argues that Butler's politics presupposes a performative subject that has real agency – just what Butler's critics have denied. The performative subject uses the 'excess' inherent in language to remake subjectivity and displace or denaturalise current configurations of power. Understood in this way, rights-claiming is a remaking of reality and expansion of the liveable, albeit without guarantees.

The final three chapters return to the fundamental terms that have always animated Butler's work and continue to do so: humanity and vulnerability. Using Butler's concepts of citationality and performativity, the contributors to this section look to photographs, movies, and television as artefacts through which meaning is instantiated and communicated. The contributors in this section offer readings of these artefacts designed to develop our understanding of 'the political' – to think politics as a way of dealing with human vulnerability. In 'This Species Which Is Not One', Kathy E. Ferguson presents Butler's enquiry into the relation between the presumptions of normative gender and sexuality and the delimitation of lives into those that qualify as 'human' and 'liveable' and those that do not. Ferguson explores these crucial issues through the text of the television series *Star Trek: Deep Space Nine*. Science fiction proves particularly appropriate to such a project because it presents imagined perspectives on 'the possible' that challenge the familiar and the supposedly unquestionable. Ferguson guides us through the heterotopic world in the drama, where an array of metaphors and analogies reconfigure the supposed securities of human psychic and physical identity as part of a reproductive cycle involving symbiosis and 'joining'. Normative sexuality is relocated from heterosexuality to timeline barriers involving separating past from present and future partners. These imaginative reconfigurations encourage contemporary readers to think more carefully, as Butler advises, about the normative violence and exclusion through which concepts of the 'human' and the 'livable life' are both constructed and enforced.

Butler has framed her responses to the events of 9/11 in terms of the precariousness of life. In this context she argues that violent vengeance both denies our vulnerability and further threatens our security. In 'Vulnerability, Vengeance, and Community' Robert E. Watkins explores Butler's arguments through a reading of *Mystic River* (dir. Eastwood, 2000). Butler's own arguments are augmented through Watkins's projection of them into a cinematic dramatisation of vulnerability and vengeance. Watkins tracks the turn towards vulnerability and community in Butler's recent work, showing how it preserves her interest in power, on the one hand, and the authoring of subjects by what precedes and exceeds them, on the other. Butler's work remains committed to the idea of bodily interdependence within society and the vulnerability of the individual as an embodied being. *Mystic River* dramatises the two main responses Butler identifies when loss or injury impinges upon us: revenge as denial, and grief as recognition. As with Butler's philosophy, Eastwood's movie is a critique of vengeance. The timeliness of Butler's message is unmistakable.

The final contributor to the volume is Timothy Kaufman-Osborn, whose 'Gender Trouble at Abu Ghraib?' returns us to Butler's originary concerns with sex, gender, and sexuality. It does so, moreover, within the very dramatic context provided by the circulation of the famous photographs taken at Abu Ghraib which emerged in 2003. These photographs – taken by US military personnel at a prison complex in Baghdad – show the abuse and torture of Iraqi prisoners in overtly sexualised 'stagings'. Kaufman-Osborn takes up the controversy among feminists over the activities of Lynndie England as depicted in the photographs, and the ensuing discussions about women, femininity, and feminism. Aligning himself with Butler, Kaufman-Osborn advises that gender should be taken seriously as a signifier, unmoored from biological sex. He argues that feminist nostalgia for rooting femininity in bodily sex generates retrograde expectations about women. In his argument persons become en-gendered through complex performative practices, just as Butler suggests. Viewing Lynndie England and the Abu Ghraib photographs in this way avoids unproductive questions about what 'men' and 'women' are like; instead, it promotes clear-minded political engagement on the terrain of political power. In particular Kaufman-Osborn reads the images and the episode as indicative of a militarised and militarising masculinism, rooted in misogyny and homophobia. He concludes that gendered practices are deployed in multiple ways, to produce discipline and subjection through sexualised violence – whether in hazing rituals, interrogation or incarceration.

Although one can locate much wider, and perhaps much more excited audiences for her writings than the field of political theory, and despite the fact that Butler does not speak exclusively or even directly to political theorists, nonetheless – wittingly or not – Butler's work certainly qualifies as political theory. And we argue that her writings demand to be read as texts of political theory, to be debated by political theorists, to be interpreted as political interventions. As can be seen clearly from the chapters summarised above, Butler's themes and enquiries bear on many of the major issues that political theorists routinely engage with in their work. These range from serious philosophical discussions – drawing on a spectrum of authorities from the classics to the postmoderns – to the most *engagé* interventions into current affairs that put her into conversation with other public intellectuals and politicians. The contributors to this volume have invested significant time and energy in their encounters with Butler, and they evince considerable enthusiasm for this agonistic engagement. As political theory itself is a broad field of study, drawing eclectically on numerous disciplines and sub-disciplines in the social sciences and humanities, we hope that the critical appreciation of Butler's work registered in this volume will have a similarly broad appeal to readers, and that her work itself will continue to engage a worldwide audience.

Part I

Phenomenology and epistemology

2 Butler's phenomenological existentialism

Diana Coole

A simple narrative is often rehearsed regarding developments in radical political philosophy; one that seems especially apposite in relation to French thought and to the debates that have enlivened post-war feminism. Its main plot involves a displacement of the existentialist and phenomenological perspectives that had dominated Continental thinking from the 1940s to the 1960s, by anti-humanist approaches that began with structuralism before proliferating in various forms of poststructuralism (notably genealogy, radical constructivism and deconstruction). The freedom and experience emphasised by the former now became objects of profound suspicion: freedom was associated with an individual subject capable of reinventing itself at will, while its experience was perceived as an untrustworthy guide in light of the latter's over-determination and saturation by ideological or discursive forms of power. Social critics accordingly turned their attention to an analysis of these impersonal structures whose constitutive capacities replaced those of agents, now conceived merely as their effects.

This narrative is both persuasive and simplistic. It is persuasive in that it accurately conveys a rather Manichean stand-off; one that was replayed among Anglophone exponents of Continental philosophy during the closing decades of the twentieth century and which resulted briefly in something of a poststructuralist orthodoxy among them. But it is simplistic because it ignores persistent traces of the previous way of thinking, which was rarely as Cartesian or as uncritically humanist as its critics suggest. As Martin Jay writes in summarising Foucault's career, 'the break with phenomenology and its concern with experience was less complete than is often assumed' (Jay 2005: 365, 391). I will argue in the case of Judith Butler's work that this common assumption has nonetheless meant that these existential and phenomenological premises have until recently endured in a twilight world, where they are effaced yet also relied upon to shore up lacunae in poststructuralism. I also suggest that from the vantage point of the early twenty-first century, the narrative has become something of an anachronism inasmuch as we are witnessing a return to these disavowed approaches. Thus Iris Young justified republication of her early phenomenological essays by contending that many of phenomenology's erstwhile critics are renewing their interest in this approach because it can 'speak from the point of view of the constituted subject's experience, in ways that complement ... the observational or interpretative methods of Foucault, Butler, or Bourdieu' (Young 2004: 8). Although it is neither feasible nor desirable simply to ignore anti-humanist concerns, it seems increasingly to be recognised that 'in taking the postmodern tale at face value, we have', as Sonia Kruks puts it, 'unwisely cut ourselves off from the rich heritage of existential thought' (Kruks 2001: 6).

Judith Butler has been a central figure in these developments, and her work seems to exemplify rather well the simple version of the story with which I began. Indeed she briefly recounts it herself (Butler 2004b: 195). While *Gender Trouble* surely remains her best-known and most influential work in feminist and queer theory, it is also an enthusiastic endorsement of the anti-humanist approaches associated with poststructuralism. It is, however, from the point of view of the more complicated account I used to criticise this narrative that I want to examine her work, and my intention here is to elicit the existential and phenomenological arguments that persist within it. My claim is that Butler's itinerary reveals all three of the narrative's phases, with the existential phenomenology that marked her early work again coming to prominence in recent essays. From this perspective *Gender Trouble* is something of an anomaly in her *oeuvre*, and one whose uncompromising poststructuralism has caused her considerable (and to some extent unnecessary) difficulties. In responding to them Butler has increasingly reverted to the earlier approach where she had not yet cut herself off from the 'rich heritage' of existentialism. But I will also show that phenomenological residues did endure even in *Gender Trouble*, albeit in a limbo of efficacy and denial and despite Butler's rather over-zealous attempts at excising them.

Does this reconstruction of existential and phenomenological themes matter? Surely it does, not least because Butler has not herself acknowledged this shift in her theoretical orientation or reflected upon its implications. She has not therefore explored sufficiently the ontological and epistemological premises of her more recent political interventions, nor explained how these are compatible with the radically constructivist claims she formerly used to reject and in whose name she still seems overtly to speak. Instead the two approaches are often simply elided or juxtaposed, although they are certainly not synonymous, nor, according to her own earlier arguments, compatible. As a consequence the later work looks at best eclectic and at worst theoretically incoherent. Although I am sympathetic to the trajectory of Butler's work I do not then believe that she can sustain the radical politics she espouses later, without questioning her avowed poststructuralist commitments and acknowledging the importance of phenomenological concepts for avoiding their shortcomings. From this perspective the earlier derivation of queer theory does not slide as imperceptibly into the New Gender Politics or into her normative concerns with the liveable life, as she might have us believe. This matters, moreover, because as long as Butler is perceived as a critic rather than an exponent of existential phenomenology, her influence on poststructuralist feminism and queer theory discourages her many followers from exploring these positions, by obscuring her own reliance upon them. Yet it is their premises that underpin much of the conceptual framework she uses in *Undoing Gender* in order to address problems concerning experience, corporeality, materiality and change as well as to redress weaknesses in her conceptions of agency, intersubjectivity, politics and society.

Returning to existence

The key themes and concepts I associate with phenomenology for the pur-poses of my argument here are as follows. First, a return to lived experience within a historical and intersubjective lifeworld; second, a non-dualist ontology that recognises the irreducible entwining of matter and meaning on every level; third, an emphasis on the contingent emergence or becoming of phenomena over time; fourth, the primacy here of the sensuous body whose corporeal engagement with the world manifests pre-linguistic although culturally mediated capacities for agency; fifth, the dialectical and bi-directional nature of the relationship between constitutive and con-stituted elements, where corporeal actors and anonymous structures are inseparable and mutually-generating processes within a complex field of forces. The 'existential' qualifier is used in this context to distinguish between the more idealist phenomenology of Husserl or Sartre and those non-Cartesian phenomenologies – the 'radical' forms Butler herself associ-ates with Beauvoir and Merleau-Ponty, and sometimes with Wittig and Bourdieu – that emphasise the generative dialectics of embodied existence as opposed to the constituting powers of consciousness. Finally, there is no illusion here that phenomenology can actually return to experience in any raw or immediate sense. The exploration of experience entails an ongoing interrogation of the discourses that have been superimposed on the life-world. In this sense existential phenomenology has a good deal in common as a critical theory with Foucauldian genealogy. What existential phenom-enology nevertheless provides is a way of paying attention to the lived details and motivations of everyday life that include its visceral, material and agentic, as well as its symbolic and structural, components. What I am contending, in short, is that such claims are compatible with, often invited by, and sometimes explicit in, Butler's earlier and later writing, while ves-tiges of them continue to operate even during her high poststructuralist phase in the early 1990s. There are also, however, unresolved tensions here.

Butler's early existentialism

In her work preceding *Gender Trouble* (1990) Butler broadly subscribed to the positions listed above. My aim in this section is to show how she derived many of her most distinctive arguments and concepts – notably performativity and even constructivism itself – from them, even though these would subsequently be presented as consequences of poststructuralist approaches (in particular of Derridean-inflected speech act theory and of Foucauldian genealogy). Butler's early interest in phenomenology is apparent in her first book, *Subjects of Desire*; a work she was manifestly reluctant to republish and effectively disowned (Butler 1999b [1987]). Although the phenomenological focus there is Hegelian rather than Husserlian, she interprets Hegel from a broadly existentialist perspective. Thus Olkowski comments on the way she 'ties Hegel's phenomenology to everyday common sense, or what she calls experience', where desire is 'found in ordinary experience' (Olkowski 1999: 40).

In a critical essay on Merleau-Ponty written shortly after, Butler went on to call for 'a feminist appropriation' of his phenomenological approach to this concrete experience. If 'the body expresses and dramatizes existential themes and these themes are gender-specific and fully historicized', she reasoned, 'then sexuality becomes a scene of cultural struggle, improvisation and innovation, a domain in which the intimate and the political converge, and a dramatic opportunity for expression, analysis and change' (Butler 1989d: 98 f.). Improvisation, expression and innovation are all existential terms, used to indicate the relative freedom of situated actors. Similar exhortations appear throughout Butler's essays during the 1980s, and it is to this terminology that *Undoing Gender* (2004b) will revert.

Just two years before *Gender Trouble* appeared, Butler published an article entitled 'Performative Acts and Gender Constitution. An Essay in Phenomenology and Feminist Theory' (1988). The polemic underlying this essay is not between phenomenology and poststructuralism but between the two (Cartesian and non-Cartesian) versions of phenomenology mentioned above. Here she maintains that already for Beauvoir and Merleau-Ponty, 'the existence of a choosing and constituting agent prior to language' had been replaced by a more dialectical 'doctrine of constitution that takes the social agent as an *object* rather than the subject of constitutive acts' (Butler 1988: 519). Indeed the previous year Butler had deemed even Sartre's work as at worst merely ambiguous here. For in his descriptions, she had explained, 'the body is lived and experienced as the context and medium for all human strivings'. Since 'all human beings strive after possibilities not yet realized, human beings are to that extent "beyond" themselves' in an '"ek-static" condition that is itself a corporeal experience' (Butler 1987b: 130). It is this 'ek-static' condition and its relationship both with embodiment and with the pursuit of possibilities associated with a limited freedom that Butler will invoke once more in *Undoing Gender* in order to explain how subjects remain beside or outside themselves, thus capable of agency without being full-blown agents (Butler 2004b: 20). Meanwhile, she commends Beauvoir for taking Sartre 'at his non-Cartesian best' and defines Beauvoir's claim that one becomes one's gender, as both 'radicalisation and concretization' of Sartre's ontology (Butler 1987b: 130). She credits her predecessor with developing Merleau-Ponty's more dialectical account of embodied acts that are both constrained and constituted by the structures their sedimented practices and habits sustain: structures that they also contest and improvise upon, thereby changing them. This dialectical field, with its agonistic reversals and mediated complexities, will also reappear in later essays in place of the more radically constructivist and unidirectional account of the 1990s.

It is in these early essays, too, that the conception of performativity emerges, along with the claim that sex is an effect of binary gender thinking rather than its origin. These are again presented as radical implications of Beauvoir's existentialism. 'If gender is a way of existing one's body', Butler deduces, and the body is 'a field of cultural possibilities both received and reinterpreted, then both sex and gender seem to be thoroughly cultural affairs' (Butler 1987b: 134; 1988: 524 f.). Because of this provenance, however, the existential body described in these early essays does not lack the material efficacy whose apparent disappearance has bothered Butler's critics since *Gender Trouble*. She provides a very satisfactory gloss of Merleau-Ponty's phenomenological account of an emergent corporeality where the phenomenal body remains a relatively open field of possibilities that are developed through its practical relationships with its world and with others.

It is this account, Butler acknowledges, that underpins Beauvoir's description of becoming, and it is from it that she derives an early definition of gender as an identity 'tenuously constituted in time' through 'a stylized repetition of acts' (Butler 1988: 519; 1990: 33). In the 'stylisation of the body' that this entails, she explains, one must understand 'the mundane way in which bodily gestures, movements, and enactments of various kinds constitute the illusion of an abiding gendered self' (Butler 1988: 519). Now, it is just this kind of contingent appearing of an emergent intercorporeal and intersubjective lifeworld that phenomenologists describe. Style means for them the becoming of relatively unified but open forms, whose parts cohere thanks to an internal but contingent affinity. It thereby indicates a non-Cartesian chiasm of meaning and matter. Style is indicative of a mode of being-in-the-world, where provisional singularities emerge to become recognisable and their corporeal way of (co-)existing is foremost in their recognition by others (Merleau-Ponty 1962: 53, 151, 186). It suggests expressiveness, openness, immanence and agentic improvisation within a structured field; the very senses of it that Butler will retrieve in *Undoing Gender* in order to describe experiences of being undone as well as possibilities for improvisation and change. It is why she could argue convincingly in 1988 (as she will in 2004) that gender is 'a basically innovative affair' despite punishments for 'unwarrranted improvisations' (Butler 1988: 531).

Butler would in fact continue to define gender by reference to style in *Gender Trouble*: as 'the repeated stylisation of the body'. She acknowledges there that gender is what Sartre 'would have' perhaps called a 'style of being', Beauvoir 'styles of the flesh' or Foucault a 'stylistics of existence' (Butler 1990: 33, 139). However, this existentialist allusion is now elided with a supplementary definition; one that seems as if it is merely enriching or paraphrasing the notion of stylisation but which actually suggests a more constructivist, unidirectional and closed process, where gender is 'a set of repeated acts within a highly rigid regulatory frame' that congeal to give it the appearance of naturalness (Butler 1990: 33). The body is now presented as a 'signifying practice'. Although none of this denies its materiality, the emphasis on repetition and signification in *Gender Trouble* does suppress the expressive, agentic and corporeal aspects of style as an experimental and relatively open process of appearing. One consequence is that the structuralist-cum-poststructuralist sense of the heterosexual matrix – where sex and gender are discursively constituted according to Butler – makes it difficult to envisage how innovations and possibilities might occur. The matrix, with its categorial reiterations and scripted performances, its discursive imperatives and its association with the incest taboo, looks too closed (McNay 2000: 35). Indeed Butler later herself concedes that the regulative schema of the heterosexual matrix 'became a kind of totalising symbolic' (Butler 1996b: 119). But it is a problem she might have avoided had the structuralist (Lacanian) and radically constructivist arguments in *Gender Trouble* not eviscerated the existentialist implications of style. At best, then, the reference to stylisation serves as a reminder there of her earlier existentialism and helps implicitly to compensate for the closures of her argument; at worst, it points to a theoretical hiatus in this most seminal of her writings.

In 1988, the idea of style had still allowed Butler plausibly to insist on the 'facticity of the material and natural dimensions' of visceral experience without any danger of implying unmediated biological causation (Butler 1988: 520). She could therefore have appealed to this ontology in responding to her critics in *Bodies that Matter*. If her reference there to a body that materialises is not entirely convincing regarding its materiality (Butler 1993: 9; Lloyd 1999b:122; Braidotti 2000: 42; McNay 2000: 44) then her earlier existentialist allusion to a dramatic body that 'is not merely matter but a continual and incessant materializing of possibilities' was considerably more persuasive, as are her allusions to Bourdieu's praxeology. The irony is that while Butler was manifestly reluctant to follow this route during the 1990s lest it tarnish her constructivist credentials, it should not have precluded her from practising the kind of detailed genealogical analyses of disciplinary power and its corporeal effects that Foucault offers in *Discipline and Punish*. Indeed in 1988 Butler was still envisioning 'a critical genealogy of gender' that relies 'on a phenomenological set of presuppositions' (Butler 1988: 530). Two years later this possibility would be foreclosed by her robust denunciation of the latter's 'humanist' presuppositions in *Gender Trouble*.

The 1988 essay does seem to end on a critical note regarding phenomenology's concern with lived experience, when Butler insists that one cannot understand compulsory heterosexuality without examining reified structures in addition to the personal experiences and individual acts that reproduce them. But this realisation is already implicit in the phenomenological notion of sedimentation (indeed Butler will accuse the phenomenological Bourdieu of *over*-emphasising its structural rigidity (Butler 1997a: 154–56)), as well as in the more dialectical account of constituted-constituting relations Butler finds there. In fact structuralist theory is itself judged in this essay to be deficient in critical resources inasmuch as it fails to describe the 'mundane manner' in which historical sediments are produced and reproduced 'within the field of bodies', and a phenomenological counter-balance is deemed a 'felicitous starting point' here (Butler 1988: 525). Finally, poststructuralism is also criticised insofar as its 'radical displacements of the subject' suggest a body that is 'passively inscribed with cultural codes': as an inert, 'lifeless recipient' of cultural relations (an ironic complaint given Butler's own vulnerability to such charges) (Butler 1988: 526). What she seems still to appreciate in existential phenomenology, then, is precisely its enduring sense of an active, expressive body with the visceral capacities sometimes to resist the constraints imposed upon it, and of everyday lives wherein contestation is nurtured. Although she already distinguishes between 'expression and performativeness' in this essay, it is only in the sense that the former suggests some prior, more natural or original, identity; it is not an objection to expressive corporeality as such.

To summarise so far, what I have found Butler describing prior to *Gender Trouble* is an existential, dialectical ontology and a phenomenological approach consonant with it, whereby experiences and structures are interwoven at both levels. In her later essays I think she returns to these positions, which had been renounced in the 1990 volume and its immediate successors, and she does so I submit because they address many of the problems thrown up by her poststructuralism. This return is evident once phenomenology's signature terminology of sedimentation, field, contingency, possibility, becoming, mediation, improvisation, expression and stylisation are identified (terms that are not in fact entirely absent even from the writing of the early 1990s). What Butler has, however, been reluctant to do is to reiterate her phenomenological commitments or explicitly to reconsider the arguments with which she would briefly but enthusiastically renounce them.

Butler's anti-humanist turn: the discursive strategies of gender trouble

The reason *Gender Trouble* seems so at odds with existential phenomenology is that its basic premise is so uncompromisingly constructivist. Instead of the complex, bi-directional mediations and open syntheses she had been describing so recently, Butler now argued that denial causes desire and prohibition constructs its own opponents: both unwittingly in the process of defining and delimiting itself and as a justification for its regulatory practices.

In Nietzschean terms: there is no doer behind the deed; no cause or origin behind the effect; no subject that supports its predicates; nothing pre-discursive or natural that lies outside discursive power. In arguing that the law produces subjectivity and desire, Butler strengthens Foucault's (and Althusser's) juridico-political sense of law that constitutes (interpellates) the obedient juridical subject, with a structuralist sense of the Law of the Father as the repressive condition for subjectivity as such, and with a more strongly linguistic sense of discursive practices that is indebted to Derrida. She also draws implicitly on Baudrillard's notion of simulacra, inasmuch as gender performances are copies for which there is no original (a source mediated by Jameson, whose own work on parody serves here as a draft for transgressive performances).

Butler's most explicit debt is, however, to Foucault. In earlier essays she had regularly cited his claim in *The History of Sexuality* that sex is a discursive category that constructs (rather than represents) sex. Foucault had referred here to a plethora of biological processes and corporeal phenomena that are reified by this categorisation. 'The notion of "sex"', he explained, 'made it possible to group together, in an artificial unity, anatomical elements, biological functions, conducts, sensations, and pleasures' (Foucault 1978: 154; quoted by Butler 1987b: 138; 1988: 524; 1990: 92). Expressed in this way, the claim is entirely compatible with the phenomenological imperative to interrogate the discourses that have been imposed on a dynamic lifeworld, while it also sustains the sense of an irreducible existential and visceral dimension that discourse reifies. In Foucault's sense of discourse, moreover, there is still a dialectical process whereby signification imposes categories that support but emerge from mundane disciplinary practices ('effective' history). It is only the first aspect of this process that Butler now emphasises. When she quotes the above passage in *Gender Trouble*, she accordingly gives the impression of a more uncompromisingly constructivist claim than Foucault suggests, and she indeed accuses him of illegitimately maintaining naturalist elements. The price she pays for this radicalism, however, is that she must continuously reassure sceptics that she is not after all oblivious to biological facts and material practices, while she will concede eventually that 'the discourse of "construction"' is not after all 'quite adequate' for explaining how the 'materiality' of sex is forcibly produced (Butler 1996b: 113; 1993, xi).

My analysis of Butler's overt turning away from her earlier phenomenological approach in *Gender Trouble* relies on two claims. First, I show how she subjects all her opponents to a series of criticisms that are drawn from a standard list of anti-humanist arguments. These are sufficiently repetitive in my view to warrant being summarised as a 'formula'. It is the application of this formula, I suggest, that allows her so summarily to dismiss even those thinkers on whose work she had formerly relied, and her criticisms here rarely do justice to the otherwise careful expositions of their work. As a consequence, I argue, second, there is a certain excess of those theories that eludes her critiques. These phenomenological vestiges do important work in quietly supporting Butler's poststructuralist arguments, and I agree with Kruks when she contends that in the 'final analysis, like Foucault, Butler operates from suppressed "existential" postulates' (Kruks 2001: 75). I suggest that her political conclusions trade on these residual existential themes, which are needed to flesh out the rather thin sense of society and of political change. The explicit claims advanced in *Gender Trouble* are nonetheless derived from the anti-humanist arguments that French thinkers had been developing since the 1960s and which Butler now refines into a critical formula that she uses to renounce the approaches and authors she had previously endorsed. This formula relies on three basic propositions.

First, Butler accuses her protagonists – existential-phenomenologists in particular – of Cartesianism, whose main legacy is oppositional thinking. This is condemned for presenting an ontological subject as the origin or cause, rather than the constructed effect (the 'fictive foundation'), of the law; for conceiving the self on the model of rational masculinity and for presuming an inert, objective body. This accusation is applied far more widely and crudely than it had been in the subtle analyses preceding *Gender Trouble*.

Second, although Derrida is only mentioned once in the body of Butler's text, inasmuch as he offers any methodological formulation of deconstruction it is applied here. Derrida presents deconstruction as a 'double gesture': once identified, oppositions are to be inverted then rendered undecidable. The second stage is crucial because it reveals the internal complicity of dualisms, where dialectical mediation and sublation are replaced by dispersal, with dissonance disorganising the entire field of meaning. It is in this sexual interworld that Butler locates the inter- and the trans-. But because 'every transgressive gesture reencloses us', Derrida warns that this deconstructive process must be continuously re-enacted (Derrida 1981: 12, 41, 42). Butler agrees. She criticises those (notably Radical Feminists) who seek merely to invert oppositions, while denouncing delusions that this revalorisation might achieve liberation.

Finally, there is the radical constructivism Butler derives from Foucault's genealogy. The main source she cites is his 1971 essay 'Nietzsche, Genealogy, History', where Foucault's main target had been the sort of emancipatory history associated with the Hegelian Dialectic. A good deal of this argument is coded within his opening assertion that genealogy 'opposes itself to the search for "origins"' (Foucault 1977: 140, 142). Although the reference is explicitly to Nietzsche's rejection of Platonic essences, Foucault's objection to origins incorporates Husserl's phenomenological aspiration to return to experience as well as teleological notions of idealised or anthropological origins that provide the model and beginning for history's *telos*. It is to subvert this redemptive humanist fable that Foucault presents genealogy as a refusal of 'monotonous finality'. And it is this mission that underpins Butler's determination to winkle out all assumptions of pre-discursive origins and the futural aspirations associated with them: they suggest to her an emancipatory – utopian and nostalgic, reifying and parochial, theological and occasionally tragic – yearning to set free some force or identity before or outside the Law. She also contends that these 'discursively and performatively instituted modes of temporality' normatively foreclose current possibilities by focusing attention on unrealisable ideals of unity and reconciliation that serve as self-justificatory fabrications in support of current interests (Butler 1990: 29, 36).

Among the many origins Butler elicits and renounces are the (radical) feminist search for an 'imaginary past' or 'origin' before patriarchy, which risks reifying women's experience; the humanist myth of the 'pregendered "person"' or of a sexual identity behind expressions of gender; natural, pre-discursive sex, sexuality or desire; 'an alternative economy of pleasures' that prefigures a non-Oedipal or post-genital politics outside the reproductive economy of the present; polymorphous perversity; bodies as yet unmarked by gender (which therefore have no 'signifiable existence'), but also the 'real' body and indeed reality or a 'truer reality' as such; dispositions and identity associated with agency; experience as 'raw' or 'naïve'; a metaphysics of substance and the subject as 'the metaphysical locus of agency' (Butler 1990: 3, 8, 25, 26, 35).

It is this threefold anti-humanist formula that is then applied almost ritualistically to individual thinkers in *Gender Trouble*. Butler had already rehearsed its application in critiques of Deleuze (whose desire for affirmation is denounced as a 'normative ideal'; an ontological universal that supports an 'emancipatory' and 'precultural eros' and an 'originary unrepressed libidinal diversity' (Olkowski 1999: 40, 43; Butler 1999b [1987]: 175, although see Butler 2004b: 198)) and Merleau-Ponty (accused of naturalising sexuality and of a silence on sexual difference that allegedly masks presuppositions regarding heterosexuality as normal and assumptions predicated on an abstract subject, although his insistence on the co-existence of sexuality and existence will later be applauded by Butler (Butler 1989d: 98; Butler 2004b: 33)). In *Gender Trouble* itself, various structuralists are taken to task on the basis of Butler's formula: Claude Lévi-Strauss, Mary Douglas, Jacques Lacan, Julia Kristeva and Luce Irigaray all fall foul of its proscriptions, even though important elements of their arguments are in fact retained (Butler 1990: 30, 37 ff., 55 ff., 80, 131). The charges against Foucault are fairly typical here: he is accused of presuming a passive, stable, self-identical body awaiting cultural inscription; of maintaining the dualism of a substantive core versus secondary attributes and of harbouring an emancipatory ideal (Butler 1990: 94 ff., 130).

Although aspects of these criticisms are persuasive, it is to their repetitive, formulaic nature to which I want to draw attention. I suggest that this strategy is especially evident, moreover, when Butler's target is the sort of existential-phenomenology from which she had derived some of her main ideas. What she tends to do here is to gloss its exponents' work in a way that leads one to anticipate their congruence with or anticipation of her own position, only to dismiss them via some rather totalising but brief invocation of the formula. This has the effect of leaving much of the summary in play, such that its uncriticised elements remain effective within her text, while occluding Butler's enduring indebtedness to this existential legacy.

This is especially the case with Beauvoir and even in *Gender Trouble* it is not easy to see where one ends and the other begins. For if the body is a situation as Beauvoir claims, Butler reasons, then there 'is no recourse to a body that has not already been interpreted by cultural meanings; hence, sex could not qualify as a prediscursive anatomical facticity. Indeed, sex, by definition, will be shown to have been gender all along' (Butler 1990: 8, 111 f). Yet Butler now alleges that Beauvoir herself fell short of this realisation and maintained a naturalist sense of sex after all: an error derived from unreconstructed Cartesian (and Christian) assumptions that sustained her mind/body dualism. She accordingly contends that Beauvoir's body is simply passive and inert, a mute facticity whose contours are a 'taken for granted ground'; that for her 'sex is immutably factic' and 'cannot be changed' (Butler 1990: 8). Yet even when she describes sexual reproduction, Beauvoir seems to anticipate the sort of pre-binary, interstitial ambiguity that Butler will ascribe to inter-sexuality and transgender. She insists on a degree of indeterminacy and contingency even at the biological level, where she alludes to 'the existence of conditions intermediate between hermaphroditism' and sexual difference and describes post-menopausal women as a 'third sex': no longer male or female but replete with renewed vitality (Beauvoir 1956: 43, 46, 47, 63; Butler 2004b: 43).

In recognising that gender is constructed, on the other hand, Beauvoir is now charged by Butler with presuming an agent or *cogito* prior to cultural signification. She saw gender as too open – too 'variable and volitional' – Butler argues, thereby suggesting that an agent chooses its identity and presuming the free, liberal subject described by Sartre (Butler 1990: 8). Yet in her 1987 'Variations on Sex and Gender' essay, Butler had explicitly distinguished Beauvoir's sense of 'choice' from this Cartesian version by referring to 'concrete cultural', 'prereflective' choice as a 'subtle and strategic project', where navigating and reconfiguring existing gendered styles and norms is possible because the body is 'a field of interpretive possibilities' (Butler 1987b: 131, 133; see Beauvoir 1956: 41, 66, 68). My point here is not merely that Beauvoir is short changed and Butler's debt to her obscured by 1990. More importantly, it is that this phenomenological ontology of becoming is the one to which Butler will revert in *Undoing Gender* in order to restore an experiential sense of possibilities, whereas in *Gender Trouble* her formula had convinced her that Beauvoir maintained a pre-discursive ideal that implicated her in the humanist metanarrative. 'But how would such a project become culturally conceivable and avoid the fate of an impossible and vain utopianism?' (Butler 1990: 112, 129, 142). Yet *The*

Second Sex had actually offered quite concrete, socialist proposals for changing women's situation and a careful phenomenology of the experiences they must negotiate: a level of sociological and experiential analysis that still seems lacking in Butler's work.

Butler acknowledges Wittig as an important figure in developing Beauvoir's radical implications, recognising that it is Wittig who describes the constitutive powers of language where repetition results in 'reality-effects' that are misperceived as facts, and Wittig who concludes that there is no sex/gender distinction because sex is already a gendered category (Butler 1990: 112, 115; 1987b: 135). Yet in her 'existential-materialist mode' Wittig, too, is dismissed in *Gender Trouble* and along very similar lines to Beauvoir (as a humanist who subscribed to a metaphysics of agency and a utopian desire for a post-genital economy grounded in a 'truer reality') (Butler 1990: 27, 117, 119, 124, 127). At the same time, Wittig remains by implication at the second stage of deconstruction: she merely inverts the binary of normal versus perverse sexuality by opposing heterosexuality to anti-Oedipal (homo)sexuality and thereby reifies the more plural opportunities she advocates. I suggest nonetheless that *Gender Trouble* implicitly trades on the existential residues of non-categorial, proliferating sexualities invoked by Wittig and that this helps to disguise political lacunae in Butler's argument that the heterosexual matrix is itself responsible for constructing the multiple and unassignable sexual identities whose existence outside the categories of the matrix remains ontologically ambiguous.

To summarise my misgivings with Butler's formula: it obscures her debts to materialist, existential and phenomenological accounts of embodied sexuality while its sweeping dismissals serve to construct their exponents as the other that delimits and defines her own constructivism. However, these existential themes continue to haunt her work, just as the 'spectre' of the law's suppressed/constructed possibilities haunts the dominant order. In the end it is Butler who constructs the dualism of the non-discursive and the discursive, whereas for existential phenomenologists they are irreducibly interwoven at every level. But at the same time, I have suggested, these suppressed themes remain efficacious in her work where they survive in the excess that eludes her formulaic criticisms and in presuppositions her radical constructivism cannot eliminate entirely. They will resurface piecemeal in Butler's later work, but without ever achieving the explicitness or coherence they had enjoyed in her writing prior to *Gender Trouble*.

What, then, were the problems with her constructivism that would encourage Butler to retrieve aspects of her phenomenological legacy? In the eyes of her critics, at least, an apparent loss of visceral materiality – and a corresponding reduction of politics to the 'merely cultural' (Butler 1998; Fraser 1998a) – was the main difficulty with *Gender Trouble*, and she ostensibly wrote *Bodies that Matter* (1993) to assuage their concerns. Laying aside the question of the validity of these concerns, it is hardly surprising that the kind of terminology Butler had used should have provoked them.

She had argued that a consequence of understanding the gendered body as performative is that it enjoys 'no ontological status apart from the various acts which constitute its reality' (Butler 1990: 136). She accordingly presented her political aim as that of resignifying and denaturalising bodily categories, with the purpose of 'parodic practices' being to disrupt categories of bodies, sex or gender through 'subversive resignification' and proliferation 'beyond the binary frame' (Butler 1990: x). It is difficult to avoid the impression that what proliferates here are categories and that bodies lack the corporeality that might resist or improvise upon them, even if this is not Butler's intention. Rather than judging whether she succeeded in disabusing her critics of their confusions, then, I want to suggest two possible reasons for the palpable exasperation that emanates from the Introduction to *Bodies that Matter*, where she summarises her rejoinders.

First, I think Butler is genuinely puzzled at some level by her critics' scepticism because she believes her work does acknowledge the presence of material factors. The reason she could sustain this belief, I suggest, is that she had never entirely abandoned her existential sense of corporeality, even though the logic of her constructivism resulted in its overt disavowal. At first Butler aims only to clear up her critics' 'confusions', insisting that while she recognises the necessity of certain biological 'facts' as '"primary" and irrefutable experiences' this does not explain their significance: 'their irrefutability in no way implies what it might mean to affirm them and through what discursive means' (Butler 1993: xi; 1996b: 113). But she also invokes Merleau-Ponty's ontology of the flesh here, in order to cite a perpetual negotiation between 'the materiality of language' and the world, where materiality and language, referent and signified, are inseparable yet irremediably different. In other words, she now draws on the ontological support eschewed in *Gender Trouble* (Butler 1993: 69). In *Excitable Speech* Butler uses Bourdieu's work similarly, to describe bodily effects of speech that exceed speakers' intentions because the body bears traces of this excess as a kind of corporeal memory. It is this sort of phenomenological sociology, she implies, that is needed to understand how norms become embodied as a corporeal style or habitus; how there can be pre-linguistic, corporeal knowing and how cultures sustain themselves through 'embodied rituals of everydayness' (Butler 1997a: 141, 152). If she will acknowledge later that she is 'not a very good materialist', in that when she writes about the body she ends up writing about language, Butler will qualify this with a claim once more indebted to Merleau-Ponty: that rather than the body being reducible to language, language 'emerges from' the body, which in turn bears its own corporeal signifiers. Insisting that performativity is about speech acts *and* bodily acts, she uses Merleau-Ponty's term 'chiasmus' to denote their complex relationship (Butler 2004b: 198). Again, this dialectical relationality or chiasmic entwining is quite different from the constructivist position, not least because there is a non-discursive, material level of existence from which discourses emerge during experience and there are thenceforth mutual incitations and constraints. It is this ontology that is impervious to the concerns of Butler's materialist critics.

The second reason for Butler's frustration arises, however, from an aporia that I think haunts all forms of radical constructivism and deconstruction, and it is a danger she had already mentioned in *Gender Trouble* when she accused Lacan of nostalgia for pre-juridical pleasure. Forever barred by the Law and unknowable from within spoken language, Butler judged that this *jouissance* functioned for Lacan like Kant's 'true noumenal reality' (Butler 1990: 56). But does she not herself fall prey to the same trap, inasmuch as her insistence on the constituting powers of discourse unwittingly constructs a discursive/non-discursive dichotomy, where the non-discursive is the limit and other of the categorial/signification and suffers from the same ontological ambiguity as Kantian noumena? (Coole 2000: 27 ff.). The result is that Butler and her critics are condemned to circle around the aporias of scepticism and dogmatism, where the ontological versus the merely discursive status of a 'real', material outside is impossible to adjudicate. An escape route had already, however, been proposed by Hegel: one must recognise an ongoing dialectic between existence and its categorisation, where there is a continuous back and forth wherein questioning, learning and engagement occur. And this is precisely the route Butler takes as she eases back into her existential and dialectical approach.

A further problem with Butler's constructivism relates to the impoverished sense of society, intersubjectivity and politics it yields. This is a limitation she has had to overcome as her work has become more politically interventionist. Politics is claimed in *Gender Trouble* to concern 'signifying practices' rather than collective life (Butler 1990: 147). Sometimes it seems to get swallowed up altogether by the sheer inertia of such practices. Yet Butler also sees the need for some more sociological referent that might explain why repetition and reification remain so resilient, and she accordingly introduces some very vague and under-theorised allusions to collective agency (the 'public'). She tells us that the sexual marking of the body is 'the result of a diffuse and active structuring of the social field' by something like a public will (Butler 1990: 131). She cites a 'mundane social audience' that performs gender while insisting on the illusion of natural gender 'in the mode of belief'. There is, she concludes, a 'collective dimension' of such acts, and the 'strategic aim of maintaining gender within its binary frame' occurs through 'tacit collective agreement' (Butler 1990: 140). But what is this agreement, and how is it negotiated? Why is it so pervasive, and what are its socio-political dynamics? We only discover that the 'public' wishes for coherence (Butler 1990: 136). Yet if it is indeed 'clear that coherence is desired', how is one to explain why and how gender is so 'tenuously' constituted and 'gender discontinuities' actually 'run rampant'? (Butler 1990:135, 140). If there is this hiatus between everyday life, with its heterogeneous expressions and experiences, on the one hand, and regulatory categories that deny and delegitimise them, on the other, then a much fuller account of how delegitimating discourses operate upon ordinary lives with which they are out of sync is surely needed to explain why contestation is so important, what it might achieve, how it is motivated and what its relationship is to the rampant forces that escape the dominant categorial power yet whose very existence it seems to construct but deny.

A further lack of theorisation however bedevils allusions to individual agency here – a problem Butler inherits from Foucault's genealogical period. She is adamant that her constructivism is not antithetical to individual agency, and she locates it 'within the possibility of a variation on ... repetition' (Butler 1990: 144, 147). However, her hostility to anything non-discursive or experiential commits her to arguing that it is not only the subject and its regulation that are constructed but also the unregulated possibilities in whose name resistance occurs, which are themselves effects of hegemonic heterosexist discourse. I suggest that what Butler offers us here, however, are merely structural *opportunities*, not *capacities*, for agency. She could have sustained the latter without subscribing to essentialist or subjectivist accounts, by acknowledging and exploring the phenomenology of agentic capacities that operate within corporeal existence and emerge within everyday life. But in *Gender Trouble* Butler is committed to a more formal, Deleuzean–Foucauldian account of dissonant repetition. As a consequence she can only maintain that the hiatus between different discourses and the 'other' they unwittingly construct offers (seemingly random) possibilities for faulty reiteration: 'The productions swerve from their original purposes and inadvertently mobilize possibilities of "subjects" that do not merely exceed the bounds of cultural intelligibility, but effectively expand the boundaries of what is, in fact, culturally intelligible' (Butler 1990: 29).

But what is this excess, and what are these mobilised subjects that require scare quotes and lack any interiority? Butler can only tell us that where order is maintained by repetition, disorder resides in a 'failure to repeat'; 'de-formity'; 'parodic repetition', that reveal the contingency, even illusoriness, of 'abiding identity' as a 'politically tenuous construction'. Here is 'a variety of incoherent configurations that in their multiplicity exceed and defy the injunction by which they are generated' (Butler 1990: 145). But can failure and regulation themselves produce such efficacious and multiplicitous excess, and what is the status of its experiential or corporeal existence? This may indeed circumscribe a 'space' or 'scene' ripe with 'possibility', but it seems to lack any means for setting them in motion. It is to grant this social field intersubjective density, then, that Butler must return to dialectical and existential-phenomenological descriptions.

The reemergence of existential and phenomenological themes

This brings me to the final – and current – phase of the narrative with which I began, and to the conclusion of my claim that in her recent work, Butler has returned – although not yet reflexively enough – to her earlier phenomenological premises. In the essays collected in *Undoing Gender* (2004b) she still insists on her constructivist credentials, yet her insistence suggests to me that she finds herself at something of a theoretical cross-roads. For example, the textbook account of 'Gender Regulations' remains overtly Foucauldian, yet the broadly contemporaneous but more politically engaged Amnesty Lecture (2002) is heavily indebted to phenomenological claims used to support the politics. Overall there is a certain eagerness, too, to distance herself from *Gender Trouble*; a work written, Butler now says, 'for a few friends' and 'too quickly' (2004b: 207, 213).

It is not possible to offer a close analysis of Butler's recent work in the space remaining, but in light of the preceding account it is apparent how many of her pre-constructivist terms and presuppositions have resurfaced. The focus on the 'livable life', for example, is saturated with existential themes. The invocation of 'livability' suggests existential, even vitalist, criteria for distinguishing between 'viable' and 'unlivable' lives, and 'existence' could probably be substituted for 'life' here. In 1987 Butler had already noted how from Beauvoir's perspective, straying outside established (gender) norms 'is in some sense to put one's very existence into question', which is pretty much her argument again now (Butler 1987b: 132; 2004b: 1). There is a renewed sense, too, of the efficacy of experience in these recent essays. For it is the 'experience' of becoming undone – of vulnerability, dependence and 'unravelling' – that can change one's sense of self and incite responses to normative life and political events. The 'different modes of living' whose possibility such experience might open are redolent of existential concerns with styles of being-in-the-world.

If experiences of being 'undone' alert subjects to contingency and thence to possibilities for renewal – for 'improvisation within a scene of constraint' – then Butler acknowledges that such concerns belong to 'a philosophy of freedom' (Butler 2004b: 1, 15, 31). But together with the focus on 'social norms' (rather than on discursive structures or regulative practices), this terminology betrays dialectical and existential premises whereby situated, embodied agents enjoy limited freedom within a structured but dynamic field (where the 'temporal and spatial' field exceeds and decentres the self) (Butler 2004b: 15). This is precisely how an earlier generation of existential phenomenologists had escaped a Cartesianism or Kantian philosophy of the subject, and it is still needed to counteract a tendency towards the liberal individualism that Butler's focus on maximising possibilities sometimes suggests. In writing that my agency is opened as a possibility for me by a world that outruns me, and that the critical task involves an interrogation of normative and conceptual constraints on my life where it is the 'constitutive sociality of the self' that grants a basis for 'thinking a [complex] political community', she draws implicitly on their ontology of an intercorporeal and intersubjective interworld. In acknowledging that the 'body implies agency' in its becoming, she is also drawing on Merleau-Ponty's reversible, reflexive flesh (Butler 2005; Coole 2005;

Merleau-Ponty 1986, ch. 4). This allows Butler to recognise that agency is socially *mediated*, not solely constituted: another dialectical term and one that suggests a relational process at odds with the earlier emphasis on subjectivity as the constituted effect of power (Butler 2004b: 21, 29, 32).

Finally, Butler argues that possibility must entail hope available to all: not as an empty abstraction, but 'apprehended phenomenologically' (Butler 2004b: 31). It is the careful analysis of unfolding events and social trajectories this entails, together with the sociological sense of a complex social field on which it relies, that suggests a more engaged politics than poststructuralism is able to sustain. It would therefore be helpful if Butler were to make explicit her return to this approach and her recognition – once more – of the existential ontology that underpins it. Inasmuch as this is complemented by detailed phenomenological and genealogical investigations of everyday life, where lived experience and structures of power are interwoven and treated as equally worthy of critical analysis, then Butler's recent work is to be applauded as a renewal of political engagement. Pulling against this possibility there is also, however, the more abstractly normative, Kantian – and recently, Levinasian – aspect of her thinking, and I hope her residual Hegelianism will encourage her to resist this.

3   Feminists know not what they do

Judith Butler's gender trouble and the limits of epistemology

Linda M.G. Zerilli

A celebrity feminist theorist of the postmodern variety goes to a conference on identity in New York City. After presenting a paper charting the demise of 'women' as a unified category, she is confronted by a hostile member of the audience who accuses her of betraying feminism. Feminism, the practice, needs a subject called women, declares the irate spectator; a subject that feminism, the theory, has dissolved in its sceptical flight from the ordinary. In a voice pitched well above the ordinary, this spectator emphatically asserts her confidence in the existence of 'real women' (like herself) and concludes by asking the speaker, 'How would you know that there are women right here in this room?' To this agitated rhetorical query the weary postmodern feminist replies rather matter-of-factly, 'Probably the same way you do'.[1]

With debates concerning the so-called category of women mercifully behind us, such scenes would appear to have little continuing significance, save as illustrations of the peculiar pathos of that particular episode in the development of American feminist theory. Once heralded as the successor to Woman (the masculinist monolith) and as the mark of a political constituency bound by a shared identity and common experience, women has lost its appeal as a category of feminist theory and as the subject of feminist praxis. Third-wave debates over the category of women more or less focused on the problem of exclusion: every theoretical and political claim to the category brings with it a normative conception of women that excludes those who do not conform. Rejected by many feminists was the idea that gender identity is the basis for a political movement of women, regardless of other social differences such as race, class, or sexuality. Likewise rejected was the idea that gender is a cultural interpretation of a biological given (sex).

To say that these debates are over, however, is by no means to declare them settled. True, the dramatic escalation of the stakes of theorising in the 1990s has yielded to a bland consensus about 'the differences among women'. But what does that consensus really mean? What kinds of shared assumptions and deep divisions does it conceal? Although the call to attend to difference helped unmask a false homogeneity in the fundamental categories of feminism, it has in turn masked the discontents of feminist theorising itself. It is as if the concept of difference were a magical substance that could not only eviscerate the legacy of exclusion in feminism but also settle fundamental questions about what theory *is* and how it relates to praxis.

Both second- and third-wave feminists have been deeply concerned with the relation between the theoretical and the practical, agreeing implicitly or explicitly with the Marxist dictum that the point is to change the world, not merely to interpret it. But they have not really clarified the relationship between interpretation and change. Proclaiming that theory ought to relate to praxis, feminists have for the most part either left the exact nature of the relation obscure or, worse, tended to define it (albeit often unwittingly) as unidirectional, with theory comprising the universal concepts that are applied in rule-like fashion to the particulars of politics. Should that one-sided relation be deemed untenable, as many feminists of the third wave hold, it seems as if our only recourse is to abandon theory and settle on mere description. But then it appears as if the price for refusing the universalising impulse of theory is the inability to say something beyond the particular case. If feminist critique entails 'the transfiguration of the commonplace', to borrow Arthur Danto's phrase, then mere description – leaving aside the whole question of whether any description is not always theory-laden – does nothing to bring particulars into an unexpected, critical relation with each other such that we can see any particular object, not to mention our own activity, anew (Danto 1981).

Likewise, if feminist critique entails taking account of the inaugural character of what Hannah Arendt calls action, then a theoretical enterprise centred on formulating hypotheses, concepts, or models that can explain and predict the regularities of sex–gender relations fails to comprehend its own subject matter and leads us to misunderstand what is at stake in our own political praxis (Arendt 1989). We need a freedom-centred mode of feminist critique that would resist the temptation to reach beyond the common to transfigure the commonplace, that is, a place outside our practices from which to form universal concepts under which to subsume particulars in the name of predicting and achieving social change. If that is the task, it should be understood in therapeutic rather than prescriptive terms. Rather than offer yet another feminist theory of sex–gender that could function as a rule to be applied to the contingencies of politics, we want to understand at once the nature of the demand for, and rejection of, such a theory.

Theory – the craving for generality?

Let us begin by clarifying the two distinct but related views of theory mentioned above: (1) theory is the critical practice of forming universal concepts that can be applied in rule-like fashion to the particulars of lived experience; (2) universal theory as such is fully bankrupt and must be replaced with the art of description that refuses to say anything beyond a particular case at hand. The tendencies are related because, as we shall see below, they both assume that the critical theoretical enterprise itself is a universalising function that illuminates particulars by subsuming them under concepts to produce a total critique. One of the reasons for the use and abuse of postcolonial feminist writings, for instance, may well be that feminists look to those writings to attenuate what appears to be the necessary consequences of this kind of enterprise, what Wittgenstein calls the 'craving for generality' and with it 'the contemptuous attitude towards the particular case' (Wittgenstein 1964: 17, 18). These uses and abuses include the production of such figures as 'The Third World Woman' (see Mohanty 1991). This craving is a product of centuries of philosophical and political thinking; it is a disposition to generalise against which feminists, working with and against that inheritance, are by no means invulnerable. What drove some feminists to produce unified categories that did not attend to the particular case was in part this craving for generality, a craving that animated the hegemonic strand of the feminist theoretical enterprise through the 1980s and into the 1990s and that continues to haunt it even today, if only in the form of its nemesis, the refusal of theory – be that scepticism or radical particularism. Barely concealed in the category of women debates is the unspoken wish that feminist theory can give, and ought to give, an exhaustive account of gender relations and provide a kind of 'super-idealised guidance' on how to change them (Pears 1988: 488). We might think of this wish as a desire for solace, a desire that would be satisfied by, and thus incessantly searches out, the perfect theory.

The phenomenal influence of Judith Butler's *Gender Trouble* in American feminist circles of the third wave speaks not only to the author's polemical brilliance but also to our desire for such a theory, even when, as in Butler's case, the theorist herself calls into question our desire for solace (Butler 1990). Is this desire unreasonable? Hasn't second-wave American feminist theory itself incited our desire for solace by generating a long chain of causal explanations of women's oppression which, if rightly understood, could be rightly remedied? Few American feminist theorists writing today would speak of the origin or cause of (all) women's suffering. But has the desire for solace, that is, for a total theory and a maxim that would tell us how to act politically, disappeared? In light of what we have learned from the 'category of women' debates, surely it is not a matter of creating once and for all a theory that would be so encompassing of the diversity of lived experience, so accurate in its account of use and effect, so final in its articulation of normative commitments, that it could in fact tell us how so to act.

Driving the tenacious but impossible idea of such a theory is a conception of politics as an instrumental, means–ends activity centred on the pursuit of group interests. This pursuit requires a coherent group (for example, women) with shared concerns. It requires as well the production of knowledge in the form of concepts that function as rules under which to make sense of the particulars of women's lives and order them, knowledge that can be used to articulate political claims and authorise them in the coinage of modern scientific rationality and its practices of justification. In light of many feminists' more or less uncritical acceptance of this conception of politics, it is not surprising that the critique of a total theory, as it was expressed in the call to attend to differences, precipitated a sense of total political crisis. The source of that crisis, in other words, lies not in the loss of women as the subject of feminism, but in a means–ends view of politics that requires such a coherent, pre-given subject. The possibility of a total theory that this understanding of politics implies treats people themselves as means to an end, as the 'passive objects of its theoretical truth', writes Cornelius Castoriadis, and the world itself as a static object: the last thing it can account for is their political activity, whatever cannot be assimilated to a closed system, namely the new (Castoriadis 1987: 69).

Following Castoriadis's critical account of the crisis of orthodox Marxism, we might say that the exposure of this total theory as a feminist pipe-dream led, in the course of the 'category of women' debates, to two different but related responses, which we might now think of as contemporary (and therefore attenuated) versions of the old philosophical battle between dogmatism and scepticism: (1) the critique of the alleged certainties of second-wave feminist theory might well be right, but we have to shut our eyes and blindly affirm them nonetheless in the interests of radical politics (for example, 'strategic essentialism'), for such politics cannot get off the ground without foundational knowledge claims and the theory that articulates them; (2) since a total (feminist) theory cannot exist, we are led to abandon the theoretical enterprise if not the feminist project itself, for the latter, to speak with Castoriadis, is now 'posited as … the blind will to transform at any price something one does not know into something one knows even less' (Castoriadis 1987: 71–72). The responses are related because, though the second is the position rejected by the first, both share the view that without a total theory there can be no conscious action whatsoever, no sense of a common project whose ideals we at once debate and fight for in someone's name. Absent the rational knowledge that allows us to think present and future social organisations as totalities and gives us at the same time a criterion permitting us to judge them, there is no feminist politics save a decisionistic one (that is, a politics devoid of any particular ideals or normative commitments). In that case, we might as well declare 'the end of feminism', for there is little to differentiate a feminist project from other political projects, including non-feminist and even anti-feminist ones. To demand that a revolutionary project (such as feminism) 'be founded on a complete theory', writes Castoriadis,

> is … to assimilate to a technique, and to posit its sphere of action – history as the possible object of a finished and exhaustive knowledge. To invert this reasoning and conclude on the basis of the impossibility

of this sort of knowledge that all lucid (that is, theoretically, critically informed), revolutionary politics is impossible amounts, finally, to a wholesale rejection of all human activity and history as unsatisfactory according to a fictitious standard.

(Castoriadis 1987: 75)

Beholden to an instrumentalist conception of politics, feminists, though most see that such knowledge is neither possible nor desirable, have a harder time seeing how feminism could possibly continue without it – or, more precisely, without something that approximates it in the sense of providing objective criteria according to which political claims could be defined, articulated, and justified. Feminists therefore find themselves tempted by dogmatism and scepticism, either affirming what they may well know is not the case (for example, 'women' is a coherent group) or denying that one can affirm anything political that one does not know (for example, speak in the name of women). And on this same logic, carried to its absurd conclusion, hinges the future of feminism on our ability to make a cognitive judgment along the lines of 'There are women in the room'.

Castoriadis's critique of the tendency to assimilate politics to a technique recalls Arendt's account of the tendency to think about politics as a form of fabrication or making. To think about politics in this way, Arendt argues, is to imagine '[t]he construction of the public space in the image of a fabricated object', that is, as an object that exists first as a model in thought, as a set of rules that guide the realisation of the model in praxis (Arendt 1989: 227). Countering this instrumentalist conception of politics with an action-centred view, Arendt claims that political actors 'know not what they do' (Arendt 1994: 23). She does not accept here the (Platonic) separation of doing and knowing and the hierarchical distinction between those who know (the philosophers or rulers) and those who do not (the demos or ruled) (Arendt 1989: 222–23). Rather, she questions the very idea that politics as action is a rule-governed activity, prefigured by theory in the form of a model, which has outcomes that can be known in advance of the actual activity itself. Political actors know not what they do, then, not because there are other theorists or philosophers who do so know, but because, when we act, we cannot predict what the action will be.

This inability to predict the outcome of political action (Arendt) or praxis (Castoriadis) is a problem only according to the requirements of a means–end conception of politics and its fictitious standard of knowledge. Both Castoriadis and Arendt question the idea that politics, as a register of human doing, requires its participants to supply, or be able to supply, a complete theory of their activity. Neither thinker associates this lack of total knowledge with the failure to think critically, with non-reflexive activities, or with the mindless compulsion of habit. Like Wittgenstein, they affirm that our rule-governed practices are underdetermined, that is, that they are neither justified all the way down nor in need of such justification to count as part of a creative and critical relation to the world. More specifically, both Arendt and Castoriadis reject the idea that politics is a means–ends activity based on practices of knowing, that is, of adducing evidence, establishing truth or falsity, providing justification or non-justification. If politics were 'a "purely rational" activity', writes Castoriadis, 'based on an exhaustive, or practically exhaustive, knowledge of its domain', then 'any question relevant for practice and arising out of this domain would be decidable' – decidable, that is, in theory and quite apart from actual praxis – and 'confined to positing in reality the means to reach the ends it aims at, and establishing the causes that would lead to the intended results' (Castoriadis 1987: 72).

Doing gender, following a rule

Butler's critical project to unmask foundationalist premises in feminism is often received as an attempt to eradicate foundations or to advance anti-foundationalism as a coherent epistemological and political position. 'Both of those positions', she rightly observes, 'belong together as different versions of foundationalism and the sceptical problematic it engenders' (Butler 1992: 7). Distancing herself (with Foucault and Derrida) from the epistemological tradition of Western philosophy, Butler's central concern is not with knowledge claims but with relations of power and their naturalisation in forms of identity. She criticises the tradition for its failure to take into account 'the rules and practices' that constitute the subject, constitute it in such a way that (gender) identity appears to be an original and abiding substance. Butler's concern is with the philosophical notion of an 'I' that stands over and against a world of objects and is master of its own discourse (Butler 1990: 144).

By contrast with this realist account, Butler writes, 'genders can be neither true nor false, but are only produced as the truth effects of a discourse of primary and stable identity' (Butler 1990: 136). If the idea of gender as a property of a subject is not an empirical proposition (true or false) but an effect of a discourse of truth and power, then critique must proceed rather differently from the way it would according to the justification problematic described above. The point can't be to prove that gender is not justified in the sense of grounded, but to show how the illusion of a ground on which we decide the true and the false of gender itself is produced and with what consequences for feminist politics (Butler 1990: 144).

How can it be, then, that Butler's *Gender Trouble* was taken by many feminists as a declaration about the 'false' or 'illusory' character of gender, as if the point of her text were to declare, in sceptical fashion, that feminists have no grounds for making political claims in the name of 'women' since we cannot say with epistemic certainty that there *are* women? That Butler's work was accused of denying the existence of 'real women' – much as the irate New York spectator held – reflects anxieties about the possibility of feminism in the face of the changing social, economic, and political realities of the late twentieth century, which deepened existing cleavages among women or created new ones. I have already suggested that these changes unsettled the rule-governed theorising of second-wave feminism. Third-wave thinkers like Butler did not cause but diagnosed – in deeply critical and non-nostalgic terms – the loss of women as a coherent, foundational category of feminist praxis. What I now want to consider is the possibility that dogmatic feminist responses to *Gender Trouble* – albeit symptomatic of the mistaken understanding of the relationship between feminist theory and praxis discussed earlier – might indicate Butler's own paradoxical entanglement in the sceptical problematic she sets out to challenge.

Rejecting the ideal of total knowledge and the notion of subject-centred reason and signification that classical scepticism assumes, Butler's critical intervention consists in an effort to expose the constitutive effects of gender as a signifying practice and the logic of exclusion that it supports (Butler 1990: 149). In a passage that puts into question the idea of an original and abiding gender identity, Butler situates critique in relation to the encounter with the extra-ordinary, the strange:

> The point here is not to seek recourse to the exceptions, the bizarre, in order merely to relativize the claims made in behalf of normal sexual life. As Freud suggests in *Three Essays on the Theory of Sexuality*, however, it is the exception, the strange, that gives us the clue to how the mundane and taken-for-granted world of sexual meanings is constituted. *Only from a self-consciously denaturalized position* can we see how the appearance of naturalness is itself constituted. The presuppositions that we make about sexed bodies, about their being one or the other, about the meanings that are said to inhere in them or to follow from being sexed in such a way *are suddenly and significantly upset* by those examples that fail to comply with the categories that naturalize and stabilize the field of bodies for us within the terms of cultural conventions. Hence, the strange, the incoherent, that which falls 'outside', gives us a way of understanding the taken-for-granted world of sexual categorization as a constructed one, indeed, as one that might well be constructed differently.
>
> (Butler 1990: 110; emphasis added)

One could hardly overstate this turn toward the 'strange', the extraordinary, in Butler's work and in the major texts of feminist theory of the 1990s. An attempt to unsettle normative conceptions of gender, perhaps to imagine other forms of life, feminist invocations of the strange such as Butler's are compelling. But is it possible that this turn to the strange ultimately re-entangles us in problematic assumptions about the nature of critical reflection discussed earlier? In the passage just cited, such reflection is understood as a 'self-consciously denaturalized position'.

What would such a position actually look like? If doubt presupposes certitude, as Wittgenstein argues, how could we possibly stand outside our form of life and judge it to be arbitrary (or, for that matter, non-arbitrary)? The point here is not to dispute the possibility of feminist critique, but to ask whether it should take the shape Butler seems to suggest. Although it may well be the case that, in certain circumstances, the strange can help us to see 'the taken-for-granted world of sexual categorization' as – if not exactly – 'constructed and mutable', it is also more often the case that the strange is simply accommodated as an anomaly to our everyday practices. If the strange is to transfigure the commonplace, we need an account that, without seeking a place outside the common (that is, the external standpoint), addresses the context in which such a transfiguration might occur. Surely it is not something in the strange as an object that enables this critical relation to the taken-for-granted, but rather its place in a network of relations with other objects that we engage as part of a practice, and this practice will involve following rules. Rather than assume that our two-sex system is 'suddenly and significantly upset' whenever we are faced with the strange, then, we should ask: what are the conditions under which (1) something or someone appears strange to us, and (2) the strange occasions critical thought?

In *Gender Trouble*, drag serves as the paradigmatic instance of the 'strange', which calls forth the act of interpretation that puts into question the naturalness of our two-sex system: '*In imitating gender, drag implicitly reveals the imitative structure of gender itself as well as its contingency*' (Butler 1990: 137; emphasis in original). Drag not only reveals to the spectator the illusion of gender as an original and abiding identity, it also serves – crucially in fact – as the paradigm for understanding gender as a performance rather than an essence, a 'stylized repetition of acts' (Butler 1990: 140). In *Bodies That Matter*, Butler, responding to the charge of voluntarism, complicates this account of performativity by distinguishing between gender as 'performative' ('the forcible citation of a norm') and drag as a 'performance' ('the parodic citation of a norm') (Butler 1993: 232). What remains, however, is the idea that drag occasions an interpretive act that allows us to see what we normally take to be an object, with inherent and abiding properties, as a contingent and mutable practice. Gender is compulsory in a way that drag is not, but both are imitative performances without an original. Thus drag, as an artistic performance, is not the faithful reproduction of a content that inheres in the original object drag supposedly imitates, but the exposure of this very idea of content as illusory. Another way of putting this point is to say that, when we do gender, we follow a rule, but this rule-following remains invisible to us; when we see drag, we become aware of the rule we are following when we do gender, hence aware of the fact that gender is a performance, not a substance. Revealed thereby, says Butler, is 'a radical contingency in the relation between sex and gender in the face of cultural configurations of causal unities that are regularly assumed to be natural and necessary' (Butler 1990: 138).

nse, then, drag occasions critical thought on Butler's account
calls for an interpretation that exposes the rule-following practice
stitutes gender: 'the various acts of gender create the idea of gender,
out those acts, there would be no gender at all' (Butler 1990: 140).
some very important way, of course, this way of thinking about
gen.... is right. Gender is a practice, just as Butler shows, and this practice
is governed by rules. The question is, what does it mean to participate in
such a practice, to follow a rule? And what would it mean to have these
rules made visible in such a way that we could obtain a critical stance on
gender as a rule-following practice? These questions must be answered
before we can decide whether drag, as an instance of the strange, has the
critical force Butler ascribes to it.

It is easy to see the convergence between Butler's performative account of
gender and Wittgenstein's notion of following a rule. Both thinkers refute
the realist notion that rules or norms have meaning apart from their application. For Butler, like Wittgenstein, meaning must be understood as a
social practice, not as something determined by individual choice. In *Bodies
That Matter*, Butler (responding to the charge of voluntarism) takes up the
challenge of how 'to understand the constitutive and compelling status of
gender norms without falling into the trap of cultural determinism' (Butler
1993: x). But why would the threat of determinism arise once we think
about gender not as 'an artifice to be taken on or taken off at will [as drag
is] and, hence, not an effect of choice', as a certain reading of *Gender
Trouble* might suggest, but rather as a reiterative and citational practice or,
in Wittgenstein's terms, as following a rule (Butler 1993: x). It is not immediately clear how we should understand the idea of the rule as something
that is constitutive and compelling (for example, 'femininity as the forcible
citation of the norm') but not determining. Butler suggests wherein the difference might lie when she claims that rule-following may fail or in some
way be incomplete. As she explains in relation to the construction of 'sex':

> [C]onstruction is neither a single act nor a causal process initiated by a
> subject and culminating in a set of fixed effects. Construction not only
> takes place in time, but is itself a temporal process which operates
> through the reiteration of norms; sex is both produced and destabilized
> in the course of this reiteration. As a sedimented effect of a reiterative
> or ritual practice, sex acquires its naturalized effect, and, yet, it is also
> by virtue of this reiteration that gaps and fissures are opened up as the
> constitutive instabilities in such constructions, as that which escapes or
> exceeds the norm, as that which cannot be wholly defined or fixed by
> the repetitive labor of that norm. This instability is the reconstituting
> possibility in the very process of repetition, the power that undoes the
> very effects by which 'sex' is stabilized, the possibility to put the con-
> solidation of norms of 'sex' into a potentially productive crisis.
>
> (Butler 1993: 10).

The undeniable appeal of this notion of failure as an inherent possibility in any reiterative or citational practice is deeply linked to an account of norms or rules as things that, were we to apply them successfully, would have precisely the deterministic consequences described above. What saves us from these consequences is the possibility of failure that inheres in the very practice of rule-following itself: the fact, as Butler explains, that every citation of a norm opens the possibility for that which 'escapes or exceeds the norm'.

Thinking about a norm (or a rule) and what it means to cite (or follow) it in this way presses Butler in the direction of positing what Derrida, in his response to John Austin's theory of the performative, calls 'the essential possibility of cases interpreted as marginal, deviant, parasitical, etc.' (Derrida 1988: 126; see also Stone 2003). Derrida's idea that the risk of failure is inherent to the speech act transforms Austin's notion of the possibility of accidents into a condition of language itself. Anomalies are not anomalous at all, but are the internal condition of all the so-called ideal cases involving no accidents. In *Excitable Speech* Butler approvingly summarises Derrida's account (Butler 1997a: 151).

But what can it mean to think about a norm (or rule) as something that exists apart from any citation of it? We could say that no such gap exists in the so-called ideal cases, that is, those in which performatives do not fail. But if failure is built into the practice of citation as the very condition of its possibility – and in such a way that we can no longer distinguish anomalies from ideal cases (as Austin did) – then it would appear as if the norm (or rule) is being construed here as something that can in fact exist apart from any citation of it. As Butler herself put it, 'every credible production must be produced according to norms of legitimacy and, hence, fail to be identical with those norms and remain at a distance from the norm itself'. This is the same point she made earlier about the reiterative practice that constructs 'sex'. It seems as if, to put this in Wittgenstein's terms, the rule is somehow independent of its application. But then we are right back to the idea of rules and rule-following that was to be questioned in the first place.

The idea of a rule as somehow determining is clearly at odds with Butler's attempt to think 'performativity in relation to transformation' (Butler 1997a: 151). Like Derrida, she wants to think at once the rule and the event, not the consolidation of the notion that certain meanings are guaranteed by the rule itself. The essential possibility of failure and the endlessly mimetic character of citationality are crucial for Butler because they reveal the 'imposture' that belongs to the performative as the condition of its own '"legitimate" working' (hence the transformative potential of drag (Butler 1997a: 151). What is this imposture if not the collapse of the space of authenticity that allows us to see that what we take to be a case of plain meaning is really the hegemony of a particular interpretation? The norm is not a rule in the sense that the realist contends (that is, determining from above every instance of its application, then, but a sedimented interpretation or application that is hegemonic and that we tend to repeat without recognising that it is we who interpret the rule in this way – but could interpret otherwise. Thanks to 'the essential possibility of deviant cases', any performative harbours other possible interpretations; it can 'break with its prior contexts', break, that is, 'with any and all prior usage' (Butler 1997a: 148). Endorsing Derrida's concern to release the performative from the social convention in which Austin would contain it, Butler writes: 'Such breaks with prior context or, indeed, with ordinary usage, are crucial to the political operation of the performative. Language takes on a non-ordinary meaning in order precisely to contest what has become sedimented in and as the ordinary' (Butler 1997a: 145).

In some sense, this account of the performative is consistent with what Stanley Cavell describes as the ability to project a word. Such projection has no objective guarantee of success based on prior usage or social convention either. But that lack of guarantee is not construed by Cavell as an essential possibility of deviancy intrinsic to the functioning of language itself. If intrinsic to anything, the failure of meaning is seen as a possibility given in the simple fact that signs only have meaning in contexts, and contexts change. Nothing can guarantee that a sign that had meaning in one context will have any, let alone the same, meaning in another (Cavell 1976: 52; 1979: 78). That, however, is less a statement about what is *nonordinary* with language in our lives than what is deeply ordinary. Abnormal cases are always possible, but they do not indicate an essential possibility of the failure of meaning as the very condition of meaning. Following Wittgenstein, we do not need to posit failure as an internal condition of language to stave off meaning determinism because the successful application of concepts does not carry with it the threat of the closure of meaning that Butler, following Derrida, seems to assume. Language is not a cage from which only the essential possibility of failure in language can save us.

The temptation to think about social transformation as requiring a break with the ordinary, where the latter stands for prior usage or social convention, is linked to the tendency to imagine that the only alternative to a hegemonic application of a rule is to see it as something that is open to transformation insofar as it can be endlessly interpreted. Wittgenstein gives voice to this tendency in the *Philosophical Investigations* (Wittgenstein 1968: §85). It seems that our only choices are to affirm that every doubt must be eliminated or else all is in doubt: any interpretation of the rule will count as understanding it. To think about rules in this way is to say, either they compel in the sense of deciding in advance of the contingencies of any actual practice how we shall act, or they leave every course of action open.

Is interpretation the best way to think about rule-following? And is it the only way of imagining social transformation and critique, a nonhegemonic application of the rule? Let us approach these questions by considering the difference Wittgenstein draws between interpreting a sign and understanding it. Interpretation (*Deutung*) is 'the substitution of one expression of the rule for another' (Wittgenstein 1968: §201). The paradox of rule-following described above follows from a failure to make this distinction. If understanding a rule were the same as interpreting it, we would need yet another interpretation of the rule to understand the rule, and so on in an infinite regress. This leads Wittgenstein to say that 'there is a way of following a rule that is not an interpretation'. This way is an immediate grasping or understanding, which shows in how we act. It is not that we never interpret a rule, but interpretation is called for only when our normal procedures break down, where there is a sense of doubt and we do not know our way about. When we apply interpretation to ordinary cases of rule-following (as Butler and Derrida do), we misunderstand what it means to follow a rule. To know how to do something (read a sign-post, play chess, calculate, or sing a tune) involves an immediate understanding or grasping exhibited through action, not an interpretation. Wouldn't the same point hold for 'doing' or 'performing' gender?

Who sees what?

Wittgenstein clarifies these points in the context of a discussion of 'two uses of the word "see"', which may give us a better sense of the problems with Butler's claims about the revelatory character of a drag performance. The notion of seeing he has in mind here is not confined to perception in the usual sense but applies as well to our ability to perceive meaning in language. Invoking the famous *Gestalt* image of the duck-rabbit, which can be seen as either a rabbit's head or a duck's, Wittgenstein draws a distinction between what he calls 'the "continuous seeing" of an aspect and the "dawning" of an aspect' (Wittgenstein 1968: 193e, 194e). To continuously see an object under an aspect, which characterises ordinary acts of perception, is to recognise it immediately as a certain kind of object, say, a picture-rabbit. To experience the dawning of an aspect, which certainly occurs but is not characteristic of ordinary acts of perception, is to see the same object, suddenly as it were, as a different kind of object, say, a picture-duck. The object has not changed, but our way of seeing it has. How is this possible?

Wittgenstein rejects arguments about the nature of perception that locate the origin or cause of a certain perception in the object itself. As he proceeds, it becomes clear that the criticism is directed at the empiricist understanding of ordinary acts of perception (which are expressed by statements such as 'I see a picture-rabbit') as entailing interpretation (which is expressed by statements such as 'I am seeing the picture-rabbit as a picture-rabbit'). Indeed, what appeared to be an inquiry into the strange experience of aspect-dawning turns out to be a critical investigation of ordinary seeing. Wittgenstein suggests that we directly perceive or have an unmediated grasp of objects; their status as a particular type of object is simply taken for granted in our actions and speech. We do not encounter things as material objects of the generic kind, things that are, initially, given to the senses and that, subsequently, must be interpreted or organised in accordance with our concepts. We do not encounter objects about which 'we form hypotheses, which may prove false', as we do when we interpret. Continuous aspect perception is a form of certainty. When I see a knife and a fork on the table, says Wittgenstein, it makes no sense to say, 'Now I am seeing this as a knife and fork.' Quite simply, 'One doesn't "take" what one recognises as the cutlery at a meal *for* cutlery; any more than one ordinarily tries to move one's mouth as one eats, or aims at moving it' (Wittgenstein 1968: 195; emphasis in original; translation altered).

But isn't that precisely the problem? – a feminist like Butler might ask. Isn't it a problem that we do not take the woman we see *for* a woman, any more than we take the fork for a fork? Isn't the whole point of feminist critique to transfigure the commonplace by putting into question the very experience of ordinary seeing? But what would it mean to think about our potentially critical relation to particular signs as requiring a fundamentally interpretive relation to all signs? Whereas Butler seems to say that interpretation is the basis of our relation to signs – only some interpretations get 'sedimented' and must be replaced by other nonordinary interpretations – Wittgenstein suggests that we normally understand without interpreting, and that is not a defect of some kind or failing on our part but the nonreflective basis of anything we might call critique. As Tully explains:

> [I]t is important not to infer from this that there must be a stock of conventional uses that are permanently beyond interpretive dispute. First, the circumstances of any particular activity of interpreting a pro-blematic sign involves the unmediated grasp of other signs, which, *eo ipso,* places them provisionally beyond interpretation. Second, it is always possible to 'step back': to call into question the regular use of these other signs and take it up as an object of interpretation.
> (Tully 2003: 39; see also Wittgenstein 1969: 204; 1967: §§234–35)

In some sense, the experience of aspect-dawning (for example, seeing the duck now as a rabbit), though reasonably rare, is important in the way Tully suggests. Through the dawning of an aspect, we become aware that we are already seeing something as something, we are engaging in continuous aspect-seeing, or we have a way of seeing at all. Wittgenstein clarifies:

> Then it is like *this*: 'I have always read the sign 'σ' as a sigma; now someone tells me it could also be an M turned round, and now I see it like that too: so I have always *seen it as* a sigma before'? That would mean that I have not merely seen the figure **1** and read it like *this*, but I have also *seen* it as *this*!
> (Wittgenstein 1980: §427)

The change of aspect shows you that you have previously seen the sign as a sigma, making you aware that you were seeing it as something at all. The important thing, however, is not to confuse this ability to see that one sees something as something with the experience of ordinary seeing, as if the interpretive moment of aspect-dawning (for example, my seeing a sigma as an M turned round) were characteristic of our ordinary life with signs (for example, is it a sigma or an M?) or corrosive of our sense of certainty when we use them (for example, it seems like a sigma, but it could be an M). The important thing is not to forget that any dawning of an aspect is always parasitic on ordinary ways of seeing rather than the overcoming of some sort of illusion (for example, seeing that the woman one sees is really performing what one thinks one sees).

The dawning of an aspect allows one to see that what one sees is not ascribable to anything in the object, but is rather based on the use of another concept. Writes Wittgenstein, '[W]hat I perceive in the dawning of an aspect is not a property of the object, but an internal relation between it and other objects' (1968: §212). When I see a sign under an aspect – be it continuous aspect-seeing or a dawning – I see it as internally related to other things. These relations are based on concepts. The seeing is immediate (grasped), not mediated (interpreted). The perspective of which I am unaware until something interrupts how I see is not itself an interpretation, nor, for that matter, is what I see now. Likewise, what I see under a change of aspect does not arise because I have placed what I saw before in doubt. If I see the sigma or the duck, I see the sigma or the duck. When I see the M or the rabbit, I see the M or the rabbit. These are not interpretations, not choices about how to see something (as if it were up for grabs), and not subject to doubt (as if I needed grounds for what I see). One might say, upon seeing the rabbit after one has been seeing the duck, 'I am seeing this rabbit as a rabbit', or 'Now that I see a rabbit I wonder if it was really a duck.' But that has to do with the language game in which seeing something as something is in play, that is, with the context in which one sees the object, not something in the object itself.

If seeing drag occasions critical thinking about gender, it is not because, being the 'hyperbolic' instantiation of gender norms, to cite Butler, drag 'brings into relief what is, after all, determined only in relation to the hyperbolic: the understated, taken-for-granted quality of heterosexual performativity' (Butler 1993: 237). For one thing, my ability to call into question any particular gender norm is parasitic on others that are provisionally beyond question. For another, there is nothing in a drag performance itself that guarantees I will see drag and gender as the same kind of object – see, that is, the drag performance as the display of what gender really is (that is, performative). It is just as likely that I will see drag when I see drag and see gender when I see gender – just as I might see the picture-rabbit, then the picture-duck, but never any necessary connection between those two objects. To see drag, after all, is to know that gender is being performed. Even if one agreed that drag incites the act of interpretation (under what conditions?), which in turn gives rise (in whom?) to critical reflection about gender norms, it does not follow that gender is like drag or that the latter exposes the fact that 'the gendered body . . . has no ontological status apart from the various acts which constitute its reality' (Butler 1990: 136).

The conditions of doubt cannot be formulated as a universalisable pro-position (Wittgenstein 1969: §§ 24, 54, 125, 247; see Law 1988: 321). It is possible, for example, to conceive a situation in which a drag performance raised existential questions about gender identity for one person, confirmed what a second already thought, and was consumed as a bawdy spectacle by a third. Whether we find ourselves raising doubts involves broad questions of context concealed by the focus on a generic object (like drag or gender or woman) viewed by an individual subject. There will be contexts in which the word *woman,* for example, will not raise questions for me (for example, when I describe to my friend, a woman, the woman sitting next to me on the plane), and there will be contexts in which that same word will raise such questions (when I hear my male colleague describe the same woman). Whether the doubts we do raise have any critical resonance beyond the merely subjective 'it-seems-to-me', moreover, involves broad questions of publicity that the focus on a generic object (for example, drag as an artistic performance with inherent subversive effects) tends to occlude.

Knowing the world, changing the world

It is the spectators and their judgements that create the public realm in which (what Butler calls) performatives have critical political effects, or not. To see this, however, will require rethinking feminist critique outside the frame both of the subject question (in which the idea of the public hardly arises, save as the enforcer of a norm) and the sceptical problematic (in which the idea of critique is synonymous with the use of the understanding and the application of concepts in a pervasive practice of interpretation, 'the essential possibility of deviant cases', and the ability to raise radical doubts). Following Wittgenstein, it is not that we cannot doubt something, as if someone or something prevented us from doing so, but that under ordinary circumstances we do not doubt it. Certainty is a doing, not a knowing: 'Why do I not satisfy myself that I have two feet when I want to get up from a chair? There is no why. I simply don't. This is how I act', writes Wittgenstein (Wittgenstein 1969: §148). A day may come when I formulate my having two feet as an empirical proposition in need of ver-ification, but within my present frame of reference I just get up and walk. The certainty expressed in statements like 'I have two hands' is fundamental to Wittgenstein's account of rule-following. There is a way of applying basic concepts that is subject neither to doubt nor justification, as it would be on a truth-conditional account. When I say 'I have two hands',' this judgment can be neither justified nor questioned for there is nothing more certain than my having two hands on the basis of which I could judge. One can imagine a language game in which doubting one's hands played a role, but that would always be in relation to a practice and thus to a context. Witt-genstein does not rule out the possibility of doubting something like the existence of one's feet or hands, but instead struggles with the question of what conditions would have to obtain for our most deeply held beliefs to be invalidated (Wittgenstein 1969: §§ 96, 97, 99; see Law 1988: 322).

In the process, however, he radically questions our (sceptically inflected) understanding of what a doubt is and under what conditions it can be raised (for example, doubting the existence of the external world or, for that matter, doubting women while sitting alone in your study writing feminist theory). What has been at issue all along, after all, is not whe-ther gender conventions are certain in the sense of being permanently beyond all dispute, but what disputing them would entail. Wittgenstein's remarks about two-thirds of the way through *On Certainty* indicate the practice of doubting I have in mind. 'After dismissing specific doubts as incoherent or unimaginable', as Jules Law observes, 'he [Wittgenstein] almost inevitably turns around and asks if after all they are not imaginable in some bizarre way' (Law 1988: 322). These doubts include everything from questioning whether he really lives in England to his name and his sex. They are raised not in the problematic form of critical reflection I have been discussing, but as imaginative exercises that involve trying to see from the perspective of another person: be it a king who believes he can make rain, a man who thinks his front door opens onto an abyss, or someone who claims he has no body (Zerilli 1998: 444–46; Wittgenstein 1969: §§ 92, 516). Something similar, I want to suggest, can be said about Butler's critical account of drag.

We *may* well see the performative character of gender when we see drag, just as Butler holds. That, however, requires not – not in the first place – the critical use of the faculty of concepts that allows us to doubt the existence of gender as 'real', but something else: the productive faculty of figuration or presentation, namely, imagination.

Radical imagination and the figures of the newly thinkable

Castoriadis's account of radical imagination and Wittgenstein's critique of rule-following are valuable resources for developing a freedom-centred feminism that would take leave of the false security of epistemology and venture out into the world of action, where we simply cannot know what we do, at least not in the ways required by a means–ends conception of politics. Such feminism would be based on the faculty of presentation (imagination) and the creation of figures of the newly thinkable rather than the faculty *of* concepts (understanding) and the ability to subsume particulars under rules. Most important, such feminism would emerge as a historically situated and collective exercise of freedom, an exercise through which we change the conditions under which things are given to us; alter, that is, the relationship of the necessary and the contingent.

This alteration neither involves nor requires attaining an external stand-point from which everything might be seen as non-necessary, contingent. Rather, it rests on the factical character of human freedom, the capacity to wrest something new from an objective state of affairs without being com-pelled to do so by a norm or rule. Changes in the meaning of gender, in other words, emerge not through the sceptical insight that gender as such is contingent and can therefore he changed (for example, we have the theory, now we can act), but through the projection of a word like women into a new context, where it is taken up by others in ways we can neither predict nor control. It is this act, and not any intrinsic stability (realism) or instability (deconstruction) in language itself, which has the potential power to change every political, worldly constellation.

As important as it is to dismantle the political pretensions of epistemol-ogy that have a way of creeping back into our thinking even after the lin-guistic turn, then, a freedom-centred feminism needs more than that. It needs also to affirm the transformative character of human practice in the absence of any external guarantees. To yield the armour of epistemology to the uncertainties of action, Arendt might say, is to find oneself face to face with the abyss of freedom. There is no objectively correct way of acting politically – say, speaking in the name of women – any more than there is of following a rule. There are no 'rules laid out to infinity', no 'line in space' and no theory that could trace it, which, if only we would follow them, lead from the oppression of the past to the liberation of the present and into the freedom of the future. Terms of political discourse like women are not fixed by something that transcends their use in actual contexts, as the gender realist would have it, but neither are they intrinsically uncertain by virtue of the ever-present possibility of failure that supposedly inheres in language as the very condition of language itself, as Butler suggests. Rather, they are created as meaningful (or not) in and through political action – that is, what *we* hold, *we* *say*. This insight suggests a less speculative and sceptical approach to feminist politics and a rather different way of thinking about claims to women as an irreducible element in such a politics. A freedom-centred feminism, after all, is concerned not with knowing (that there are women) as such, but with doing – with world-building, beginning anew.

Note

1 Readers will recognise in this anecdote the pathos of third-wave debates about the category of women. As I argue below, these debates took for granted the idea that one can doubt the existence of women as the sceptic doubts the existence of empirical objects such as tables and chairs.

Part II
Feminism and philosophy

4 'French theory' goes to France

Trouble *dans le genre* and 'materialist'
feminism – a conversation *manqué*

Lisa Jane Disch

Judith Butler's *Gender Trouble* appeared in its first French translation in spring 2005. It comes as something of a 'delayed broadcast', as Eric Fassin puts it in his preface to the volume (2005c: 5). Not only did the French-language edition take fifteen years to appear, it was preceded by translations of four of Butler's later works.[1] From the perspective of an American feminist scholar the delay is puzzling. *Gender Trouble*, of all Butler's work, is the one that we think of as the most French. Teresa de Lauretis attributes this impression to a clever marketing strategy that sold Butler's text to a nearly worldwide audience as a 'feminist intervention in the field of French philosophy' (2005: 57). French intellectuals regard the book as typically American. *Gender Trouble* stands as an exemplary work of what they have taken to calling 'French Theory', a moniker they leave in English, capitalise and put in quotes to signal that it is 'a creation *ex nihilo* of the American university' (Cusset 2003: 36).

Although Cusset seems to endorse this intention by calling it a 'creative misunderstanding', the overall tenor of the debate suggests otherwise (2003: 15). The implication seems to be that whatever we Americans do with French texts is merely 'French', which is to say citational through and through. What we have taken for an exotic import is nothing but home-grown pretension. A 'body of comments by Anglo-American writers' who insist on '"putting in dialogue" people who have nothing to say to each other' (Delphy 1995: 198, 214).

Fassin himself broaches the matter of 'French Theory' by posing an avowedly indelicate question: why 'import American thought in reverse – in this case, why translate Butler?' (2005: 6–7). His answer is that her fifteen-year old critique made a timely intervention into a debate provoked by two struggles in the French National Assembly that brought the 'presumption of hetero-sexuality' to light (2005: 7). One of these was to recognise gay and lesbian domestic partnerships or PaCS (*Pacte civil de solidarité*), and the other was to institute gender parity in the legislature (2005: 12). That French con-servatives, including women, had come out in support of parity in the name of an essentialist ideology of sexual difference and complementarity created a favourable discursive context in which to recognise PaCS but accord them

second-class status in comparison with 'families'. Whereas the PaCS legislation did grant *select* benefits to same-sex (and opposite-sex) domestic
partners, it also delineated a set of privileges exclusive to 'families' – access
to fertility treatment, adoption services, French residency and citizenship
(Raissiguier 2002). In light of these struggles, Fassin recommends Butler to
her French audience as a queer theorist for their times.

Certainly Butler has influenced the development of queer theory in
France. What is striking is that Fassin says little of her relationship to feminism there, particularly as Butler steadfastly maintains that she is first and
foremost a 'feminist theorist' whose 'commitments to feminism are probably
my primary commitments' (1994: 32). Stevi Jackson, a British scholar who
has written extensively on French materialist feminist theory, is one of a few
feminist scholars to address this question. Her verdict may explain Fassin's
silence. She charges that Butler's 'radical deconstruction of gender ... owes
much to materialist feminism without itself being materialist' (1995: 13). To
Jackson, Butler has done something more egregious than inventing 'French
Theory': she *re-invents* French materialist feminism without proper
acknowledgement.

This is a charge worth exploring. If Jackson is correct, Butler is not quite
the innovator that she and Fassin believe her to be. There is already an
indigenous body of work that, to recall de Lauretis, makes 'a feminist
intervention into the field of French philosophy'. Had the preface to the
French version of *Gender Trouble* been written by a French materialist
feminist, she might have posed a question even more indelicate than that of
Fassin. It might have gone something like this: who needs Butler when we
already have Monique Wittig?

Butler trouble

Butler herself is well aware of *Gender Trouble*'s reputation among critics of
'French Theory'. In the preface she wrote in June 1999 for the tenth-
anniversary edition, she engaged the charge. She characterised the text as
being 'rooted in "French Theory"' (1999a: x). She admitted that it combines
the works of authors who 'had few alliances with one another' and would
'rarely, if ever' be read together by French intellectuals. She conceded that
this 'intellectual promiscuity' comes off 'precisely as American', and puts it
'at a significant distance from France and from the life of theory in France'
(1999a: x).

What to make of this? Is it a confession? To whom would it be addressed?
Does Butler mean to apologise to American feminists for having sold her
work to them under a false brand? Could she be making amends to a
hoped-for French readership (at the time she wrote the preface there was no
French translation in sight)? I would be tempted to take Butler's preface
straightforwardly, as an act of contrition for posing as a 'French Theorist' if
not for a couple of telling details.

First, the very phrase 'French Theory' cites a French protocol. The capital letters and quotation marks are the French way to make fun of Americans who set themselves apart by citing what they pass off as French. It is noteworthy that Butler follows this protocol in the tenth-anniversary preface because she does not do so in the preface she wrote eight months earlier for the 1999 paperback reissue of her dissertation book, *Subjects of Desire: Hegelian Reflections in Twentieth-Century France.*

There she speaks of her intellectual debt to French thinkers without quotation marks, capitals, or apology. If anything, she apologises for the fact that this text was not quite French enough, having been published 'too early, pressured by the job market', as Butler was just becoming 'open to French theory in a way that I mainly resisted while at Yale' (1999b: viii). Looking back on her too-hasty dissertation revisions from the position of enunciation that *Gender Trouble* had accorded her, Butler instructs her readers that the chapters she added on Deleuze, Lacan and Foucault were written before she was 'quite prepared to make the theoretical moves' that a 'more complex consideration' of those authors would require (1999b: viii). That sophistication would come 'in the writing of *Gender Trouble*', which this preface recommends as the achievement of a legitimate intellectual approach based on 'critical theory in the French vein' (1999b: viii).

Just one year later, can Butler have meant to mock that same work as no longer French theory but 'French Theory'? Can 'critical theory in the French vein' have been demoted to 'apparent Francocentrism' in the space of twelve months? What if she is citing 'French Theory' *as* French *argot*? This would mean that she is actually speaking French (even though the words appear to be English). By picking up the French protocol, Butler demonstrated not that she was 'distant' from French intellectual debates but that she was *au courant*.

Second, even if Butler cites the French, she refuses their terms of debate. She does not concede that *Gender Trouble* invents 'French Theory' but says that it is *'rooted'* in it (1999b: x; emphasis added). The very notion that intellectual traditions cannot be remade outside their contexts of origin rests on an academic nationalism to which the French themselves do not subscribe – at least not when it is they who do the importing. The career of Hegel in twentieth-century France is a case in point. Just imagine how a French intellectual would react to a German *Existenzphilosoph* who put French 'existentialism' in scare quotes.

Butler sees herself engaged in what French intellectuals have also practised: the invention of theory 'at the site where cultural horizons meet, where the demand for translation is acute and its promise of success, uncertain' (1999b: ix). Her tenth-anniversary preface does not apologise for *Gender Trouble* but affirms it as a work 'of cultural translation' that brought 'poststructuralist theory ... to bear on US theories of gender and the political predicaments of *feminism*' (1999b: viii–ix; emphasis added). This answer, a powerful riposte to the first charge, recalls the second to mind.

The invention that Butler does claim – a critical approach to gender influenced by twentieth-century French philosophy – Jackson would say that materialist feminists had already patented.

Troubling materialism

> The category of sex is the political category that founds society as heterosexual . . .

Monique Wittig (1992: 5)

This statement, from the 1976 essay 'The Straight Mind', is one of Wittig's striking contributions to what Christine Delphy was the first to call 'materialist feminism', a rich body of thought created in the 1980s by feminist scholars who had participated in the French Women's Liberation Movement. Materialist feminism is distinctive because: it was produced by participants in a collective who read, re-stated, and built on one another's work; it defied, precisely by virtue of this collaborative way of working, the enervating (and commonplace American) separations of 'theoretical' v. 'empirical' scholarship, academic theory v. political practice. This was scholarship written to advance, and *to be read by* participants in, a political movement. Most important, French materialist feminism made a distinctive contribution to the field of political theory that has been largely overlooked.

Wittig put it best in that 1976 essay when she wrote: 'thought based on the primacy of difference is the thought of domination' (Wittig 1992: 4). Although this insight has nothing like the currency of the catchphrase that emerged from US feminism – 'the personal is political' – to my mind it not only rivals but exceeds that phrase in critical power. The French materialist feminists should be heralded for analysing women's oppression not in terms of sexual difference but *against* it. This is not to say that they were indifferent to difference (as they were charged by some feminist academics in the United States who misrecognised them as 'liberal' feminists). They analysed sexual oppression together with racial oppression as exemplifying the dynamics whereby modern hierarchal societies produce 'natural' groups.

This put their feminism in stark contrast to the first round of feminist social science in the US academy, which presumed gender 'difference' as an empirical object of study. At the same time as American feminists in the social sciences were busy documenting the differences between men's and women's psychologies, ethical orientations, public v. private spheres of influence, and 'ways of knowing', the French materialists were calling into question the very notion that sexual difference can be taken as fact. They understood this very idea to be the effect rather than the origin of gender oppression. Their feminism was, in Delphy's words, 'first and foremost non-naturalist' (2001: 7).

To these feminists in France, materialist analysis of sex difference (and later, gender) was not about women, not their 'difference', or 'interests', or 'ethic'. On the contrary, as Delphy explained, 'subjection should be put at the heart of the analysis of the situation of subjugated persons and categories, as opposed to their other characteristics, physical characteristics that do not explain subjection, or other characteristics that are generally the result of subjection ... emphasis should be placed *on the opposition* and not on each of the terms' (2001: 25–26; emphasis added). A peculiar materialism indeed! These French feminists began not by affirming the 'reality' of women's different labour and experience but by doubting that those differences 'are *there*, anterior to their social use' (2001: 13). They set themselves against the very things that US feminists' focus on personal 'experience' often encouraged: romanticising (straight middle-class) womanhood, resurrecting empiricism, and feeding a fundamentalist attachment to sexual difference in feminism's name (Grant 1993). This was materialist analysis premised on a discursive conception of power as consisting of a 'relationship between *division* and *hierarchy*' (Delphy 1993: 1). For Delphy, as for Laclau and Mouffe, the social is a field without positive terms where 'to be something is always not to be something else' (Laclau and Mouffe 1985: 128). Difference is not the 'substrate' of hierarchy but its *effect* (Delphy 1993: 27).

The insight about difference that Wittig summed up with the economy of words that is her signature did eventually reach American shores – but not as a distinctively feminist export. It was heralded as a tenet of contemporary French 'postmodern' or 'poststructuralist' philosophy that ingenious Yankees took credit for putting to work in feminist politics. Jane Gallop, who by her own admission was one of the most entrepreneurial, has reflected on the way that American feminist literary critics made their reputations by doing 'French-style literary theory' which 'by 1981 or so ... had become the most prestigious, the "highest" discourse in American literary studies' (1992: 47). This infuriated Delphy and her colleagues, not only because they were not properly credited by their Anglo-American counterparts but also because they were cast has having missed the boat that launched from their own shores!

In effect, academic feminists in the US put French theoretical insights to work to divide French feminists into two camps. There were the psychoanalytically influenced thinkers who qualified (in Jane Gallop's words) as 'peculiarly French' (1992: 41). And then there were the legatees of Beauvoir who were presumed to advocate equality in the American style: equality posing as universal that actually privileged all things masculine and denigrated the feminine. Gallop explains that what seemed so 'French' about '*écriture feminine*' at the time was precisely that 'rather than vying for token status, trying to be recognized as good as men (and thus "different from most other women"), "French feminism" claimed that Everywoman already could produce the high culturally privileged writing' (1992: 46). In hindsight, Gallop acknowledges that 'those of us American feminist academics who were clever enough or lucky enough to be associated with "French feminism"' made tokens of themselves: '[we] were rewarded and accepted as literary theorists: "encouraged to see [ourselves] as different from most other [feminist critics], as exceptionally talented and deserving; and to separate [ourselves] from the wider [feminist] condition"' (1992: 47).[2]

Delphy saw it differently. She charged Anglo-American scholars who represented *écriture feminine* as peculiarly 'French' with selling the intellectual equivalent of snake oil: this was essentialism 'made in USA' lent cachet by an exotic brand (Kraus 2005: 171). As Cynthia Kraus has argued, this construction could work only because Delphy refused to acknowledge the existence in France of self-identified feminist proponents of 'difference feminism' (2005: 174).[3] That first marketing ploy was so successful that it paved the way for Butler to perform what Delphy saw as an even more intricate sleight of hand: to deploy one American construct ('French Theory') to discredit the essentialism of another one ('French Feminism'), as if that essentialism had been French all along (Delphy 1995: 210–13; Varikas 1993). For the select American feminists who can master this move, the pay-off is lucrative. It is they who become 'peculiarly French' in contrast to both American feminists of a lesser academic pedigree and to French feminists who have let their intellectual wardrobes fall out of fashion.

In an impassioned polemic that came out in 1995 in *Yale French Studies*, Delphy responded to these moves by protesting that the 'invention of French Feminism' is sheer American 'imperialism' (1995: 192). This charge probably took more than a few US feminists by surprise, as it was they who were feeling intellectually colonised by French philosophy. Many anthologies of feminist work produced from the mid-1980s to late 1990s registered the rifts that were created within feminist and women's studies by the advent of French critical philosophy.[4] These concerns found expression in the debates that took place under the rubric of 'feminism v. postmodernism', a framing that, at its most paranoid, positions US feminists as being silenced by high theory that arrives from outside (Alarcón 1990; Christian 1987).

Delphy's charge repositions feminists in France, specifically the *Questions Féministes* collective, as having been silenced and even defrauded by a feminism that is the illegitimate offspring of 'French Theory'. She charges that the need to invent that tradition inaugurated an essentialist way of reading so that in the writings of US scholars, 'French authors – male or female, feminist or not – [were] almost never compared to their Anglo-American counterparts, however similar, but only to other French writers, however different' (1995: 215). With Delphy's prompting, I mean to return in earnest to the indelicate question I put in the mouths of the French materialists earlier in this essay: Who needs Butler when we already have Wittig?

Dangerous liaisons

The Women's Liberation Movement (MLF) in France erupted slightly after that in the US and was, in fact, named by the French media by analogy to its counterpart (Kaufmann-McCall 1983: 283). The French movement may have started later but, theoretically speaking, it was more advanced. The MLF explored a 'materialist' approach from the start, whereas US feminist academics waited until the 1990s for the emergence of a 'non-naturalist' feminism. It was not Wittig but Butler who cleared our palate of the cloying aftertaste of 'difference' feminism. We may think we are indebted to *Gender Trouble* for showing us that 'sex ... [has] been gender from the start' (Butler 1990: 113). Wittig and her colleagues would say that materialist feminists got there first. Already in 1981 they were demonstrating that 'what we take for the cause or origin of oppression is in fact only the *mark* imposed by the oppressor' (Wittig 1992: 11).

And Butler would say that Wittig is correct – at least in part. Butler acknowledges Wittig as a predecessor. In fact, she uses Wittig's powerful statement – 'the category of sex is the political category that founds society as heterosexual' – as an epigraph to the first chapter of *Gender Trouble*. Butler credits Wittig with 'delineat[ing] the performative construction of gender within the material practices of culture [by] disputing the temporality of those explanations that would confuse "cause" with "result"' (1990: 25). She applauds Wittig's reference to the idea of sex as 'mark' (which Wittig attributes explicitly to Collette Guillaumin's 1977 essay 'Race and Nature: The System of Marks' (Guillaumin 1988)) as 'a phrase that suggests the intertextual space that links Wittig with Foucault' (1990: 25). She even goes so far as to attribute one of her own signature phrases – that sex is 'gender from the start' – to Wittig's article 'One is Not Born a Woman'.

Even as Butler extends one hand to Wittig as an ally, she pushes her away with the other. There may be intimations of a theory of performative subjectivity in her work, but Wittig needs a Butler to point them out to her. Left to her own devices, Wittig defines 'the feminine' as 'an "attribute" of a gender', subscribes to a voluntarist and instrumental view of language, and succumbs to an 'existential-materialist' predisposition to 'presume the subject, the person, to have a presocial and pregendered integrity' (1990: 26, 29).

What to make of Butler's intellectual relationship to Wittig? It is tempting to read the two as having little in common, Wittig being a thinker whose radicalism is overshadowed by her commitments to humanism. Nancy Fraser casts Wittig in these terms. She situates her on the 'equality' side of the 'difference' debate that preoccupied US feminist academics in the 1980s for her 'feminist commitment to universalism and ... negative view of difference' (1992: 7). De Lauretis has called attention to the 'paradox' in the fact that 'Wittig, who had first proposed the disappearance of women, was herself cast in the essentialist, passé, or humanist camp' (2005: 56). Although Butler recognises more ambiguity in Wittig's relation to humanism than does Fraser, ultimately she faults Wittig for the paradox that de Lauretis would pin on her. Butler concludes that Wittig only 'appears to dispute the metaphysics of substance', while nonetheless retaining the 'humanist subject, the individual, as the metaphysical locus of agency'

(1990: 25). Is this a cynical gesture, an erasure of Wittig that allows Butler to make room for her own originality? Or is there some fruitful disagreement between them?

Linda Zerilli (2005) would say that there is such a disagreement, and that she would side with Wittig. She pits the two against each other as exemplars of feminism as a 'skeptical practice' (Butler) and as a 'rhetorical practice' (Wittig) (Zerilli 2005: 91). She assesses Butler's tendentious reading of Wittig as symptomatic of Butler's own preoccupation with the problem of 'epistemology' that plagued academic feminism from the mid-1980s throughout the 1990s. This claim is surprising because Butler is nothing if not adamant that there is no ground beyond power from which to critique it. Nonetheless, Zerilli contends that Butler shares one assumption with the feminists that she so powerfully criticised. They, who were 'steadfast in rejecting as ideological any claim to know the universal subject or to define its interests', nonetheless could not help defining the project of feminism as a project of knowledge; they optimistically sought 'objective criteria according to which political claims could be defined, articulated, and justified' (2005: 37). Butler, as Zerilli describes her, inverts the paradigm. Hers is not an optimism but a radical scepticism that treats 'sexual difference as if it were only a matter of truth and practices of knowing' and, so, imagines that the first task of theory must be to 'critique ... our customary ways of acting and thinking' (2005: 207, nn. 24, 39).

Zerilli counters that scepticism cannot be viable as a political practice without exactly the sort of 'external standpoint' that Butler's anti-foundationalism disallows: a position outside of *meaning* (i.e. 'human *praxis*') 'from which to see cultural artifacts and practices like sex and gender as wholly constructed' (2005: 72). Zerilli contends that Butler expects drag to work exactly this way. She deploys it as an 'instance of the strange' that, by making visible the rules that we follow 'when we do gender', takes the 'form of an empirical proposition that gives the lie to an established truth like naturalized sex difference' (2005: 47, 61). Zerilli's point is that feminists cannot expect to pry sex and gender apart by the force of doubt alone. To act as if this were so (which she accuses Butler of doing) is just as typical of what she calls 'feminism in the age of science' as the preoccupation with epistemology that Butler so thoroughly rejected (2005: 207, n. 24).

What disappoints Zerilli about Butler's recourse to drag and other strange figures is that scepticism is not what feminist politics needs. However persuasively we feminist theorists manage to establish that sex difference is unknowable as an object, however well we demonstrate that it 'exists' only under specific conditions of gender domination, sexual difference will continue to count for something. In the world we twenty-first century feminists inhabit, it is still 'rooted in relatively stable modes of human praxis' (2005: 72). What it takes to counter this is not 'an appropriately denaturalized position from which to doubt what we think we see but *an alternative figure of the thinkable*' that 'offers a new way of seeing that allows us to gain a different perspective on an empirical object that has not (necessarily) changed' (2005: 62). This is precisely the contribution of Wittig, whom Zerilli credits with 'lead[ing] before the eyes (with images and metaphors) the radical reformulation of the social contract' (2005: 70). As Zerilli reads her, Wittig puts not 'sex into doubt' but *doubt* into doubt (2005: 71).

Zerilli finds this achievement in Wittig's difficult *Les Guérillères*, a utopian novel that Zerilli contends, taking her lead from Wittig, has been frequently misinterpreted, especially by its English-speaking readers who suffered the unfortunate translation of a central term. The novel depicts the overthrow (*renversement*) of a social order founded on the patriarchal social contract. Although Zerilli emphasises that Wittig distinguishes her work from others of this genre, such as *Herland* or *Woman on the Edge of Time*, by her 'refusal' to install a feminist utopia 'in its place', many readers assimilated her work to this genre (Zerilli 2005: 80). Christine Fauré (who, of course, read the text in its original language) characterised *Les Guérillères* as crystallising the 'desire' for 'a new utopia: a society of women possessing the distinctive features of a homogeneous and harmonious community' (1981: 31).

Zerilli perceptively argues that Wittig's use of irony to mock the communitarian impulse rendered her book subject to such misreading. There are, for example, the 'feminaries' that Wittig introduces to satirise the desire within feminism for founding figures and founding documents. Documents of the early women's liberation struggle composed of 'rhapsodies on the female genitals', and 'playful retellings of the dominant myths of the heterosexual order from a minority point of view', the younger characters mock the 'feminalies' as movement juvenilia. Zerilli emphasises: 'Once necessary to an earlier generation of *guérillères*, the feminaries are read aloud for sheer amusement by a later generation ... for they represent an inverted and outdated symbolic practice' (2005: 81). In light of Zerilli's reading, the passage that Fauré cites in support of her own looks like a joke on exactly these lines. It describes the *guérillères* forming a society of women: 'Moved by a common impulse, we all stood to seek gropingly the even flow, the exultant unity of the Internationale. An *aged grizzled old woman* sobbed like a child. Alexandra Kollontai could hardly restrain her tears' (Fauré 1981: 83–84, citing Wittig 1971: 144; emphasis added). Zerilli would read this not as Wittig's endorsing 'the exultant unity of the Internationale' but mocking the older generation of *guérillères* who understood their struggle in such 'outdated' unitary terms.

This mockery is the destructive moment of *renversement*. Its refigurative moment comes in one of the most misunderstood tactics of the text – Wittig's repetition of 'an entirely ordinary pronoun *elles*' (2005: 89). Normally, *elles* signifies in opposition to *ils*. It stands for a particular collective plurality, a 'they' composed exclusively of women. By contrast, *ils* can stand, variously, for a collective plurality that is male, mixed gender, or that has no literal members at all but is abstract and authoritative, the 'they' of 'they say'. Zerilli explains that lacking the 'lexical equivalent for *elles*', the translator chose 'the women' (2005: 88). That word choice so obscured what Wittig was trying to do that she wrote an essay to correct it. Wittig explained that she meant the pronoun *elles* to stand not in opposition to *ils* but in its place. Her aim was not to 'feminize the world' but 'to universalize the point of view of *elles*' (Wittig 1992: 85). *Elles*, which Wittig calls the 'axis of *Les Guérillères*', would not simply turn sexual difference on its head; it sought to make 'the categories of sex obsolete in language' by violating the custom that limits *elles* to a collective female subject while permitting *ils* to stand for collective public authority in general (Wittig 1992: 84–85).

Zerilli underscores how this 'strange use of an entirely ordinary pronoun' could be so powerful by linking it to another important figure in Wittig's repertoire: the Trojan Horse. This is a simile for radical writing that does not aim to 'represent ... the minority point of view' (like the 'feminaries') but, as Wittig herself explained in 'The Mark of Gender' (the essay she wrote in 1985 in response to the English translation of *Les Guérillères*), to alter the 'system of reference' that positions it as particularised and minor (Wittig 1992: 79). What Wittig insists on with the Trojan Horse is that a radical work 'will be situated in the ordinary', not – as Zerilli maintains both feminist epistemology and Butler would have it – in an outside or strange viewpoint (2005: 77). Zerilli explains, 'recognition of the ordinary (the familiar forms of the horse) is what allows the strange to do its subversive work. Otherwise it remains strange (an off color, outsized, barbaric mass of wood to which no one would lay claim), nothing more' (Zerilli 2005: 79). This is the signal difference between Wittig's 'rhetorical practice' and Butler's 'skeptical practice'. Wittig demonstrates that it is not necessary to 'first reveal that sex is contingent and then act to change it' but that it is only 'through the ingenious practice of action that we alter – and become aware, really, of the possibility of altering – the relation of the necessary and the contingent' (Zerilli 2005: 91). In short, 'Wittig does not try to get outside heterosexuality – there is no outside, as she recognizes – but to disrupt it from within' (Zerilli 2005: 208, n. 28).

Does my mind look straight in this?

Few of Wittig's readers would agree. Not only Butler, but also many who are sympathetic to the materialist feminist project perceive the very project of Wittig's political essays to be to search for a standpoint outside heterosexuality from which to destabilise it. The very paragraph in 'The Mark of Gender' from which Zerilli draws her reading of '*elles*' continues with Wittig declaring that she 'set up *elles* in the text as the absolute subject of the world ... I wanted to produce a shock for the reader entering a text in which *elles* by its unique presence constitutes an assault, yes, even for female readers ... Word by Word, *elles* establishes itself as a sovereign subject' (Wittig 1992: 85). There are clearly *two* moves here which bespeak a telling ambiguity in Wittig's work. The first, which Zerilli so perceptively explicates, is that *'elles'* is a Trojan Horse. The second, which Zerilli glosses over (despite quoting the paragraph in its entirety), is that *'elles'* is a sovereign standpoint from which to call heterosexuality into question. *Contra* Zerilli, Wittig not only seeks such a position, she believes that she has found it.

Witness her signal polemic, 'The Straight Mind', published in 1981, whose infamous last line seems to declare its independence from all things heterosexual: 'Lesbians are not women' (1992: 32). It is too easy to read this piece as a manifesto – a political summons calling all who oppose sexual domination to unite as lesbians. Granted, it may well have been heard that way, especially given that it was first delivered orally at the Modern Language Association meeting in 1980. And it was certainly read that way, given that it was first published in a February 1980 issue of *Questions Féministes* that was devoted to the question of 'political' lesbianism (Duchen 1984: 26). This was not an abstract question. The exchange touched off a passionate debate that continued for over a year, and would ultimately divide the 'Radical Lesbians of Jussieu', who regarded 'radical lesbianism as a political position and heterosexuality as a patriarchal strategy', from members of the *Questions Féministes* collective who resisted this move as an 'insidious and extremely dangerous reversal of "the personal is political"' (Duchen 1984: 31, 34). Wittig sided with the Radical Lesbians, breaking with the part of the original *Questions Féministes* collective (including Delphy and Beauvoir) that went on to found *Nouvelle Questions Féministes* in 1981 (Leonard and Adkins 1996: 2, 20, n. 4).

Can Wittig's 'Straight Mind' be no more than a manifesto? Not if there is any merit to Zerilli's reading (and I think there is). There is no Trojan Horse radicalism in calling a minority to ride the hobby horse of identity politics. A richer interpretation suggests itself in light of the insights Zerilli draws from *Les Guérillères*: that 'The Straight Mind' is a similar effort to 'make the categories of sex obsolete in language' (Wittig 1992: 85). This would make it an anti-manifesto, not a summons to unite in terms of a common identity but a call to effect a common divestment. The idea is to 'break off the heterosexual contract' by rupturing the connection between identity and sexual difference.

Wittig addresses this call to distinct parts of her audience in turn, first to 'lesbians and gay men' and then to 'women'. To the first, she charges, 'if we, as lesbians and gay men, continue to speak of ourselves and to conceive of ourselves as women and as men, we are instrumental in maintaining heterosexuality' (1992: 30). Is this scepticism? Does Wittig expect that people can simply doubt who they are? No. It is the prelude to an 'alternative figure of the thinkable'. Wittig puts this forward by a radical disarticulation of the man/woman conceptual pair. She interrogates her listeners: 'Can we redeem *slave*? Can we redeem *nigger, negress*? How is *woman* different? Will we continue to write *white, master, man*?' (1992: 30).

On its face, the question is offensive. Can Wittig really mean to elide the relations of oppression that distinguish 'woman' from 'slave'? Can she, a citizen of a colonial power, be unaware of white women's participation in racism and colonialism? Perhaps this is metonymy, not metaphor; the link is associative rather than comparative. Wittig is trying to displace gender – the man/woman couplet – from a sexual frame of reference that nature is said to justify and resituate it in a context of oppression that nothing can redeem. To do this, she must decouple man/woman because insofar as these two terms are wedded to each other (as it were), they cannot but naturalise sexual difference and normalise heterosexuality. Their pairing inevitably suggests that sex grounds gender, that opposites attract, and that hetero-sexuality is not just a social norm but a natural mandate. Wittig proposes a rival chain of association – slave, nigger, negress woman: white master man – that cannot but shock the 'straight mind' because it engenders a linguistic universe in which 'woman' calls to mind not 'man' but 'slave' and where 'man' leads directly to 'master'. Wouldn't it be something if 'woman' called forth the same panic as 'nigger'?

In the infamous closing paragraph, Wittig turns to address women, spe-cifically feminists. She launches an argument that could have been the model for the opening pages of *Gender Trouble*:

> What is woman? Panic, general alarm for an active defense. Frankly, it is a problem that lesbians do not have because of a change of perspective, and it would be incorrect to say that lesbians associate, make love, live with women, for 'woman' has meaning only in heterosexual systems of thought and heterosexual economic systems. Lesbians are not women.
>
> (Wittig 1992: 32)

This pronouncement can be read to operate both literally and symbolically. Speaking literally, lesbians are not women because they do not fulfil tradi-tional gender roles. Speaking symbolically, they are not 'gendered' because 'lesbian' does not call 'man' to mind. Wittig goes for shock value again in suggesting that *neither should it make us think of 'woman'*. Her objective, once again, is to *displace* the (hetero)sexual frame of reference, not merely to shift it from the axis of difference (man/woman) to that of sameness (woman/woman).

'Lesbians are not women.' This is to say that 'lesbian' is not legible in the terms of a social and symbolic economy of sexual difference. Lesbians nei-ther violate the imperative to identify with the one sex and desire the other nor conform to it. 'Lesbian' is neither the One (same) nor the other (dif-ferent). If a lesbian is a Trojan Horse, then Wittig's pronouncement – 'Les-bians are not women' – functions like *'elles'*. It concludes her address with a ruse, an enigmatic suggestion that cloaks a war machine in the guise of a tribute. Can Wittig help it if her audience took up this suggestion in the most straightforward possible way, as a separatist call to arms?

'Lesbians are not women.' By what discursive alchemy should this come to mean, '(Only) Lesbians are feminists'? How does *being* something come to be prerequisite to *doing* something? By the alchemy of what John Mowitt describes as the 'essentially nostalgic' equation of agency with 'the agent – that is, an entity capable of asserting its will, or acting in accord with its desire, in any and all circumstances' (2002: 51, 56). This conflation makes 'being' prerequisite to 'doing'. Mowitt calls it nostalgic because it is the move of theorist who cannot accept the 'theoretical and political advances' since 1968 that have shown voluntarist theories to be inadequate to the task of analysing and fostering political change, and who retreats 'in quest of an entity who can make decisions about political choices and be responsible for them' (Mowitt 2002: 51).

Wittig both is and is not on such a quest. As Zerilli has demonstrated, the power of *'elles'* was its 'combining two existing concepts that are not normally related (for example, the feminine gender and the universal voice)' to make possible a new position from which to speak and act (2005: 91). This was undercut by the translator's assumption that it named an agent. Yet, this assumption was not entirely unwarranted. Wittig herself designated *'elles'* to be the 'absolute subject of the world'. I would not say, with Butler, that this proves that Wittig clings to the 'humanist subject' as the 'locus of agency' (1990: 25). As I have argued, Wittig disorients the subject of humanism by depriving it of its axis in sexual difference, challenging the common sense that to know oneself is to know oneself as a 'man' or a 'woman'.

Persons are not born but made

Even so, there is undoubtedly a strain of nostalgia for the agent in Wittig. And this is why, even though we have Wittig, we would still need Butler. It is the contribution of Butler's later work on 'insurrectionary' speech acts to broach the possibility of agency without fantasising 'the restoration of a sovereign autonomy in speech' (1997a: 145, 150).

Butler builds this account, as Karen Zivi also shows in her contribution to this volume, on the concept of performativity: the *'bodily* gestures, movements, and styles of various kinds' (Butler 1990: 140; emphasis added) whose repetition over time stabilises the 'effects of gender' and the 'materiality of sex' (1993: x). Butler went out of her way to emphasise that such ritual repetition establishes 'a practical sense for the body, not only a sense of what the body is, but how it can or cannot negotiate space, its "location" in terms of prevailing cultural coordinates' (1997a: 159–60). This repetition is crucial to stabilising the sex/gender distinction together with securing the boundaries of the various other fictive domains (private/public; nature/ society; interior/exterior) from which the juridical 'person' of liberal politics draws not just the illusion of *being* an agent but the 'nostalgic' notion that being is *prerequisite* to doing. Given how Butler emphasises the 'somatic dimension' of gender (1997a: 5), it is odd that her appropriation of performativity is so often read as reducing gender to a 'discursive' construct (de Lauretis 2005: 56). Karen Barad puts it well when she writes that 'performativity, properly construed, is not an invitation to turn everything (including material bodies) into words; on the contrary, performativity is precisely a contestation of the excessive power granted to language to determine what is real' (2003: 802).

The concept 'performativity' gives Butler a way to think about how the juridical 'persons' of modern liberal democracies inhabit – take possession of and come to be possessed by – the bodies whose 'work' paradoxically both constitutes us as rights-bearers and grounds our claim to rights. John Locke famously captured this double bind with his phrase 'property in our own persons', a formulation that demonstrates how property not only follows from personhood but is its requisite. Whereas Locke moves quickly to focus on the question of securing the 'property' that 'persons' acquire by their autonomous agency, Butler is captivated by the work that it takes to *be* a 'person' who can be regarded as an agent. Her concern is with what Samuel A. Chambers aptly terms the 'normative violence' involved in sustaining the illusion that one has a title to oneself and to what one takes in from the world (2007).

Butler's critique of the 'normative violence' of straightness in her earlier work seeks to undo what Mowitt calls 'nostalgic' agency by other means. Reading 'straightness' against the grain of its connotations as 'upright' and 'responsible', she proposes to see it as the symptom of the disavowed loss that is written into masculinity and femininity by the Oedipal narrative (Disch 1999). This disavowal, the price that an 'agent' pays for self-possession, takes a toll on political movements that it is Butler's concern, as a political theorist, to spell out. She argues that when identities premised on disavowal become politicised, they tend to imagine that the only trustworthy ally is a 'straight' ally, and, so, to issue in movements that are more or less violently separatist. As Butler emphasises, 'heterosexuality does not have a monopoly' on such 'exclusionary logics' (1993: 112). On the contrary,

> they can characterize and sustain gay and lesbian identity positions which constitute themselves through the production and repudiation of a heterosexual Other; this logic is reiterated in that failure to recognise bisexuality as well as in the normativising interpretation of bisexuality as a kind of failure of loyalty or lack of commitment – two cruel strategies of erasure.
>
> (Butler 1993: 112)

This is precisely the sort of exclusion that feminist activists in France who opposed 'political lesbianism' were trying to call attention to (cf. Butler 1990: 127–28).

How much more ironic it is, then, that Jackson and Delphy should accuse Butler of stripping the 'materiality' out of feminism. Butler merely insists, as Delphy did in response to the radical lesbians, that bodies (no less than 'experience') are sustained by and complicit with the forces that any oppositional politics seeks to transform. Butler's point is not to deny the materiality of bodies but to pry agency out of the hands of the agent. She prompts a shift of focus from mythologising individual heroes towards analysing the systematic relations of both complicity and defiance that make insurrectionary acts possible. For Butler, there is no escape from patriarchy. Lesbian *or* heterosexual (Butler would add bisexual or transgendered), one *can* resist its terms – but *only* from within.

Notes

1 *Psychic Life of Power* appeared in 2002; *Antigone's Claim* in 2003; and *Excitable Speech* and *Precarious Life* in 2004.
2 Gallop inserts the square brackets because she is reworking a passage from Adrienne Rich's indictment of 'token' women in a commencement speech that Rich delivered at Smith College in 1979.
3 Kraus argues that Delphy's impassioned polemic has a double purpose. It is at once a 'critique' of the American representation of French feminism and a salvo in an ongoing 'crisis of representation' taking place '*among* feminists here and now [in France]' over the right to stand for feminism (2005: 167). Delphy sets up *écriture féminine* as an exclusively American invention, in order to 'produce' materialist feminism as the genuine article: 'a product *made in France: French Feminism made in France*' (2005: 171; emphasis in original).
4 See DeLauretis (1986); Fraser and Nicholson (1990); Hirsch and Keller (1990); Weed (1989).

5 Acclaim for *Antigone's Claim* reclaimed (or, Steiner contra Butler)

John E. Seery

I read Judith Butler's *Antigone's Claim* shortly after it appeared in print in 2000. A long-time admirer of Butler's oeuvre, I've also expressed several lingering points of reservation about her overall work, especially concerning the possible politics thereof (Seery 1999). But *Antigone's Claim* won me over without complaint. Its style alone seemed to be an improvement: spare, readable, accessible, luculent. And here she was proffering an interpretation not of another near-contemporary philosopher, but of a classical text, no less one that has attracted legions of learned readers into its pages. Butler reviews some of the most important modern readings for feminist purposes – Hegel's, Irigaray's, and Lacan's – and deftly distinguishes her own reading from the rest. I took her emphasis on incest to be stunningly insightful, its unspoken gothic connection to heteronormativity to be nothing less than brilliant, and her portrayal of Antigone's living death to be hauntingly profound. For two years running I made it a point to teach *Antigone*, along with *Antigone's Claim*, in two of my courses (Classical Political Theory and Contemporary Political Theory). I told my friends, anyone who would listen to me, that Butler's book was one of the most important pieces of scholarship in the last fifty years – indeed, that such a reading of a classic text comes around only once every 2500 years or so. I had become a Judith Butler fan, not just a cautiously appreciative onlooker.

Ah, but this would not turn out to be an extended love letter to Judith Butler, nor the beginning of a coming-out confessional. Rather, I now feel jilted. Butler takes to task feminist statists who look to *Antigone* as their defiant heroine in good part, because, she says, they typically re-enact certain acts of partial blindness in their appropriations of the play. Their main blind spot is to understand Creon and Antigone as opposites (public–private, male–female, reason–emotion, secular–sacred), a reading that can be attributed largely to Hegel. So far so good. Yet I discovered that I had acceded too uncritically to Butler's analysis. After reading George Steiner's (1984) *Antigones* – a source she cites – and returning to Hegel's (1977) *Phenomenology of Spirit*, I quickly became disappointed with Butler's own bold claims. Her bravura act of drawing attention to others' blind spots surely raises the general epistemic question of whether any Sophoclean interpreter ought to presume that she occupies a place of relative blindness-avoidance, and yet Butler seems to be claiming for herself some significant exemption from being snared in an Oedipean legacy. But more, on review, I started observing glaring blind spots in Butler's own analysis, to which I myself had been blind, and thus the blind had been leading the blind, all under the guise of a truth-teller supposedly leading the way. In the following chapter I want to explore some of these oversights in three interrelated areas – Butler's general reading of Hegel, her reading of Hegel's reading of (feminist) irony, and her reading of death and tragedy. I'm not claiming to be presenting a rival exposé, but rather I will juxtapose some of Steiner's analysis to Butler's, which may cast some light on her larger project of demasking some of the blindness that constitutes heteronormativity (and I thereby reprise some of my earlier anxieties about the political future of her post-structuralist projections).

Butler reads Hegel

A principal thesis of *Antigone's Claim* is that Hegel's reading of the play has bequeathed to subsequent interpreters, especially state-feminists, a separatist, oppositional, and territorialist understanding of the relationship between a 'kinship' realm and that of the state: 'The Hegelian legacy of *Antigone* interpretation appears to assume the separability of kinship and the state, even as it posits an essential relation between them' (Butler 2000a: 5). Interpreters struggle to stabilise Antigone as the characterological representative of kinship ties (and Creon as her state counterpart) – yet such readings must somehow ignore the incest in her own family history, most notably and infamously that between her father and her mother; and must also overlook a good deal of textual and dramatic evidence indicating mightily erotic overtures toward her brother Polyneices. If anything, contends Butler, Antigone ought to be viewed as the representative of aberrant kinship relations, or at least as a figure whose life and death mark the limits of intelligibility about family identities and obligations. The question for Butler, then, is why so many readings of *Antigone* ignore or repress the incestuous thematics of the play – but she doesn't pose that question as a question. Rather, she cites that collective elision as a fact, lending to her readers more than just an impression that the scholarly community of Sophoclean interpreters on the whole either ignore incest altogether or else, to the extent that they entertain such readings, 'insist' that no incest between Antigone and Polyneices is present:

> How interesting, then, that so many of the readings of Sophocles' play insist that there is no incestuous love here, and one wonders whether the reading of the play does not in those instances become the very

occasion for the insistence of the rule to take place: there is no incest here, and cannot be.

(Butler 2000a: 17)

She names Martha Nussbaum, Jacques Lacan, Pierre Vernant and Pierre Vidal-Naquet as interpreters who apparently re-enact the incest taboo in their own interpretive activity and commentary. But it is again Hegel whom Butler names as the chief culprit/architect in this ongoing activity of incest excision and oversight and taboo-enforcement: 'Hegel makes the most dramatic of such gestures when he insists that there is only absence of desire between brother and sister' (Butler 2000a: 17). In an apparent effort to strike some measure of scholarly balance, Butler seems to concede, in a footnote, that some folks have indeed read a bit of incest into the play: 'See also George Steiner's brief discussion of incestuous sibling bonds from 1780 to 1914 in *Antigones*, pp. 12–15' (Butler 2000a: 87, n. 18). Note that in an earlier footnote Butler credits Steiner with a 'nearly exhaustive treatment of the figure of Antigone', but she does so in keeping with an insistence on a distinction between her own reading of the 'textual appearance' of Antigone as opposed to subsequent readings of the 'figure' of Antigone (Butler 2000a: 83, n. 2). Note also that she portrays Steiner's discussion as 'brief' and confined to a specific time period and mentions Goethe's critique of Hegel on incest in another footnote (Butler 2000a: 13, n. 1).

My buried suspicions about Butler's presentation awakened into an irritation, beginning with her footnoted and abbreviated summary of Steiner's book. Steiner, as I read him, doesn't confine his discussion of incest in the nineteenth century to a mere section of his book, pp. 12–15, nor does he confine his discussion of incest to the nineteenth century – instead, he is clearly preoccupied with incestuous readings throughout his book, and throughout the ages. Incest is his central motif, the conspicuous point, the punch line, the kicker, to the whole book (Rank 1926, cited in Steiner 1984: 13, n. 1). After an extended discussion of others' portrayals of Antigone's incestuous overtures toward Polyneices, Steiner writes:

> The incest motif is integral to Greek mythology precisely because this mythology encodes the presumably gradual, disputatious evolution of kinship conventions, terms, and taboos; precisely because, as I have suggested, the 'figures' who appear and act in the 'foundational' myths (the myths of linguistic systematisation and social ordinance) are also those 'figures of speech' in and through which the root categories of gender, of mutual relation, of exogamic or endogamic status, are made visible and articulate.

(Steiner 1984: 158)

Steiner insists that the incest cannot be confined to Oedipal framings; incest informs the sibling relationships of the play as well, and he spends a good number of pages exploring more sexually explicit latter-day treatments of Antigone's relationship with her brother: 'It may be that the notion of incest between brother and sister is structurally unavoidable in the figural-semantic fabric of the Oedipus tangle' (Steiner 1984: 160). But Steiner goes even further and points out an incestuous web, signalled in the text, linking Ismene to the Antigone and Polyneices scandal: 'Again, Antigone's "provocation", to Ismene for every syllable in this opening speech is simultaneously a calling and a challenge, aims at the unique scandal and sanctification of kinship in the lineage of Oedipus' (Steiner 1984: 209). The story of sibling incest, Steiner underscores, is an old one:

> Originally, and the concept of 'origins' is itself in part a mythical one, much of mythology may have been a compelling formulation of the uncertainties, of the atavistic embarrassments attached to the courses of kinship and of familial organization via incest. Antigone and Ismene are the sisters and children of Oedipus. This dark knot links them with the monstrous necessities of human origins (whom but their sisters could Cain and Abel wed?). But this anarchic commonality, in its turn an enormity, cuts them off from the accepted norms of evolved mankind. With the context of the myth, their kinship is an outrage.
>
> (Steiner 1984; 208)

Did Butler read another book, or did she just not read this one well? Whatever the explanation, her all-too-brief summary of *Antigones* is misleading. I don't think it can be chalked up to mere sloppiness or carelessness or overstatement. As we'll see, Steiner's book indirectly yet prominently inspires Butler with the central question that she poses at the outset of her concluding chapter, 'Promiscuous Obedience': 'In George Steiner's study of the historical appropriations of Antigone, he poses a controversial question he does not pursue: What would happen if psychoanalysis were to have taken Antigone rather than Oedipus as its point of departure' (Butler 2000a: 57). To say the least, his book figures large in her book; it's more than a mere scholarly citation. And more, even that indirect appropriation in 'Promiscuous Obedience' represents, I'll argue, a key misreading or mischaracterisation of Steiner's project. I propose that Butler's book reveals her own act of minimising and containing Steiner's understanding of incest, and that her own repeated acts of incest-minimalisation cast doubt on her larger project of demasking heteronormativity.

It begins with her reading of Hegel. Butler attempts to contain Hegel's reading of incest, insisting that he 'insists' there can be no incest. First, Butler rehearses Hegel's depiction of Antigone in the *Phenomenology* as a woman whose relationship to citizenship can only be vicarious, mediated through her brother – and Antigone can do so in this way, she says, 'because, according to Hegel, there is ostensibly no desire in that relationship' (Butler 2000a: 13). She initially portrays Hegel as simply not explaining explicitly why brother–sister incest would disqualify Antigone for vicarious state recognition via her brother. She then reads some kind of implicit recognition on Hegel's part that an incest taboo somehow supports kinship, but he never says that explicitly, she notes. Rather, she continues, he claims that the 'blood' relation makes desire impossible between brother and sister. By the end of that short paragraph of analysis, an all-too-quick hermeneutics of Hegel's possible hints, evasions, and silences, Butler now declares emphatically: 'Thus Antigone does not desire her brother, according to Hegel, and so the *Phenomenology* becomes the textual instrument of the prohibition against incest, effecting what it cannot name, what it subsequently misnames through the figure of blood' (Butler 2000a: 13).

Three pages later Butler calls this supposedly unspoken denial of incest of Hegel's 'the most dramatic of gestures' (Butler 2000a: 17).

Steiner reads Hegel

Let's compare Steiner's reading of Hegel on the same material. Steiner underscores the historicity and overall movement of Hegel's account, all of which suggests, for the time being (and thus for the analysis of the play in a Greek context), that Hegel is possessed not only with depicting a march toward ultimate resolution but, rather, with portraying 'the contradictoriness of being itself', to use Lukacs's phrase (Steiner 1984: 23). Wherever, then, Hegel depicts a synchronically 'oppositional' relationship between, say, the family and the state, one must realise that these are historically inter-related, intermixed terms, as if frozen snapshots in a moving narrative. So, too, with brother to sister incest. Butler reads Hegel's account as merely stabilising kinship relations, a static, oppositional account (which is, in effect, to de-Hegel Hegel). Steiner emphasises, in contrast, the 'sublated' or *aufgehoben* aspects of that formulation (according to which historical moments are 'overcome' or 'transcended' but also incorporated and never completely eliminated in the subsequent modality):

> Inside the family, continues Hegel, one relationship is privileged above all others by virtue of the immediacy and purity of its ethical substance. It is that between brother and sister. Again, Hegel's contracted, lyric argument is shot through with the presence of Antigone. Brother and sister are of the same blood, as husband and wife are not. There is between them no compulsion of sexuality or, if there is such compulsion (Hegel implicitly concedes the possibility), it has been overcome.
>
> (Steiner 1984: 33)

Butler sees no acknowledgment of desire whatsoever, whereas Steiner sees that as an implicit, but necessary concession in Hegel's scheme of things. He reads the *Phenomenology* as acknowledging sibling incest rather than denying it:

Direct intimations of incest (such as those of the scholiast), let alone representations, are extremely rare in the 'Antigones'. But often, in encounters between Antigone and Polyneices, the idiom, the aura, of the incestuous, are active immediately beneath the surface. We have seen this to be the case throughout Hegel's experiencings of the Sophoclean text.

(Steiner 1984: 160)

Even if we grant Butler's minimalist reading of the *Phenomenology* as plausible, we ought to press her for not at least acknowledging Steiner's rival reading of the same material, if only to dispute it. Or, we wonder why Butler doesn't make more of an acknowledgment in her exegesis that her own rendering is highly contestable, if not polemical. Her partial, tendentious, one-sided reading of Hegel, however, doesn't stop there. On page 31 of *Antigone's Claim* she begins a close reading of Hegel's supposed reading of Antigone. Throughout, Butler reads (imagines? projects?) Antigone as dipping in and out of Hegel's narrative of 'The Ethical Life' in the *Phenomenology*, and she basically rebukes Hegel for at times effacing Antigone's individuality by leaving her unnamed, and yet at other times for transmuting her particularity into a universality, also unnamed (she scolds him both coming and going). Yet if one reads the *Phenomenology* for oneself, one could forward a credible reading that, for all of the merits of Butler's spirited intervention, she is nonetheless the person constructing the very attributions and evasions in Hegel's text that she assigns so adamantly to Hegel. She starts out that part of her book announcing that Hegel is discussing Antigone in this section of the *Phenomenology*, and yet 'in fact, she remains largely unnamed in this section, merely prefigured through most of the discussion' (Butler 2000a: 31). Hegel is discussing the self who acts against the law, and Butler claims that 'Then, without advance warning, Hegel appears to introduce Antigone without naming her' (Butler 2000a: 31). The remark has to do with a person who breaks human law in following divine law, or who breaks divine law in following human law – and for some reason Butler assumes that Antigone must alone be that culprit in Hegel's eyes. But in her discursive account of Hegel's discursive account, Butler contends that Hegel suddenly shifts his attention to Oedipus, again without explicit signposts in the text: 'This leads him to the figure of Oedipus throughout the following route' (Butler 2000a: 31–2). Butler spends several paragraphs looking at Hegel's apparent contrast between Oedipus's crime and Antigone's crime (the one place, I might point out, in this section of the *Phenomenology* where Hegel names Antigone explicitly – and he names her overall only twice). She then contends that Hegel is again in crisis control mode:

Hegel points to this moment, almost founders upon it, but is quick to contain its scandalous consequence. He distinguishes Oedipus from Antigone, establishing the excusability of his crime, the inexcusability of

hers. He does this precisely by ridding her action of any unconscious
motivation, and identifying her with a fully conscious act.

(Butler 2000a: 33)

And then Butler spends several pages discussing how Antigone 'acknowledges her deed', and compounds the crime through public speech.

Another reading of the same material might, however, reveal Butler as the
person engaging in scandal-avoidance (via *hineinlesen*). Steiner spends a fair
bit of time reproducing Søren Kierkegaard's reading of the play and of
Hegel's reading. According to Kierkegaard, the key difference between
Antigone and Oedipus is that Antigone knows the truth of her incestuous
past (and present), whereas Oedipus likely remained in the dark. Somehow,
when Butler re-creates Hegel's contrast between Oedipus and Antigone, she
doesn't consider the issue as one of consciousness about incest. Rather, hers
is an asymmetrical reading – comparing Oedipus' unconscious relation to
his incestuous deed with Antigone's outward 'deed' of burying her brother
and talking about it. At that moment in her own text, Butler seems (to me)
to de-scandalise Antigone's relationship to Polyneices, making this issue of
Antigone's 'guilt' and the possible Hegelian excusability or inexcusability
thereof merely one of burying the dead or not, somehow divorced now from
Antigone's own possible complicity in an Oedipean legacy. For Kirkegaard,
Antigone harbours a secret, a secret that she cannot 'admit' in public; and
Butler's discussion about Hegel's discussion of Antigone's refusal to admit
guilt takes up that issue only on grounds of whether a woman ought to
appear repentant before the state (Butler 2000a: 34–35). Somehow, at this
point, incest drops out of Butler's consideration (of Hegel's discussion) of
Antigone's possible criminality, and instead she confines the issue as merely
one of Antigone's womanhood *vis-à-vis* the state (setting up Hegel for
allegedly construing the conflict too narrowly).

Surprisingly, for someone who claims that she is reprising (or discovering)
an incestuous reading of Antigone against those who ignore it or insist
otherwise, Butler doesn't really explore the nature of the incest, and in fact
pays little heed to it. Her own book re-creates its minimisation – reproducing, re-performing and reinforcing the taboo, relegating it to the margins of
her account – a charge she levels against others. For instance, she seldom
connects the incest to a death motif or to the tragedy of the play. Rather,
she alludes to some generalized 'desire' that Antigone might hold for Polyneices (albeit distinguishing her reading from Lacan's), which would somehow help explain her uncompromising attachment to him (and the reasons
for her refusing motherhood or marriage as solution to the woes) (Butler
2000a: 53–55). Yet, somehow Butler doesn't explain why desire or eroticism
for Polyneices as a live body would extend to his corpse, i.e. why incest
would dovetail into necrophilia. Steiner, in contrast, points out that Antigone's language of most intimate immediacy toward Polyneices consistently
invokes death imagery: line 73, where Antigone says that she 'will lie beside

Polyneices', who is 'the dear one' (Steiner 1984: 158). In her own death song she alludes to Polyneices' marriage to Argia as an alliance fatal to herself. Steiner explores Rotrou's account of Antigone that draws on the phallic imagery of Eteocles' sword blade, a suggestion that the brotherly rivalry was in good part an offspring of jealousy – for Antigone (Steiner 1984: 162). And he examines at some length Antigone's 'bird-cry' over Polyneices' body, a commingling of nuptial and maternalist imageries, which also prefigure her future barrenness (the empty nest, the empty bed) (Steiner 1984: 223–29). Moreover, Steiner explores the syntax in Antigone's opening words to Ismene, which, he contends, gesture towards a fusion and enact it, a fusion of four doomed siblings – Antigone, Ismene, Polyneices, Eteocles – which 'ominously but also ecstatically perpetuates the unspeakable cohesions of kinship in the House of Laius' (Steiner 1984: 211–13). Perhaps because Butler always treats Hegel's account of Antigone's religiosity as a stereotypical stand-in for feminised, privatised, emotive kinship attachments, she seldom explores the underworldly and deathly imagery that consistently frames the sibling scandal – and that scandal isn't very scandalous under her pen (Steiner 1984: 23). She quotes lines 891–3, which directly link the tomb with a bridal chamber – but she interprets those lines as a 'figurative' marriage with one's kin who are already dead (Butler 2000a: 76). Butler returns to these lines (891–3), now an example of Antigone's scandalising the public with her wavering gender – but thereby Butler seems to be shying away from the incest connection. She submits that Antigone's love towards her father and brother can be consummated only by its obliteration (Butler 2000a: 76). Returning to a discussion of *Antigone* in her chapter 'Bodily Confessions' in *Undoing Gender*, Butler again oddly reassures her reader that Antigone's 'crime is not exactly a sexual one, although her relation to Polyneices is intense, if not overdetermined by incestuous meaning' (Butler 2004: 166). A few pages later she raises this point about Antigone's sexual relationship to Polyneices only as an open question: 'She loves her brother, says, in fact, she wants to "lie with him", and so pursues death, which she also calls her "bridal chamber" in order to be with him forever. She is the child of incest, but how does incest run through her own desire?' (Butler 2004: 169).

Kinship trouble

Butler comments that it is important to separate the issue of Antigone's supposedly tragic barrenness from the incest question – those matters can and should be de-coupled, she insists:

> It is no doubt important, on the one hand, to refuse her conclusion that to be without a child is itself a tragic fate, and, on the other hand, to refuse the conclusion that the incest taboo must be undone in order for love to freely flourish everywhere.
>
> (Butler 2000a: 24)

She quickly qualifies that 'the aim' here is not the celebration of 'incestuous practice' (Butler 2000a: 24). Rather, for Butler, Antigone's 'predicament' is somehow a more generalised 'crisis of kinship': 'What social arrangements can be recognised as legitimate love, and which human losses can be explicitly grieved as real and consequential loss?' (Butler 2000a: 24). Antigone's situation, Butler contends, 'prefigures' the situation of those today 'who cannot publicly grieve the losses from AIDS, for instance' (Butler 2000a: 24). For Butler, the play's scandal, Antigone's 'living tomb', isn't really about incest per se, it's about ('emblematises') the melancholy of the public sphere and 'heterosexual fatality' (Butler 2000a: 81, 82) – although she adds that Antigone is 'not quite a queer heroine' (Butler 2000a: 72). Butler suggests a possible conclusion that Antigone's 'tragic fate' is 'the tragic fate of any and all who would transgress the lines of kinship that confer intelligibility on culture' (Butler 2000a: 72). Antigone's tale provides a springboard for Butler, in other words, for addressing a range of contemporary issues that are sort-of related to incest.

In attacking state-feminists' narrowly reformist, legalistic purview and drawing attention to far wider cultural/linguistic/political discontents, Butler presses Antigone into service as melancholic stand-in for any and all persons who are marginalised under the terms of heteronormativity (even though they may not fully realise it). But that expanded (and domesticated?) reading of Antigone's possible legacy also requires that Butler retreat from the particularities of incest. That move may therefore make Butler vulnerable to the charge, similar to that which she levels against Hegel, that she effaces Antigone's particularity in order to use her example to map out a new future. It's crucial to her outlook, then, that she not read the play as a thoroughgoing tragedy, or at least the tragic elements can be (for our purposes) contested, contained, and controlled. Instead of a collision of fates, Butler must partially de-criminalise Antigone's act, separating her public defiance of burial from her knowledge of (and overtures towards) incest at that point. She challenges Hegel on his depiction of Antigone as a fully conscious agent and instead submits that Antigone is an exemplar of a plaintive and confused cultural intelligibility about kinship-as-such (Butler 2000a: 77). But note, in contrast, Kierkegaard's rival reading of Antigone's 'living death' (which Steiner treats at some length). Antigone, for Kierkegaard, experiences 'true tragic sorrow' (*sande tragiske Sorg*) (Steiner 1984: 57). Her tragic guilt is inherited guilt. She is of the 'living dead' because of her secret knowledge of Oedipus' catastrophe and her own relation to this catastrophe (Steiner 1984: 59–60). Now-dead Oedipus is celebrated by the *polis*, but Antigone 'is, twice over, a stranger in the house of being' (Steiner 1984: 60). She cannot grieve openly about his secret, nor her own. Moreover, she is in love – with Haemon. Kierkegaard believes that her love for Haemon is no ordinary love; the depths of her soul suggest to Kierkegaard that she is capable of immense love. But she cannot share her innermost being – her sacred secret – with her lover; and thus she cannot do justice to the total love she feels toward him. She must die, thus forsaking both marriage and motherhood: 'Only her death can arrest the pollution (the inherited guilt) which the disclosure of her secret and the consummation of her love would, fatally, transmit to succeeding generations' (Steiner 1984: 61). For Kirkegaard, Antigone is fully aware that she forsakes marriage and motherhood in favour of death. For Hegel, any contributions that Antigone ultimately makes to the public realm must be *via negativa*, by way of death and tragedy: 'The publicly manifest spirit has the root of its power in the underworld' (Hegel 1977: 287). For Butler, however, Antigone must be a less-than-conscious agent whose refusal of heterosexual closure through marriage and childbearing must remain to herself murky and occluded, instead of deliberate and intentional. This maternalist forbearance is also suggested in her name, construed as anti-generation (Butler 2000a: 22). And instead, Butler reserves for herself the intelligibility that 'exceeds' Antigone's life and makes her story no longer a heterosexual tragedy but 'the occasion for a new field of the human' that promises forth an 'unprecedented future' (Butler 2000a: 82).

Before we are swept away by this extremely uplifting language, a little more scrutiny of how Butler performs this dazzling legerdemain, of turning a Greek tragedy into a promising political programme, may be in order. As mentioned, her final chapter 'Promiscuous Obedience' begins with a question that she claims Steiner poses but does not pursue: What would happen if psychoanalysis were to have taken Antigone rather than Oedipus as its point of departure? Her analysis is powerfully insightful and suggestive: the Oedipean story portrays gender and 'kinship trouble' as a curse of one's genealogical past, bequeathing a dark legacy that insidiously demands as part of its narrative that such a taboo past must necessarily be forgotten, overcome, and resolved via heterosexualised futures (Butler 2000a: 62). The Oedipean mandate establishes normative family relations via the background threat of sexual horror and kinship chaos. In contrast, writes Butler: 'The Antigonean revision of psychoanalytic theory might put into question the assumption that the incest taboo legitimates and normalises kinship based in biological reproduction and the heterosexualisation of the family' (Butler 2000a: 66). Such analysis might provide alternative understandings of the 'curse', thus laying out the 'possibility of an aberrant future', questioning for instance the fiction of family bloodlines and thereby de-instituting heteronormativity such that 'alternative kinship arrangements' won't necessarily lead to tragedy again (Butler 2000a: 70). But Butler's ingenious analysis represents, it seems to me, a slight but possibly symptomatic mischaracterisation of Steiner on the question 'he does not pursue' (Butler 2000a: 57). Steiner's paragraph in question is this:

Between the 1790s and the start of the twentieth century, the radical lines of kinship run horizontally, as between brothers and sisters. In the Freudian construct they run vertically, as between children and parents.

The Oedipus complex is one of inescapable verticality. The shift is momentous; with it Oedipus replaces Antigone. As we saw, it can be dated c. 1905. But it is the earlier paradigm which concerns us now.

(Steiner 1984: 18)

Steiner, to my interpretive eye, is saying here that between the eighteenth and twentieth centuries, radical depictions of incest shift from horizontal (inter-sibling) tales to vertical (parent–child) tales, from one kind of incest to another. Butler, interjecting her reading of Freud here, suggests that Steiner is suggesting a shift from incest-acknowledgement to incest-repression (and *faux*-resolution). We've seen that she already minimises Steiner's extensive cataloguing of eighteenth- and nineteenth-century Antigonean incest. Why would it be necessary for Butler to portray twentieth-century psychic life and analysis as almost as thoroughly incest-averse, so much so that she apparently refuses to acknowledge Steiner's unrestrained scholarship if only as an exception?

Steiner, later in his book, seems to agree with Butler's unargued point that Freudian returns to Greek myths serve more often than not to console and stabilise rather than to unsettle:

Implicit in Freud's method is the assumption – it defines his conservatism – that the indispensable mapping has been done, that the contribution of modern psychology and social thought to our understanding of the springs of man is a methodological and possibly a therapeutic one, but not a refutation of the antique.

(Steiner 1984: 125)

Yet Steiner describes Freud elsewhere as a 'lucid student of Sophocles', especially on conveying the 'undecidable finalities of conflict at work in Antigone and beyond it' (Steiner 1984: 254). And more, his account of Oedipus, and the Freudian tracking thereof, points finally to an 'unmatched economy of terror' rather than a happy-ever-after homecoming motif (Steiner 1984: 298). Steiner even regards Freud's Oedipalism as an exercise in self-incest – an idea you just don't find anywhere in Butler's comparatively sanitised account:

He [Oedipus] thinks his acts to inescapable finality; he acts his thoughts to the liminal logic of absolute self-perception which is, also, and of necessity, blindness. There is in this perfect intellection, of which Freud's self-analysis was a conscious mimesis, an incest more radical than that of blood.

(Steiner 1984: 299)

Whoa! In no way could one read Steiner's book and contend that it portrays or implies that twentieth-century Oedipean accounts promote, after all, incest-repression or resolution. Indeed, like Butler's, Steiner's book is a cautionary tale about post-Oedipal blind spots and the cursed tragedies they seem to prefigure:

> We are, proclaim psychoanalysis and structural anthropology, *les enfants d'Oedipe* ... More and more, we can come to understand in the modernist movements in the West a hunger for 'beginnings', for a return to archaic, essentially Greek, sources. This will to homecoming, to the fusion of past and present, has been vivid in the representations of the tragic politics of our age.
>
> (Steiner 1984: 285)

But the re-telling of these tales doesn't, for Steiner, reiterate, re-enact, and perpetuate the hidden secrets and taboos; instead they showcase and expose them. To be sure, Steiner doesn't offer an obvious antidote or resistance to these allegedly archetypal curses, though he does find in Antigone a 'latent challenge' to the inevitability of the tragedy, namely certain opportunities for a 'reciprocal intelligibility' of key characters that might withstand some of their meanness (Steiner 1984: 299). But he certainly offers no political programme, just a provisional meditation. Again in contrast, Butler offers her bold reading of Antigone as politically auspicious, not just deconstructive, as if we could someday become – critically de-linking kinship and biological reproduction – *les enfants d'Antigone* – the children (as it were) of a dead virgin.

Politics and post-structuralism

Butler wraps up her book with a discussion of the idea of 'a constitutive outside', a recurring concept in many of her books and which may provide the key to understanding her entire Antigonean analysis (and its possible discontents). Just before the end of the book she challenges Hannah Arendt for her apparent acceptance in *The Human Condition* of a public–private distinction, traceable to the ancient Greeks. She faults Arendt for failing to describe 'precisely the way in which the boundaries of the public and political sphere were secured through the production of a constitutive outside' (Butler 2000a: 82). The 'constitutive outside' she identifies includes a number of sometimes-separable, sometimes-overlapping constituencies – slaves, women, and children – but she nonetheless lumps all of these groups (e.g. both kin and slave) into an aggregate singularity. They are all excluded from the public sphere of property-holding males, another singularised group that is not to be disaggregated in her account. The two groups mirror one another, as inside and outside, as norm and aberrant – and Butler wants to challenge the stability of the very conceptual and linguistic framework that renders these terms into binaries in the first place (as it were) and then re-enacts and reinforces them. I want to call attention to the fact that

Butler (here and elsewhere) always uses the term constitutive outside in the singular, rather than plural. She doesn't say 'constitutive outsides', or 'one of many elements excluded from but contributory to the mainstream', but instead deploys a rhetoric that ties this excluded singularity integrally to the formation, the constitution, of the main normativised group itself, as a symbiosis. My concern is that whenever Butler uses this term constitutive outside, always in the singular – as in *the* constitutive outside – she is using language that should be identified as structuralist rather than post-structuralist. A few times Butler uses the term 'radical outside', suggesting degrees of outsidership, but she doesn't explore or clarify radical versus non-radical outsidership (Butler 2000a: 29). Poststructuralism, as I understand it (while not insisting here on a foundational definition), has attempted to understand the many, multi-faceted elements within a linguistic system that contribute to signification, to the ongoing crystallisations and permutations, pushes and pulls, of identity and difference. While part of Butler surely wants to treat 'kinship' as a collective, pluralised signifier, it typically becomes under her pen a repository category – time and again she has to shoehorn inconvenient remainders into its ambit, marking it thereby as an all-encompassing 'otherness' to the state. Soon enough she starts reverting to a dichotomous analysis overall – deploying and reinforcing rather than contesting and re-describing certain operative binaries: norm-aberrant (or 'poor copy' of the norm), insider–outsider, excluded–included, legitimate–illegitimate – all of which certainly recall an erstwhile structuralist approach (Butler 2000a: 78). My question for *Antigone's Claim* is whether or to what degree Butler has forced, in Procrustean fashion, many unmanageable details, some relating and some not relating to incest, into basically a crude, very rough-hewn 'queer–straight' binary that lurks just underneath and throughout. Incest becomes the metonym for 'the' constitutive outside to a sweepingly trans-historical heteronormativity. One could object and point out, without pedantic nit-picking, that 'outsider' sexualised practices and strategies vary greatly, over time and place; and merely unsettling a presumed distinction between kinship and incest doesn't go very far in addressing the wide range of possibilities (to name but a few!): adultery, miscegenation, polygamy, bigamy, paedophilia, necrophilia, bestiality, zoophilia, cannibalism, divorce, concubinage (of various types), enslavement (of various types), fetishism (of various types), harlotry (of various types), monstrosity (ditto), sadism, masochism, sadomasochism, algolagnism, masturbation (*à la* Diogenes), trans-sexualism, transgenderism, transvestitism, hermaphroditism, pseudo-hermaphroditism, androgyny, gynandry, voyeurism, narcissism, coprophilia, scotophilia, erotomania, nymphomania, and so on. Note the use of 'fundamental' here: 'These various modes in which the Oedipal mandate fails to produce normative family all risk entering into the metonymy of that moralised sexual horror that is perhaps most fundamentally associated with incest' (Butler 2000a: 71). But Butler uses *Antigone* as a broadside that goes way beyond an endeavour of chipping away merely one element in the project of de-instituting heteronormativity – rather, she proclaims effusively (albeit in the conditional, 'If kinship is the precondition of the human, then … ') that Antigone is 'the occasion for a new field of the human' (Butler 2000a: 82).

Compare, again, Steiner's more measured analysis and ambitions. Much of what he says is compatible with Butler's customary concern about the performative claims of speech-acts, yet he also presents a more historicising, evolutionary account. In the process of analysing *Antigone*, Steiner recognises and deploys more than one salient binary, sounding finally more post-structuralist than structuralist, and certainly more so than Butler in *Antigone's Claim*. So, too, is Steiner centrally preoccupied with 'gender trouble', but, while not quiescent in his own gender politics, he probably would remain sceptical about Butler's vision of an 'unprecedented future' wherein 'gender is displaced' (Butler 2000a: 82).

I've belaboured Steiner as a partial foil to Butler in order to suggest that, insofar as he outflanks Butler on her own terrain of analysing incest-inflected speech practices, he demonstrates and virtually concedes the difficulties of generating a directional politics out of post-structuralist complexity. He doesn't contend that an Antigonean exposé of incest supposedly at the heart of heterosexist family grammar might hold a perlocutionary key to changing the world. How could like-minded Butler, in contrast, entertain seriously such a flight of fancy? I believe that Butler in *Antigone's Claim* has actually abandoned a post-structuralist analysis and instead has reverted to an awkwardly structuralist, quasi-Hegelian outlook, whereby the negation of a negative is supposed to lay the basis for movement toward someplace positive. She offers a caricatured account of Hegel's analysis of *Antigone* in order to distance herself from Hegel's legacy, but it is really she who presents statically oppositional language in her schematic emplotment of a new future. As much as I still accept, or regard as uncannily brilliant, many of her intellectual and exegetical moves in *Antigone's Claim*, and while I agree heartily with what I take to be her ultimate political-cultural aims, intentions, and visions, I'm no longer convinced that her particular approach is strategic. It's not going to win over many hearts and minds that need winning over. True enough, it may make a good bit of intellectual sense to reveal that, for instance, 'aberration is at the heart of the heterosexual norm', or that a masked gothic otherness lurks behind all mainstream practices. But these sweeping insights deserve further scrutiny and resistance. My worry is that, politically, they invite us back into, and never really get us beyond, simplistic, oppositional, invidious, zero-sum, competitive, mutually exclusive rather than mutually interdependent terms and outlooks. Progressive theorists and activists might start to believe that they must, first and foremost, somehow 'de-institute heteronormativity' as a global initiative in order to help marginalised persons and peoples – all humankind, actually – survive and feel safe and valued. The logic is awfully negative: we have to challenge the taboo on incest as a way of unsettling concepts of kinship as a way of opening up more possibilities for alternative family practices. That circumvolutory strategy not only taints virtually all hetero-sexuals as repressed incest-mongerers, but it likens and aligns too closely alternative practices to sexualised horror and chaos – it replicates the logic it wants to displace – and then pits inside against outside, pretty much as one perversity against its alleged Other, albeit all now debased and debili-tated. Butler's qualifying or backtracking from her ostensibly panoramic or globalising analysis comes only in a footnote: 'It has been one strategy here to argue that the incest taboo does not always produce normative family, but it is perhaps more important to realize that the normative family that it does produce is not always what it seems' (Butler 2000a: 95, n. 9). And I am well aware that Butler makes the same charge against some 1970s radical socialists and subsequent Lacanians (Butler 75–6). Sure, no position there-after can hail itself sanctimoniously as foundational, but nothing remains very attractive or compelling under Butler's depreciating influence, either. Her attempt to link heteronormativity across the board with incest-as-taboo is tantamount to a political smear campaign, where if you sling enough mud, some of it might stick. How did post-structuralism (if that's what it is or supposed to be) become an exercise in negative politics? (You don't see much generosity and magnanimity performed in Butler's text; it's almost all disputatious and captious.) Would it not be a better strategy to suggest somehow, via a culturally deepened and genuine pluralism as opposed to a thin and state-based pluralism, that alternative family structures can pro-ductively and happily (if agonistically) coexist with their supposed adver-saries (and vice versa), that many such co-extensive practices can simultaneously be viable and life-affirming and robustly attractive, rather than foundering fundamentally on background exclusion and horror? Maybe the problem with Butler's approach is that it begins with tragedy, trying then to read tragedy against itself, and there's a real question whether it successfully acquits itself of tragedy. Myself, I've never been able to recommend a salutary politics from a tragic perspective except by way of irony – and Butler is no ironist here. She reads *Antigone* in a way so that subsequent readers might avoid the encoding of alternative kinship arrangements as somehow cursed and tragic from the outset; but whether that reading supports her contrapositive proposition – prompting move-ment toward 'a highly constructivist and malleable account of social law informing matters of sexual regulation' – strikes me now, not as fated to fail, but as just dubious (Butler 2000a: 75).

Part III
Capitalism and culture

Missing poststructuralism, missing Foucault

Butler and Fraser on capitalism and the regulation of sexuality

Anna Marie Smith

When American liberals think about the politics of sexuality, their ideas are usually framed in individualistic and narrow terms. Many defenders of reproductive rights aggressively oppose the bans on late-term abortions, mandatory parental consent, and compulsory waiting-period laws, but for all their important work on these issues, they often neglect the economic dimension of reproductive rights. Less attention is given to the legislation that prohibits Medicaid funding for abortion and the welfare policies that severely violate the privacy rights of poor single mothers. In another domain, liberal homosexual activists often champion reforms such as same-sex marriage in exclusively bourgeois terms. They insist that lesbian and gay couples should be able to share their employee benefits just like their heterosexual counterparts, but they rarely discuss the fact that many lesbians and gays – and many Americans, for that matter – do not have access to adequate benefit packages in the first place, and they tend to ignore the fact that homophobia contributes to the over-representation of sexual minorities within the lowest income bracket. As for issues such as the privatisation of health care and the elimination of welfare rights,[1] liberal homosexual leaders either remain completely silent or, worse, express their enthusiastic support for the neo-liberal agenda. Indeed, the differences between such organisations as the Log Cabin Republicans, the Lambda Legal Defense Fund, and the Human Rights Campaign Fund on the one hand and the much more progressive National Lesbian and Gay Task Force on the other became much more sharply drawn when US President Bill Clinton dragged the political centre to the right in the 1990s, and they remain significant under the Bush administration. Given this tendency within liberal circles to compartmentalise and depoliticise social problems, it is absolutely crucial to the radical democratic project that we consistently emphasise a multi-sectoral approach to human rights. We need to refuse, in explicit terms, the liberal tactic of bracketing questions relating to economic justice, and we need to situate our cultural analyses of 'identity politics' within political economy contexts, through references to issues such as the distribution of wealth, employment trends, urban planning, and welfare policies. One alternative to the liberal depoliticisation strategy is of course provided by orthodox leftist thinkers. However, their solution is hardly promising, for they simply remove cultural phenomena from the political agenda altogether. As Judith Butler points out in her article 'Merely Cultural', economistic leftists have aggressively attacked cultural studies scholars on the grounds that the latter have virtually abandoned the terrain of economic justice in favour of 'identity politics'.[2] While privileging the economic as a distinct and foundational sphere and hailing class-based struggles as primary, economistic leftists have relegated the new social movements to what they regard as the largely irrelevant cultural sphere. Further, they have attacked cultural politics as 'factionalising, identitarian and particularistic' (Butler 1997c: 265).

The leftist class-centric critique of identity politics was particularly prominent in the work of Gitlin, Hobsbawm, and Rorty during the mid-1990s (Gitlin 1995; Hobsbawm 1996; Rorty 1998). It is not clear, however, that their polarising view – one that constructs two distinct and opposed spheres, the new social movements versus class politics – would have as much credibility in the American Left today. We are currently witnessing a paradigm shift as American leftists work across the labour–new social movement divide in projects as diverse as service-worker organising drives, international workers' solidarity initiatives, living wage campaigns, the students' anti-sweatshop movement, the anti-World Trade Organization and the anti-World Bank protests, and the burgeoning immigrants' rights movement.

The exchange between Judith Butler (1997) and Nancy Fraser (1997a, 1997b) on the relationship between capitalism and the regulation of sexuality is extremely valuable, for it presents two other alternatives to the liberal approach. Their texts not only return our attention to the challenge of combining the perspectives of cultural studies and political economy, they also contain important proposals for moving beyond the orthodox leftist impasse. Furthermore, the Butler–Fraser debate is deeply informed by the authors' respective theoretical paradigms. For these reasons, this debate deserves our close attention and critical analysis.

Butler on the regulation of sexuality and capitalism: too much Derrida or not enough?

Butler begins her critique of economistic leftist thought with the observation that the very distinction between material and cultural life is highly suspect. In traditional Marxist theory, for example, racism and sexism are given some attention, but only insofar as the oppression of racial minorities and women produces a recognisably 'economic' effect. Traditional Marxists would address the disproportionate concentration of blacks and Latinos among the poor, the unemployed, and the unskilled, but they would tend to ignore the fact that blacks of all classes are subjected to racist exclusions and representations. For Butler, however, economistic leftists are particularly dismissive where lesbian and gay politics are concerned. 'Considered inessential to what is most pressing in material life, *queer politics is regularly figured by the orthodoxy as the cultural extreme of politicisation*' (Butler 1997c: 270; emphasis in original).

Although Fraser is certainly not an economistic leftist, Butler nevertheless takes aim at her work at this juncture in her argument. In *Justice Interruptus*, Fraser constructs a distinction between what she calls the politics of distribution and the politics of recognition. She argues that we can improve our understanding of hierarchical social relations in modern capitalist societies and the current dilemmas facing progressive movements by building an imaginary terrain in which power relations take the form of two fundamental structures. On one axis, the social hierarchies are fundamentally economic in nature; the least powerful groups on this axis are subjected to socio-economic injustices such as exploitation, economic marginalisation, and deprivation. On the second axis, the hierarchical structure is organised in terms of recognition. The least powerful are faced with cultural and symbolic forms of exclusion such as cultural domination, non-recognition, and disrespect (Fraser 1997b: 13–14). Fraser admits that in concrete historical conditions, the two axes are thoroughly intertwined; actual subordinate subjects experience both types of oppression, and actual movements combine both types of justice claims (Fraser 1997b: 15, 32; see also Fraser 1998b). She nevertheless contends that we can usefully enhance our arguments about justice by considering her ideal types – the abstract subjects who would experience the greatest forms of injustice in her imaginary model. Working within the paradigm of Weberian social theory on this point, Fraser is not advancing any normative claims about the 'idealtypical' subject; the 'ideal type' is simply an abstract construction that is deployed for heuristic purposes. We will return to the problem of constructing the 'ideal type' below.

On the axis of distribution, the ideal-typical subject who endures the worst form of injustice is the working class. Fraser suggests that we consider the homosexual as the ideal-typical subject who suffers the greatest form of injustice on the axis of recognition. While Fraser recognises that homophobic discrimination clearly violates the rights of lesbians and gays, she points out that they can be found in every socioeconomic bracket, that they do not occupy any specific location within the division of labour, and that they do not constitute an exploited economic class. For these reasons, Fraser concludes that 'the injustice they suffer is quintessentially a matter of recognition' (Fraser 1997b: 18).

From Butler's perspective, we should reject Fraser's model because capitalism necessarily intertwines itself with the perpetuation of compulsory patriarchal heterosexuality. Butler contends that Fraser risks ignoring the gains made by socialist feminists and leftist psychoanalytic thinkers in the 1970s and 1980s. She points out that they saw the 'regulation of sexuality' not as ahistorical and natural but as 'systematically tied to the mode of production proper to the functioning of political economy' (Butler 1997c: 272). For her part, Butler states:

> Struggles to transform the social field of sexuality do not become central to political economy to the extent that they can be directly tied to questions of unpaid and exploited labor, but rather because they cannot be understood without an expansion of the 'economic' sphere itself to include both the reproduction of goods as well as the social reproduction of persons.
>
> (Butler 1997c: 272).

Butler's critique attacks the very foundation of Fraser's framework, for she argues that the distinction between the two dimensions of injustice – distribution and recognition – is itself problematic. Her argument is both empirical and theoretical in nature. Empirically, she gives several examples of the economic dimensions of homophobic discrimination. The point that lesbians and gays are systematically denied, on the basis of our sexuality, equal access to economic resources is not a trivial one. There is substantial evidence that homophobia is in fact having a direct impact on the distribution of life chances in contemporary American society (Badgett 1997; Black *et al.* 2000; Smith 2004).

By speaking explicitly in terms of analytic separations, ideal types, and heuristic devices, however, Fraser has already anticipated the marshalling of empirical evidence that would demonstrate that specific groups suffer simultaneously from both distributional and recognition-oriented injustices. As such, Butler's theoretical argument is more important than her citations of empirical data. Butler attempts to demonstrate that even on an analytical plane, we cannot separate the two spheres – the politics of distribution and the politics of recognition – since, by its very nature, the economic sphere always already has the cultural sphere within itself as its condition of possibility. 'Sexuality must be understood as part of that mode of production [as defined in Marxist political economy]' (Butler 1997c: 273), and 'the economic, tied to the reproductive, is necessarily linked to the reproduction of heterosexuality' (Butler 1997c: 274). Where the condition of homosexuals is concerned, 'the operations of homophobia are central to the functioning of political economy' (Butler 1997c: 274). From this perspective, then, normative heterosexuality and the two-gender system are not epiphenomena; they are 'essential to the functioning of the sexual order of political economy' (Butler 1997c: 274).

In her reply, Fraser states that although she finds deconstruction useful in examining the complexities of identity politics and recognition, she does 'not find deconstruction useful at the level on which Butler invokes it here, namely the level of social theory' (Fraser 1997a: 289). Butler does in fact deploy a classic Derridean interpretative strategy in her argument. She attempts to demonstrate that the economic cannot be analytically separated from the cultural because the latter operates as the 'constitutive outside' of the former – or, in other words, because the cultural is the condition of possibility for the economic. Butler's argument, however, actually bears a closer resemblance to structuralist Marxist thought. There are many similarities, for example, between Althusser's approach to ideology and the stable, systematic and predictive dimensions of Butler's formulation ('the cultural' always functions as the supplementary constitutive 'outside' for the economic 'inside', and homophobia is always central to the operation of political economy) (Althusser 1971). Whereas for Althusser, the economic necessarily depends upon the ideological for its reproduction, for Butler, the economic necessarily depends upon the cultural. In this sense, Butler's position becomes vulnerable to the theoretical critiques that have been directed against the totalistic aspects of Althusser's work.

Butler's argument that the cultural is the condition of possibility for the economic is also problematic from an empirical point of view. In some cases, we might find it useful to emphasise the ways in which the state operates in capitalist societies with a relative degree of autonomy from the economic, legitimates itself as utterly external to the economic, and yet plays a key role in the constitution of the economic in the latter's very origin (for a theoretical approach to the relation between state and capital that is deeply influenced by post-Marxism and poststructuralism, see Jessop 1990, especially parts 3 and 4). A given welfare reform, for example, may produce significant economic effects; it might put pressure on the lowest wages in the labour markets or it might increase the household incomes of the poorest consumers. That same reform, however, may not have been produced exclusively by the economic – it may not, in other words, simply be a product of the class struggle, for it may also be conditioned by the existing official apparatus. Social movements struggling for specific reforms sometimes benefit more from the opportunities created by specific institutional arrangements – a weak central government, a relatively undeveloped administrative bureaucracy, domestic wartime measures, a multiple party system, and so on – than they do from their links with ascendant class fractions (see Skocpol 1995; and more generally Jessop 1990).

It is only by subsuming the entire field of social policy under 'the cultural' (Althusser himself makes a similarly sweeping gesture when he creates the category 'ideological state apparatuses') that Butler's culturalist position can accommodate institutional analysis. Once again, however, such an argument would expose Butler to anti-totalistic criticism. If we adopted this approach, we would have to forgo any consideration of the historical specificity of particular legislative initiatives, administrative procedural rules, and court decisions in favour of an overriding presumption that official institutions and hegemonic cultural discourses organically work together in a perfectly harmonious manner. This is not to ignore the fact that 'cultural' issues – race, gender, sexuality, family relations, and so on – are sometimes so deeply intertwined with the state that it becomes difficult to make definitive distinctions between their effects. Welfare policies, for example, are often shaped by cultural phenomena such as moral panics about black women's promiscuity, 'super-predators', the under-class, teenage pregnancy, and so on, but these panics can be perpetuated, legitimated, reconstructed and remobilised by official discourse as well. See, for example, the pathologisation of the poor, female-headed black family in the 'Moynihan Report' (United States Department of Labor, Office of Policy Planning and Research 1965), and more generally Gwendolyn Mink's research on the racial, gendered, and moralistic dimension of welfare policy (Mink 1998).

In any event, the heterogeneous character of the cultural, the complex interweaving of cultural elements and official discourse, and the conditioning effects of state institutions are such that we cannot assume in advance that a single cultural instance, such as homophobia, will always be central to the functioning of political economy. Butler also cites, with approval, highly problematic functionalist arguments in which the social is constructed as a closed organic system. She refers, for example, to the socialist feminists who use psychoanalytic theory to demonstrate that 'kinship operate[s] to reproduce persons in social forms that serve the interest of capital' (Butler 1997c: 271–72). Like functionalism, poststructuralism undermines the possibility of an autonomous, fully self-conscious, and instrumentalist subject that is prior to a given formation. A deconstructive approach cannot, however, be reconciled with functionalism's organicist and totalistic dimensions (for a critique of functionalism, see Giddens 1977 and Poulantzas 1973). Butler's text is fundamentally at odds with itself in this respect. She juxtaposes references to organicist models of the social with the argument that patriarchal heterosexuality is a fragile and incomplete formation that remains vulnerable to radical forms of resistance – rather than the vehicle of an omnipotent totality (Butler 1997c: 276). In sum, it could be argued that Fraser's criticism would be more effective if it were inverted. The problem with 'Merely Cultural' is not that it illegitimately introduces deconstruction into the terrain of social theory, but that its social theory is insufficiently poststructuralist.

Capitalism and the regulation of sexuality: poststructuralist historical methodology at work

A deconstructive approach would treat socialist feminist theory in a provisional manner. For example, it would construct the domestic labour thesis (the idea that capital depends upon unpaid domestic labour performed principally by women to keep wages low) not as a universal law but as a sensitising concept. Feminist theorists, queer-studies students, and students of political economy should consider the possibility that there might be a mutually constitutive relation between the regulation of sexuality and the reproduction of capitalist relations in specific contexts, but such a relation would have to be demonstrated with reference to specific historical cases through structured empirical research. If we then considered the resulting case studies together, we should expect to find uneven patterns of similarities, continuities, and discontinuities – what Wittgenstein would call 'family resemblances' – rather than the perfect repetition of a universal rule (Wittgenstein 1958; for methodological remarks about the study of the relation between capitalism and racism, see Hall 1980). If Butler errs on the side of claiming a necessary interdependence between the regulation of sexuality and capitalism, Fraser goes too far in the opposite direction, for she contends that sexual relations have become relatively 'decoupled' from the economic structure in modern capitalist societies (Fraser 1997: 284; Fraser 1998b: 21). Both of these arguments are flawed insofar as their epochal and overly sweeping metaphors are antithetical to historically specific institutional analysis and the study of race, class, gender, sexual, and national differences. Socialist feminist theory has clearly played an important role in the empirical research projects of historians such as Weeks (1981) and Scott (1988b). Their work shares with socialist feminist theory the rejection of a naturalistic or instinctual approach to sexuality in favour of historically specific social constructionism. But because socialist feminist theory is treated in their texts as the source of sensitising concepts rather than a predictive model, the complex and contradictory issues in the relation between capital and the regulation of sexuality are brought to the fore. Whereas Butler posits a close 'fit' between the needs of capital and the promotion of patriarchal heterosexuality, Scott demonstrates that such a perfect correspondence between the two structures never actually took place.

The relation between capital and hegemonic official discourse on sexuality is contingent: while the regulation of sexuality is certainly shaped by prevailing economic relations, it is never fully determined by it. Conversely, a specific capitalist formation never simply 'requires' a particular sexual regime. This remains the case even where consumerism has become a powerful cultural presence. Notwithstanding the fact that major events in today's lesbian, bisexual, gay, and transgendered community are produced with the assistance of substantial and blatant corporate sponsorship – to the extent that someone attending a large-scale Pride Day celebration might reasonably conclude that 'gay rights' is just another niche market commodity – sexual subjects continue to experiment with different forms of self-definition in various ways that both complement and contradict consumerised identities (Weeks 1995).

At the same barricades?

It is of course true that Butler and Fraser generally occupy the same political positions on capitalism and homophobia. Both strongly endorse the radical democratic pluralist agenda that would combine socialist egalitarianism with radical antiracist, feminist, and queer politics. In this sense, it is entirely possible that we would find both of them at the same barricades in specific political contexts. There are, nevertheless, several differences between them on the question of political practice. In Fraser's work, the political subject is implicitly constructed in a rational, instrumental, and voluntarist manner. It is perhaps the case that Fraser is too close to the rationalistic and individualistic dimensions of Weber's methodology. Weber maintained that sociological research must assume that the subject – which for him is the individual – is capable of engaging in subjectively meaningful rational action. He admits that the individual is in fact rarely fully conscious of the subjective meaning behind his or her action and often acts on impulse, out of habit, on the basis of imperfect information, and/or in an irrational manner. Weber nevertheless concludes that the ideal type of meaningful action by the individual must be used by the sociologist as a heuristic device to produce a systematic study of rational self-conscious meaning (Weber 1978: 1, 13–18, 1, 21–22; Weber 1949: 42). The Foucaultian warnings about the seductive lure that is exercised by normalising institutions and the constitutive effects that they may have on the subject's identity are missing. Fraser's argument in favour of what she calls 'transformative redistribution' and 'transformative recognition' is grounded on a set of conclusions that she draws from her abstract analysis and defends in cost-benefit terms. She states that as 'real-world' subjects realise that concrete social structures actually operate in a manner that is roughly analogous to her dual-axes system, they 'should prefer' her political agenda (Fraser 1997b: 32). In those cases in which distribution and recognition injustices intersect, the combination of the two 'transformative' projects would be 'more attractive still' (Fraser 1997b: 32).

Where individuals remain recalcitrant, Fraser advocates a remarkably behaviourist course of remedial action. She states, for example, that 'for this scenario [transformative redistribution and transformative recognition] to be psychologically and politically feasible requires that all people be weaned from their attachment to current cultural constructions of their interests and identities' (Fraser 1997b: 31). She evokes psychological terminology as well to describe the ways in which liberal reformist and socialist approaches to redistribution can have different symbolic effects (welfare-state policies can stigmatise the poor; socialist policies can promote solidarity, for example). Fraser states that these two approaches can exercise 'different subliminal dynamics of recognition' (Fraser 1997b: 26). In her reply to Butler, Fraser underlines the fact that she considers homophobic injuries and economic deprivation as equally serious forms of injustice. The precise logic of her remarks about political practice nevertheless remains voluntaristic in nature. Having explained that 'economic heterosexism' is rooted exclusively in status-based exclusion, she states, 'change the relations of recognition and the maldistribution would disappear' (Fraser 1997a: 283).

How can we actually defeat our reactionary enemies and achieve this radical transformation? How should Fraser's general argument about recognition and redistribution be put into practice in a specific historical-institutional context? Under what conditions would subjects find themselves drawn to Fraser's progressive course of action? What if radical social change requires more than simply convincing existing subjects on the basis of rational arguments that it is in their best interest to fight oppression and exploitation? What if there are no fully self-conscious subjects who can disentangle themselves entirely from the seduction of assimilatory political incitements and coolly decide between 'affirmative' and 'transformative' strategies? What if 'ideology' and 'the unconscious' often play important roles in shaping the subject's investment in a political position? What if the attainment of a political goal requires not just the mobilisation of existing subjects but the difficult work of bringing a whole new subject into being in the first place? And even if we do successfully instigate the formation of subjects who will engage in a 'transformative' politics that properly combines redistributive and recognition struggles, what if the effects of bio-power normalisation – or what Weber would call bureaucratic routinisation (Weber 1978: 1, 246–54, and 2, 956–1005, 2, 1121–23, 2, 1148–57) – are so profound that a specific political campaign based on consciously avowed progressive intentions ultimately leads to the construction of institutions that contribute to new forms of injustice and unfreedom over the long term? How can we guard against assimilation, insider politics, careerism, co-optation, and corruption?

For example, taken on its own, Fraser's approach would not give us all the tools we need to address the same-sex marriage debate. What would the 'transformative' solution to this question actually mean in the contemporary conditions of South Africa, Australia, France, Canada, or the United States? While it is true that economic globalisation, the international marketing of American cultural commodities, migration, and travel are nurturing transnational sexual cultures, lesbian and gay rights still remain profoundly shaped by the particular legal and constitutional frameworks specific to each nation-state. Fraser admits that we would need to conduct a case-by-case study of the specific institutional features of a given status injury before we could determine the best remedy (Fraser 2000: 115). Her arguments about same-sex marriage, however, suggest that the role in her model for such a historically specific institutional analysis is quite limited. Referring to the privileging of heterosexuals in family law, she suggests that this form of heterosexism could be eliminated either by legalising same-sex marriage or by de-institutionalising heterosexual marriage and assigning entitlements and benefits on other bases, such as individual citizenship. For Fraser, the differences between these two approaches are insignificant: 'Although there may be good reasons for preferring one of these approaches to the other, in principle both of them would promote sexual parity and redress this instance of misrecognition' (Fraser 2000: 115).

It is indeed possible that same-sex marriage might significantly disrupt patriarchal heterosexuality in one institutional context. In another, however, it might enlarge the privileged married class and contribute to the further marginalisation of the unmarried class. As an isolated reform, same-sex marriage would not change the ways in which contemporary American welfare policies target single mothers for moral discipline on the basis of their marital status (see, for example, Smith 2007), nor would it do anything to ensure equal access to benefits for those individuals whose sexual practices and alternative kinship structures do not conform to the cohabiting monogamous couple model. In some conditions, the institutionalisation of same-sex marriage – an apparently progressive reform – might actually contribute to new forms of domination. See, for example, Valerie Lehr's critique of same-sex marriage as a fundamentally liberal-individualist reform that would not only perpetuate the exclusion of nonconformists but would also redirect energies away from broader campaigns against right-wing forces. The danger here is that such a reform could appear as a fundamental democratic victory when it might actually leave existing relations between the citizen's intimate life, civil society, and the state basically intact, and when it would do very little to challenge the eviscerated definition of the public good that currently prevails in American politics (Lehr 1999).

It is also implied in Fraser's argument that we are capable of sorting out our preferences and arguments in a rational manner. But surely the mere mention of marriage, of all things, resonates with profound unconscious investments for straights and queers alike. And given the history of sexual regulation in the United States, those investments might extend far beyond the terrain of gender and sexuality; they might also be entangled with religious, racial, and class-oriented elements as well. Can we be certain that everyone is navigating this debate in purely rational terms? It is extremely unlikely, for example, that we will ever persuade elements of the religious Right to accept same-sex marriage on the basis of rational arguments about human rights and equal participation. Those folks passionately believe that we, the queers, are evil – period. Given the intransigence of their position, we will need to redouble explicitly antagonistic struggles against religious fundamentalism to dismantle heterosexism. The advance of queer rights in this respect will require intensive adversarial political strategies; rational deliberation tactics, on their own, would be insufficient.

And what about the proponents of same-sex marriage within the lesbian and gay community? Many queer commentators have pointed out the right-wing shift toward corporate media celebration and moralism among leading homosexual intellectuals, activists, and institutions in the United States (see, for example, Schulman 1998; Cohen 1999; Warner 1999). What if the demand for same-sex marriage has emerged as a movement priority in the context of this shift, and what if it has been produced in part by a non-feminist or even anti-feminist discourse that has failed to question the limitations of existing family law? Such a failure is of course entirely understandable. While we have seen some gains, such as the adoption of same-sex benefits policies by private corporations, the passage of local and state anti-discrimination measures and hate crimes laws, the striking down of state sodomy laws, a smattering of 'positive images' in the media, and the same-sex marriage victory in Massachusetts, American lesbian and gays still have to contend with the 'don't ask, don't tell' military policy, the Defense of Marriage Act, hostile family law courts in child custody cases, the impact of the AIDS crisis, and a steady stream of state-level homophobic initiatives. The politics of 'feasible' and 'pragmatic' 'small steps' can be very attractive in the face of such contradictions, and such an approach is especially compelling now that Clintonism has institutionalised an extreme pessimism vis-à-vis the role of government among liberals and centrists. The turn to the right among lesbian and gay activists – and the way in which progressive feminist arguments about the family are suppressed in key leadership sites – would require extensive discussion in its own right. For our purposes here, however, it should be noted that Fraser's approach does not give us the tools we need to analyse the way in which some demands become hegemonic within a given social movement – to the extent that they appear to sum up its entire identity – while others are neglected. What if a pariah group came into being as a social movement in part by inhabiting, through analogy, already authorised discourses that identify forms of discrimination against other groups and provide for official remedies for those wrongs? (For a similar argument, see Brown 1995.) What if that emerging movement's own identity then became deeply informed by the terms of that official anti-discrimination discourse, even though the latter offered only a strictly limited way of thinking about democracy? For all its impoverished approach to politics, the authorised anti-discrimination discourse would at least provide some promise that the movement's 'own voice' would be heard. In fact, the movement leadership might find that some small gains could actually be won if it phrased its demands according to the official anti-discrimination discourse's terms. What if, however, those gains flowed primarily to the most privileged members of the minority community in question, causing the community's elite to take an increasing interest in promoting a movement leadership that operated exclusively within existing legal and political frameworks? A disconnection between the conditions of the least privileged members of the minority community and the agenda of the elite leadership coalition would probably develop, especially if no formal democratic structures were in place through which that leadership could be held accountable to the community as a whole.

And what if that movement was all the while placed under extreme pressures as its members continued to endure expulsions from their birth families (one of the defining features of homophobia) and systematic forms of discrimination? In these conditions, it is entirely possible that the movement leadership would tend to invest in the authorised way of thinking about discrimination and that it would tend to neglect the fact that its community also has roots in nonconformist traditions that cannot be easily reconciled with official discourse. Further, it is likely that the movement leadership would not prioritise a critical interrogation of the official approach to discrimination. But if this were indeed the case, then factions at the margins of the group who deviated from this subjectivation/co-optation process would not be given an equal voice in setting the movement's agenda; creative coalitions with other progressive critics of the authorised anti-discrimination discourse would not be formed; and very little investment would be made in the nurturing of new approaches to democratic politics.

This theoretical narrative itself remains overly schematic – there is a world of difference between the Human Rights Campaign Fund's endorsement of Senator Al D'Amato and the principled work being carried out by the National Lesbian and Gay Task Force. We should nevertheless carefully consider the implications of the shift toward an increasingly conservative, pro-corporate, moralistic, and single-issue-oriented form of homosexual activism when we assess the various anti-homophobia strategies that are currently available to us. Fraser's assessment of the remedies for heterosexism does not take into account the fact that a reform such as same-sex marriage may not be a neutral vehicle that merely delivers specific goods to an already fully constituted subject. Indeed, if we took Butler's performative theory of identity formation seriously, we would have to consider the fact that a reform might do more than to say 'yes' or 'no' to a pre-constituted subject; a reform might also effectively invite a new subject – a new movement or at least a new variant of an existing movement – into being.

To the extent that a given reform actually did exert this sort of interpellation effect, and did contribute to the constitution of a new subject, the latter's identity would in a sense be at least somewhat prepared in advance. The precise character of the reform in question would tend to shape the movement's parameters. The emerging movement would tend to be disposed toward a fairly restricted set of political practices that more or less resembled the specific reform discourse, and it would tend to dismiss alternative possibilities as incoherent. In short, a reform such as same-sex marriage could contribute – in a complex, mediated, indirect, and contingent manner – to the hegemonic status of conservative elements within an otherwise promising social movement. We need to make sure that the toolboxes of progressive social movements include more than abstract normative arguments about distribution and recognition. We also need to provide structured empirical research about specific historical configurations and to build sophisticated theories that address the problems of bureaucratic routinisation, institutional normalisation, and the incitement of assimilation and co-optation.

Butler, Foucault and scepticism in politics

With her Foucaultian approach to political theory, Butler consistently addresses a question that has become absolutely crucial in our contemporary conditions: how can contemporary progressive social movements successfully negotiate the insidious lures of the institutions that give rise to the movements' formation and political practice but threaten even the most promising campaigns with colonisation and self-betrayal at the same time? Butler has quite rightly attacked economistic leftists for their reductionism and dismissive position on sexual politics. However, there is an enormous potential for dialogue between Butler and leftist thinkers like Frances Fox Piven who have consistently warned against the tremendous capacity of the American political system and state apparatus to lure popular protest movements into an assimilatory and self-regulatory process of institutionalisation and depoliticisation (Piven and Cloward 1979). It is perhaps one of Butler's most important contributions to political theory that she has consistently approached the analysis of subjectivation from a perspective that is thoroughly informed by a Foucaultian scepticism about the possibility of a fully self-conscious rational actor who achieves a complete mastery of institutions and the unconscious. Indeed, queer theory is particularly well situated to make this specific contribution to political theory since the effects of bio-power institutions are at their most insidious where the contemporary deployment of sexuality is concerned.

Notes

1 The Personal Responsibility Act, signed by President Clinton in 1996, eliminates the statutory right to welfare assistance; under the current regime, welfare is a discretionary privilege that is determined almost exclusively by each state.

2 Butler first presented 'Merely Cultural' as a paper at the Rethinking Marxism conference held in Amherst, Massachusetts, in December 1996. One of the appendices in Rorty's text, 'The Inspirational Value of Great Works of Literature' (125–40), is a slightly revised version of a talk that was delivered at the annual meeting of the Modern Language Association in December 1995 and published in *Raritan* 16 (summer 1996): 8–17.

7 Towards a cultural politics of vulnerability

Precarious lives and ungrievable deaths

Moya Lloyd

For a long time now I have been interested in what I see to be a particular tension in the work of Judith Butler. This is the tension between her explicit commitment to producing 'ontology itself as a contested field' by exposing how particular ontological claims are constructed and then circulate (Butler in Meijer and Prins 1998: 279; see also White 2000) *and* Butler's own unacknowledged ontological presuppositions. In previous work I have explored this tension in terms of the relation between agency and performativity-as-citationality in order to raise questions about Butler's approach for an understanding of political intervention and change (Lloyd 2007a). Here my focus is somewhat different. I am interested in the ethics that Butler has begun to develop in writings such as *Precarious Life*, which will be my main focus, *Undoing Gender* and *Giving an Account of Oneself*. In short, this is an ethics, indeed a potentially global ethics, which issues out of a common human experience of vulnerability, and particularly vulnerability to violence. What interests me are the ontological assumptions that ground this ethics.

My argument is two-fold: first, that Butler's account of ethics relies upon an idea of the ek-static subject that itself depends upon an *unproblematised* and *unexamined* ontological claim concerning the desire for existence; and, second, that even at those moments when Butler attempts to rethink this desire in social terms, she does not go far enough. This is because Butler fails to engage adequately with the historicity of the social, that is, with the historical practices that constitute the social.

I have an additional reason for exploring Butler's work on ethics. As a thinker who in 2000 confessed to 'worrying about the turn to ethics' on the grounds that 'ethics displaces from politics' (Butler in Butler and Connolly 2000: 5), I am interested in whether this worry has dissipated or whether Butler's attitude towards ethics and politics (and, specifically, the relation between them) has altered. So I will spend some time towards the end of this chapter considering how Butler appears to conceptualise the connection between ethics and politics in the texts published after 2000.

Mourning and politics

Precarious Life, published in 2004, contains a series of essays in which Butler reflects on politics in the aftermath of the events of September 11, 2001 ('9/11'). In particular, she is concerned with the political opportunity that was lost when, instead of attempting to 'redefine itself as part of the global community', the US 'heightened nationalist discourse, extended surveillance mechanisms, suspended constitutional rights and developed forms of explicit and implicit censorship' as public criticism came to be all but silenced (Butler 2004a: xi).[1] So what was the lost political opportunity in question? It was, Butler asserts, a chance to acknowledge the fact of human interdependency (that my life depends on 'people I do not know and may never know'); to reflect on the relation between human vulnerability and violence; and to consider 'what, politically, might be made of grief besides a cry for war' (2004a: xii). '9/11', that is, furnished an occasion on which to 'start to imagine a world in which violence might be minimized, in which an inevitable interdependency becomes acknowledged as the basis for a global political community' (Butler 2004a: xii–xiii). Although the US administration eschewed this opportunity, Butler does not. In *Precarious Life*, she ponders, to borrow from the book's subtitle, 'the powers of mourning and violence'.

Butler's interest in grief and mourning is not new. It is explored in detail, for instance, in *Antigone's Claim*. Here, drawing on arguments first advanced in *Gender Trouble*, and developed in *Bodies that Matter* and *The Psychic Life of Power*, she explores how heteronormative sexuality works to restrict the public expressions of grief amongst sexual minorities. Moreover, via the story of Antigone, Butler tackles the issue of what happens when against the edict of the state an individual (Antigone) attempts publicly to mourn for a person deemed ungrievable, unmournable by the state and indeed, whose very body it constructs as unburiable. (Recall that the ruler Creon forbids the burial of Polyneices.) In the essay 'Violence, Mourning, Politics', contained in *Precarious Life*, Butler extends this analysis of mourning in new directions. She not only considers how conventions or norms of mourning are shaped by power relations (a thesis already encap-sulated in her arguments in *Antigone's Claim* and elsewhere).[2] She now speculates about how the experience of mourning might open up 'another kind of normative aspiration within the field of politics' (Butler 2004a: 26); specifically, an opportunity for rethinking politics, and particularly interna-tional politics, in a less aggressive, more ethical mode. In saying this it is important to be aware that Butler is not interested in developing an account of grief or mourning *per se*. She is interested in them only because they expose the precariousness of life and our vulnerability to the Other. Grief and mourning, that is, are symptomatic of the interdependent nature of human existence. So how does this argument work?

In the act of 'undergoing' grief and mourning, Butler surmises, 'some-thing about who we are is revealed, something that delineates the ties we have to others', moreover 'that shows us that *these ties constitute who we are*, ties or bonds that compose us' (2004a: 22, my emphasis). It is not only that loss makes a 'tenuous "we" of us all' (Butler 2004a: 20) since at some time we will all experience the loss of someone (through death, or simply through separation). It is not even that loss and vulnerability are effects of 'being socially constituted bodies, attached to others, at risk of losing those attachments, exposed to others, at risk of violence by virtue of that exposure' (Butler 2004a: 20). What is critical is that grief and mourning are forms of 'dispossession' (Butler 2004a: 28): when loss occurs, that is, 'I think I have lost "you" only to discover that "I" have gone missing as well' (Butler 2004a: 22).[3] Loss reveals the subject's dependence on an other for its own sense of self and thus for its continued existence. With the dispossession that follows the loss of the other, a transformation in the self takes place. I am no longer what I was. It is precisely at the moments when one body is undone by another – and for Butler the body is central to her conceptualisation of vulnerability since it is the body that exposes us or opens us up to the other: to their gaze, their touch, their violence (Butler 2004b: 21) – that human existence is explicitly exposed as one of interdependence. Vitally, it is this porosity to the other (a corporeal porosity) that is also the source of an ethical connection with the other.

Although grief is often assumed to be privatising, Butler demurs. She argues that actually, mourning 'furnishes a sense of political community of a complex order' by foregrounding 'the relational ties that have implications for theorizing fundamental dependency and *ethical responsibility*' (Butler 20004a: 22, my emphasis). Loss exposes the fact that the one thing that all humans share is a physical dependence on other humans for their survival. Clearly violence – individual or state-sponsored; pre-emptive or retaliatory – is one of the principal means by which that survival is put at risk. In order to counter such violence, and to acknowledge ethically the fact of our being 'invariably in community' (Butler 2004a: 27) with the other, what Butler suggests is the development of a 'point of identification with suffering itself' (2004a: 30). Instead of denying human vulnerability, in order to recognise it, losses must be grieved. The difficulty, of course, is that not all human lives are deemed to be worthy of grief; indeed, not all deaths count as deaths deserving public acknowledgement. It depends on the social norms regulating the scene of recognition (Butler 2005a). Bearing this in mind, from an ethical perspective identifying with suffering has to be allied, for Butler, with a certain critical reflexivity about the ways in which particular lives figure as more vulnerable or more valuable than others; in short, as more human than others (Butler 2004a: 30). Making grief into a resource for either ethics or politics invites the question: 'Who counts as human? Whose lives count as lives? ... What *makes for a grievable life?*' (Butler 2004a: 20).

It is Butler's emphasis in *Precarious Life* on the regulatory production of the human and the kinds of normative violence that are operative in ranking who can be mourned or grieved, and more broadly, who counts, that I find most compelling. Butler marshals plenty of examples to demonstrate what she calls 'a differential allocation of grievability' at work in the world today. She compares the public grief ensuing in the US over the death of journalist Daniel Pearl with the *San Francisco Chronicle*'s refusal (on the basis that it would cause offence) to publish either obituaries or memorials for a group of dead Palestinian women and children killed by Israeli troops. She exposes how the unmournability of specific lives serves to dehumanise them and thus to effect a form of normative violence against them, a violence, that is, that cannot be seen as violence because we cannot see such lives as lives at all. Finally, she identifies how mourning as an act of nation building is predicated upon a process of 'national melancholia', wherein certain deaths are disavowed as deaths. Her point, of course, is not just that the norms defining who counts (in all the senses just noted: mournability, grievability, liveability and recognisability as human) are socially conditioned; it is also that such normatively driven accounting also serves a variety of political purposes.

I am also persuaded by her contention that the experience (both individual and collective) of mourning might motivate people to act politically. Certainly grief at losing a son or daughter in the armed forces serving in Iraq since 2003 has galvanised parents to become active members of the antiwar movement on both sides of the Atlantic (McRobbie 2006: 85, n. 2). Take, for instance, Reg Keys of 'Military Families Against the War', who stood against Tony Blair in Sedgefield in the 2005 General Election, campaigning under the strapline 'War-torn families unite'. Moreover, it is also clear that there are already many instances at work of an ethical or political identification with suffering of the kind that Butler advocates. Butler herself cites two particularly potent examples. First, she explores how the 'shock, outrage, remorse and grief' produced by the circulation of photos of Vietnamese children being burned and killed by napalm, photos the US public 'were not supposed to see', was pivotal in turning the tide of public opinion against the Vietnam War (Butler 2004a: 150). The US public (or at least sectors thereof) identified with the vulnerability, indeed destruction, of the lives on view and expressed ethical outrage at their (continued) treatment. Second, she touches very briefly upon the activities of Women in Black as an example of feminist opposition to militarism. What is noteworthy about this network is precisely that the silent vigils it holds in cities throughout the world exemplify the very identification with suffering that Butler's ethics advocates: when women, that is, reflect on their own suffering and the suffering of other women who have 'been raped, tortured or killed in concentration camps, women who have disappeared, whose loved ones have disappeared or have been killed, whose homes have been demolished'.[4]

Butler, however, is not simply concerned with reflecting on the kinds of human accounting that prioritise certain lives and that negate particular deaths. She is positing an ethics of responsibility towards the other based on vulnerability. This account of vulnerability draws on arguments that Butler makes in *Psychic Life* about primary dependency and is thus intrinsically connected to the idea of ek-stasis that she deploys throughout her work. Obviously there is much that could, and should, be said about this ethics. I will restrict myself, however, to highlighting what I perceive to be two of its problems. The first concerns the ontological assumptions underpinning Butler's discussion of human vulnerability as it relates to the idea of ek-stasis. The second relates to Butler's understanding of the social, which I will argue is too thin.

Ek-static subjectivity

Butler's first treatment of the idea of ek-static subjectivity comes in *Subjects of Desire*, when she describes the relation between desire and self-consciousness in Hegel's *Phenomenology*. Like the myopic 'Mr. Magoo whose automobile careening through the neighbor's chicken coop always seems to land on all four wheels', ready to travel somewhere else to fail all over again (Butler 1999b: 21), the journeying consciousness according to Butler is not a subject progressing neatly from one 'ontological place to another' on its way to journey's end. It is the narrative of a consciousness that is perpetually outside itself; the narrative of an 'ek-static' subject, a subject that, because negativity is 'essential to self-actualization', must 'suffer its own loss of identity again and again in order to realize its fullest sense of self' (Butler 1999b: 13).

When Butler returns to ek-stasis in *Precarious Life*, which is the rendition that I am concerned with, she defines it as 'literally, to be outside oneself'. Helpfully, she furnishes various examples of what this means: 'to be transported beyond oneself by a passion, but also to be *beside oneself* with rage or grief' (Butler 2004a: 24). The movement outside the self that characterizes ek-stasis is, she surmises, a movement that is potentially transformative of the self. It is, to borrow a phrase from *Giving an Account of Oneself* (where Butler is describing recognition as a process of ek-stasis), the means 'by which I become other than what I was and so cease to be able to return to what I was' (2005a: 27). The idea of being outside oneself also has a second related connotation: for it indicates that the self 'invariably loses itself in the Other who secures that self's existence' (Butler 2004b: 149). Otherness, that is, is constitutive of selfhood. In order to understand the significance of this idea for Butler's understanding of the vulnerability that she sees as fundamental to – indeed 'ineradicable' from (Butler 2004a: xiv) – human life and sociality, I want to reprise briefly the argument that she makes in *The Psychic Life of Power*. I have two reasons for doing so: first, because it is here, I contend, that most of the co-ordinates of her increasingly complex account of ek-stasis are laid out, and second, because it is this account that informs the discussion of primary vulnerability in *Precarious Life*.[5]

The context for Butler's discussion in *Psychic Life* is her articulation of a psychoanalytically informed theory of subjectivity, a theory that I now want to sketch. There are three key elements to this theory. First, Butler begins by considering primary human dependency. Her argument is very simple: in infancy all subjects develop a 'passionate attachment' to those on whom they depend for life: If 'the child is to persist in a psychic and social sense', Butler notes, 'there must be dependency and the formation of attachment: there is no possibility of not loving, where love is bound up with the requirements for life' (Butler 1997b: 8). Although this initial dependency, or 'primary passion', is not political 'in any usual sense' it is important for Butler principally because it 'conditions the political formation and regulation of subjects', becoming 'the means of their subjection' (1997b: 7). Out of a 'desire to survive' (Butler 1997b: 7) subjects are perpetually willing to submit to their own subordination.

Second, she highlights the role of foreclosure in the formation of the subject, specifically the foreclosure of certain kinds of passionate attachment or 'impossible' loves. 'If the subject is produced through foreclosure', she notes, 'then the subject is produced by a condition from which it is, by definition, separated and differentiated' (Butler 1997b: 9). Far from being an autonomous subject, the psychic subject is thus a dependent subject, a subject that is produced in subordination and whose continued subordination is essential to its continued existence. While primary attachments are essential to the survival of the child, if the subject is to emerge fully then they must ultimately be disavowed. That is, the subject must disavow its dependency on the Other in order to become a subject (even though the impossible loves that it disavows continue to haunt it, threatening it with its own unravelling). And so, some aspects of who we 'are' are pre-conscious: they are both unknown and unknowable to us.

The final element is her (Freudian) conception of melancholia, an idea already outlined in detail in *Gender Trouble* and developed in subsequent works. Melancholia, as Butler understands it, is the means by which a lost object, instead of being let go of, as in mourning (though of course Freud ultimately drops the distinction between mourning and melancholia), is incorporated 'into the very structure of the ego' (Butler 1990: 57). Thus an act of identification takes place in which the melancholic subject incorporates the lost object into its own ego such that its ego is constituted by that identification, the result of which is the creation of 'a new structure of identity' in which certain qualities of the lost other are permanently internalised in the ego (Butler 1990: 58). In a particularly provocative and suggestive move in her earlier texts, Butler applies this process specifically to heterosexuality, contending that heterosexuality is based upon a similar melancholic process in which, because of a prior prohibition on homosexuality, lost homosexual love objects are incorporated into the ego and an identification set up with them. Hence the so-called 'never-never' structure of gendered identity (Butler 1990: 69) that recurs throughout her work: 'the

"I never loved her, and I never lost her", uttered by a woman, the "I never loved him, I never lost him", uttered by a man' (Butler 1997b: 138). In *Psychic Life*, however, Butler also links melancholia more specifically to the formation of conscience and guilt, to suggest that a subject's very capacity for reflexivity is itself an effect of disavowal, foreclosure and the installation of the other within the ego. What is critical here is that it is loss – and its survival – that is essential to the inauguration of the subject.

Together all of these elements suggest a self that is never quite knowable to itself because of what it must disavow, a process Diana Fuss captures nicely when she notes that '[b]y incorporating the spectral remains of the dearly departed love-object, the subject vampiristically comes to life' (1995: 1). This is a self that is, moreover, always susceptible to subordination by any Other who promises to guarantee its survival or 'continued existence' (Fuss 1995: 7); and who through its potential to suffer loss is always potentially open to the transformations brought about by melancholia.

Butler does not simply limit her account of this ek-static process to the kinds of interactions humans have with other humans from birth. Subjectivity is equally an effect of encounters with the social world, broadly conceived. As Butler puts it in *Undoing Gender*: 'one's persistence as an "I" through time, depends fundamentally on a social norm that exceeds that "I", that positions that "I" ec-statically, outside of itself in a world of complex and historically changing norms' (2004b: 32). From this she concludes that 'in our very ability to persist, we are dependent on what is outside of us, on a broader sociality, and this dependency is the basis of our endurance and survivability' (Butler 2004b: 32). Indeed, the very fact that one comes into a world already configured by certain norms that 'precede and exceed me' (Butler 2004b: 32) suggests that any sense of self must always already be a social self, an historically conditioned self, a self governed by the regulatory norms that determine what makes a culturally intelligible subject and what allows for a liveable life. This accords with her argument in *Psychic Life* where she explores how the topography of the psyche is configured according to certain prevailing social norms, and is thereby configured according to the operations of power.[6]

If we relate the foregoing discussion to the concerns that motivate Butler in *Precarious Life*, we can see how the relation to the Other (widely understood) conditions the nature of the self that is formed, and how the social world itself impinges on, or more accurately is constitutive of, subjectivity in particular, regulated ways. We can also thus discern a site of critique: against the norms that limit who counts. A conundrum nevertheless remains. If, as Butler writes, '*the ec-static character of our existence is essential to the possibility of persisting as human*' (2004b: 33), since we depend on things external to us (others, norms and so on) in order to be, then what is it about relationality, ek-stasis or our vulnerability to the other that would lead us to a non-violent encounter with them rather than to a course of self-preservation whatever the cost? What is it in the experience of vulnerability, in other words, that might lead us to treat the Other, indeed any Other wherever and whoever they are, as deserving an ethical response from us, moreover a response that reveals our own potential vulnerability at their hands? To try to make sense of these questions, it is necessary, I think, to return to *Psychic Life*.

Butler's debt to Spinoza

There is a paradox at the heart of *The Psychic Life of Power* that I have always found slightly perplexing. This is Butler's debt to Spinoza.[7] *Psychic Life* is a book that seeks to explain its own paradox, the paradox of subjection. Deriving from Foucault's notion of *assujetissement*, this is the contention that the subject depends for its existence upon its continued subordination by power. Why, Butler wants to know, is this subject 'passionately attached' to the conditions of its own subjection? Or, as she puts it, 'What is the psychic form that power takes?' (Butler 1997b: 2). Part of her answer, and the part I want to dwell on here, is that the desire for its continued subjection by power is the result of 'a *prior* desire for social existence' (Butler 1997b: 19, my emphasis), or what Spinoza called the *conatus*, the contention that 'desire is always the desire to persist in one's own being' (Butler 1997b: 28; see also Butler 2004b: 32 and Spinoza 1955: 136). There is, of course, something deeply problematic about this debt to Spinoza, for, as Butler recognises in *Subjects of Desire*, the Substance, of which the *conatus* is an attribute, is a 'metaphysical' substance (1999b: 12). Furthermore, in *Psychic Life* she observes that Spinoza promotes a 'metaphysical monism' (Butler 1997b: 28). The Spinozan desire for existence is a metaphysical desire, a desire that transcends culture, language and politics. And so she proposes in *Psychic Life* 'to recast' this metaphysical idea as a 'more pliable notion of social being', rendering it as 'something that can be brokered only within the risky terms of social life' (Butler 1997b: 28). It is here that the tension noted at the beginning of this chapter (between Butler's deconstruction of particular ontological claims and her own ontological assumptions) enters. For while the terms by which persistence – or survival – is made possible are *social* terms, that is, norms that are the contingent effects of specific power relations, the desire for existence itself, as she deploys it, appears not to be. This is clear from her characterisation of it. The desire for existence, she notes, is a desire that is 'exploited by regulatory power' (Butler 1997b: 19), a desire with the 'capacity' to 'be withdrawn and to reattach' under different modes of subjection (Butler 1997b: 62), a 'desire to survive, "to be"', which is a 'pervasively exploitable desire' (Butler 1997b: 7). For desire to be exploited – or exploitable – by power implies, of course, that it pre-exists power and is thus not one of its effects. Likewise, the notion that desire can withdraw and reattach suggests also that it is a substance with capacities independent of power. Truncating an argument developed at more length elsewhere (Lloyd 2007b), it means that the desire

for existence appears to operate as an *a priori* universal that transcends and/
or precedes culture and society.

It would be wrong, in my view, to see this emphasis on Spinoza's *conatus*
as so much detritus in her thought that is eventually vacuumed away, to be
replaced by a more resolutely constructionist idea of desire. Rather the
'desire to survive', as she often terms it, is an idea that persists into her
most recent work. In *Undoing Gender*, for instance, she explicitly claims that
'the Spinozan *conatus* remains at the core of my work' (Butler 2004b: 198),
explaining in a later essay in the same volume both what excited her about
his work, namely 'the extrapolation of emotional states from the primary
persistence of the *conatus* in human beings' and why it was so important to
her: it allowed for 'a form of vitalism that persists even in despair' (Butler
2004b: 235). Moreover, her increasing emphasis on what I call the 'politics
of survival' is predicated, in my view, on this idea, albeit mediated through
Hegel's understanding of desire as the desire for recognition. The crucial
point is that problems similar to those found in *Psychic Life* – attributing to
the desire to exist certain qualities *prior* to its imbrication in power
relations – are carried over into this later work. For here what interests
Butler is the way that social norms of recognition are configured such that
the desire 'to persist in one's own being' is denied to certain individuals
(Butler 2004b: 31). In other words, it is the norms of recognition that she
subjects to critical scrutiny, *not* the desire for existence as such. As with her
earlier discussion, Butler never interrogates the 'status' of this Spinozan
precept (Chambers 2003: 147). She thus continues to use it as an explanation for the paradox of subjection (why the subject accepts its own subordination by power) and, by extension, a politics of survival. But now she
also appears to deploy it as an explanation for an ethics of responsibility
towards the other. What, therefore, is relation between the desire for existence and the idea of a non-violent relation with the other?

A partial answer is perhaps supplied in *Undoing Gender*, when Butler
notes that for Spinoza 'This [conscious and persistent] being desires not
only to persist in its own being but ... to live in a world in which it both
reflects the value of others' lives as well as its own' (2004b: 235). If, when
Butler takes over Spinoza's idea of the *conatus*, she also takes over his idea
of a dualistic ethics where ethical or 'virtuous actions' can be subdivided
into two types, those arising from tenacity or *'animositas'*, that is, 'the desire
whereby every man strives to preserve his own being', and those from
'highmindedness' or *'generositas'*, that is, 'the desire whereby every man
endeavours ... to aid other men and unite them to himself in friendship'
(Spinoza, 1955: 172–73), then there is a possible explanation for the ethical
relation to the other that she envisages. This is one where, as for Spinoza,
the 'virtuous person does not merely pursue private advantage, but seeks to
cooperate with others' (Garrett 1995: 872). There is some reinforcement for
this view when, in a conversation with William Connolly, discussing the
possibilities of a 'new sense of ethics' that might emerge from ek-static

relationality, Butler notes that this new ethics 'involves paradoxically, both a persisting in one's being (Spinoza) and a certain humility, or a recognition that persistence requires humility, and that humility, when offered to others, becomes a generosity' (Butler in Butler and Connolly 2000: 5–6). Whether the desire for existence and the generosity that Butler alludes to are two distinct qualities, or whether, as critics have suggested of Spinoza, cooperation with the other ultimately reduces to an act of self-preservation guided by the belief that assisting the other guarantees one's own survival (an ethical egoism), is a moot point. Either way, the idea of the *conatus* as universal and pre-discursive appears to be at the heart of Butler's ethics.

Why is this so significant? The justification that Butler offers for her efforts to critique the ontological is that ontological claims define what or who qualifies as real. Ontology is thus intrinsically connected, for Butler, with power. Ontological claims function to generate hierarchies, to subordinate, to exclude and to create 'domains of unthinkability' (Butler in Meijer and Prins 1998: 280). Contesting them is thus a way of contesting who counts as real – which persons, which kinds of lives and so forth. It is an expressly political move. The fact, therefore, that Butler deploys an ontological claim of her own *without contesting its validity or scope* is potentially problematic, for, according to the logic of her own argument, such unproblematised claims work in the interests of power, limiting who or what counts. Assuming rather than problematising the ontological nature of the desire for existence means, for instance, that lacking such a desire becomes unthinkable. To construe the Spinozan *conatus* as a principle that pre-exists subjection, as Butler does, is thus to commit the very same theoretical error of which she accuses *inter alia* Lacan, Žižek, Foucault, and Kristeva: that by siting a particular element or quality (be that the Imaginary, the Real, heterogeneous bodily pleasures, or the semiotic) outside of culture, they effectively immunise that notion from critique and also, crucially, from political transformation.[8]

When Butler neglects to account for the 'discursive and social production' of the desire to exist in either *Psychic Life* (Chambers, 2003: 147) or her more recent work, she too places that idea beyond critique and outside of politics. This, in my view, is a mistake. What is required, instead, is an exploration of the desire for existence as a discursive construction or cultural practice operating according to and constituted by certain historically specific norms and power relations. This is necessary not only in order to be able to assess the potential costs (and benefits) of an ethics (or, indeed, an account of subjectivity) that takes this postulate as its starting-point. It is also necessary to overcome the limits that this assumed connection between the *conatus* (as an ontological presupposition) and ethics sets on our ability to think the possible. Here I want to turn my attention to my final concern. Earlier I noted that Butler proposed to 'recast' Spinoza's essentially metaphysical notion of the *conatus* into a 'more pliable notion of social being' (Butler 1997b: 28). My question in what follows is whether Butler's understanding of the social would allow her to 'recast' this idea in such a way as to accommodate my demand for an account of the desire for existence that is able to acknowledge not just its discursivity but also its historicity. To set the scene, I briefly reflect on the link for Butler between ethics and politics.

Ethics and politics

In her introduction to the *Judith Butler Reader*, Sarah Salih surmises that one of the themes that 'may be said to characterize Butler's work as a whole ... is the ethical impetus to extend the norms by which "humans" are permitted to conduct livable lives in socially recognized spheres' (2004: 4). Is it, in fact, judicious to read Butler's discussions of heteronormativity in *Gender Trouble*, say, or her account of the resignificatory potential of hate-speech in *Excitable Speech*, in terms of such an ethics? Certainly both texts, in different ways, are concerned with forms of normative violence that produce only certain subjects as viable and culturally intelligible, and their speech as publicly acceptable speech, but is it accurate to interpret this concern as an ethical rather than political concern? I would suggest not. Both texts, it seems to me, are fundamentally political texts, the only difference being that the former foregrounds a subversive politics while the latter advocates a resignificatory politics.

There is clear support for such an interpretation in the remark I reported earlier, where Butler declares her resistance to ethics on the grounds that it displaces politics. She elaborates thus: a political approach takes 'the use of power as a point of departure for a critical analysis', a move that 'is substantially different from an ethical framework' (Butler in Butler and Connolly 2000: 5). This suggests to me that Butler would read her own work *prior to* 2000 as addressing *political* rather than ethical issues. But what of the statement itself? There is something slightly odd about it. In setting up an opposition between ethics and politics, Butler *appears* to suggest that ethics is apolitical insofar as it is not inflected, conditioned or underpinned by power relations. For a thinker whose work draws on Foucault's this is a peculiar statement to make, for, as he showed in his final writings, social norms shape in a variety of ways the kinds of ethical relations that are possible (as well as thinkable and allowable) with both self and Other. And, to be fair, Butler acknowledges as much with regard to Foucault, at least, not just in the conversation from which her remark is extracted but also in *Giving an Account of Oneself*. Given her expressed ambivalence towards ethical frameworks, what is to be made of her own recent foray into ethics? Does it testify to a willingness to adopt an apparently apolitical position in order to think about self–other relations? Or, is the ethics that Butler articulates better thought of as an ethico-politics, or politicised ethics, that is, an ethical framework that takes power as its starting point?

Although for reasons of spatial economy I am unable to pursue this argument very far, I think her engagement with the work of Emmanuel Levinas is instructive here. When Butler turns to Levinas she does so, she contends, in order to elaborate the significance of Levinas's idea of ethics 'in the context of today' (Butler 2004a: 140). There are two particular aspects of his thought that are relevant. She notes, through the idea of the face, 'he gives us a way of thinking about the relationship between representation and humanization', and, in addition, he 'offers, within a tradition of Jewish philosophy, an account of the relationship between violence and ethics that has some important implications for thinking through what an ethic of Jewish non-violence might be' (Butler 2004a: 140). I want to pause briefly to consider the first of these claims. Instead of subjecting to critical scrutiny the idea of the face as the means by which others make ethical demands on us, Butler simply concurs with it. Although she disagrees with Levinas about the nature of the address the face makes (he sees it as accusatory; she does not), she seems to accept unquestioningly that it is on the basis of our 'primary susceptibility to the action and the face of the other, the full ambivalence of the unwanted address' that 'exposure to injury *and* our responsibility for the Other' are constituted (Butler 2005a: 91). What she then does is show how Levinas's work lends itself to an exploration of how particular 'faces' are produced. And so Butler discusses how photographs in the *New York Times* of young Afghani women throwing off their burkas were used to 'humanise' those women for an American readership; their humanisation being not a recognition of the agonies and pains they suffered during the US invasion and thus of the precariousness of their lives, but of their 'liberation' as they divested themselves of their repression, symbolised by their throwing off of their burkas. Their bare faces symbolising, according to Butler, 'successfully exported American cultural progress' (Butler 2004a: 142). She also looks at how certain faces are produced as 'evil' – the faces of Osama bin Laden, Yasser Arafat, and Saddam Hussein – and how this construction of them according to dominant cultural norms works to dehumanise them, and all like them (Butler 2004a: 141f.).

It is, I propose, this same approach that has largely characterised to date her discussion of the relation between ethics and politics in general. She concentrates, that is, on exploring how power circumscribes the kinds of ethical encounters that take place – how existing normative frames operate to regulate and determine who counts (and how they count), as well as who is derealised in the process. At the same time, however, she appears to take for granted the existence of the ethical imperative, by which I mean the factor or principle that makes possible the ethical encounter. This is what happens with the idea of the *conatus* and the impulse of 'generosity' towards the other that arises from ek-stasis; it is also what happens when she accepts Levinas's idea of the face (the ethical demand of the other on the subject). On these occasions, therefore, Butler argues *as if* the ethical imperative is *apolitical* (because it is presented as prediscursive and, thus, as not predicated on power relations) and *as if* ethical encounters in determinate contexts are political (because they operate through power relations and normative violence). Although it would be wrong to dismiss Butler's concern with lived ethical conduct and how the norms that govern recognition operate differentially throughout society, as noted earlier, the dependence of her ethical theory on certain unexamined prediscursive assumptions needs to be redressed. Does Butler's work provide the resources to offer a plausible account of the discursive and social construction of the desire to exist (of desire 'recast', as it were)? My argument is that, ultimately, it does not. This is because of the impoverished conception of the social with which Butler works.

Social and political

As Kirsten Campbell points out in relation to Butler's discussion of the Lacanian Symbolic, one of the difficulties with Butler's thinking here is that 'the "social", the "cultural", the "symbolic" and the "norm" are not clear and distinct conceptual categories in her work' (Campbell 2002: 647). Indeed, Butler appears to use them all synonymously. What Campbell locates as a problem with the idea of the Symbolic is, I think, a more extensive problem pervading both Butler's understanding of language and resignification, and, more to the point here, her understanding of politics, ethics and emotions. One of the oppositions that sustains Butler's work is that between the social and/or cultural on the one hand, and *a priori* universals that transcend or precede culture and society, on the other. Although Butler's aim, as Laclau contends, may well be to expose these 'structural determination[s]', as he calls them, as culturally and historically contingent products (2000: 188), it is how she goes about this that is the issue. In this respect, it is not just that Butler's own work relies, as I have suggested, on certain universal ontological or metaphysical claims of its own. It is that her understanding of the social is too narrow and undifferentiated to do the work that she wants it to, because it is insufficiently historicised. When Butler deploys the term 'social', whether in relation to norms, culture, or language, it signals a contingent effect circumscribed by power. What she does not do, however, is pay sufficient attention to the *historical* conditions of emergence of these particular effects. She does not, that is, examine the historical practices that themselves generate the social.

So to demonstrate that the desire to exist is a thoroughly social rather than metaphysical desire (or, even, one simply affected by social arrangements) Butler must, in my view, do rather more than contend that the form that this desire takes depends upon the material context in which it is articulated, and that consequently shapes it or gives it a determinate meaning. She has to address the historicity of this idea. She has to examine the actual historical conditions of its emergence. She needs, in other words, to minimise what might be thought of her quasi-Derridean impulse to explore ontological conditions of possibility (in this case of an ethical relation with the other with, recall, the capacity to reconfigure international relations, and which is based on the abstract notion of a desire to exist) and to maximise the Nietzschean–Foucauldian imperative to examine precisely the kinds of assumptions this desire is predicated upon, the discourses it is locked into, the norms that configure it (and that it configures) and the implications it has for particular practices.[9] Only then will she be able to create the potential for a critique of the desire for existence as a social artefact, and thus to open up a space for rethinking the relation between desire, existence, survival and the human. Only then will she be able to explore fully what I have tentatively called a *cultural politics* of vulnerability.

Notes

1 This was the time, recall, of the Guantanamo detentions, the Patriot Act, and the establishment of the Office for Homeland Security.
2 Intriguingly, Butler never considers how the act/experience of mourning itself may be conventional; she simply adopts Freud's account of what takes place psychologically in mourning and melancholia.
3 Arguably for Butler other emotions might be equally dispossessing, such as love, desire, anger and so forth, since all reveal one's dependence on the Other. While I agree with this, in principle, what bothers me about Butler's approach is that she does not consider how particular emotions themselves are culturally constituted. Indeed, as it stands, she seems to accord them a certain naturalism by assuming that they are experiences that we all have or are capable of having because we all experience love and desire and so on. She does not, that is, explore how particular emotions are produced as the effects of certain socially constituted discourses, practices, and power relations, and how, as such, their shape might differ under different conditions and how those entitled to experience them might also be culturally determined. Indeed, she appears far more concerned with the human ontological condition (of dependence and vulnerability) than with what Chambers has called the 'ontic practices of emotion' (personal correspondence with the author). If this is the case, then it is precisely this concern that generates the tension in her work outlined at the outset of this chapter: between her deconstruction of ontological claims and her own unexamined ontological assumptions.
4 'Women in Black', http://www.womeninblack.net/mission.html (first accessed 25/04/06). Women in Black began in Israel in 1988 when women began protesting against Israel's Occupation of the West Bank and Gaza. The network subsequently spread. Since 1991 women in Belgrade have held weekly vigils; Women in Black New York have held weekly vigils since 1993.
5 The links between *Psychic Life* and *Precarious Life* are manifold. There is the shared lexicon, the explicit anticipation in the former of an ethics based on the desire to be, the central place accorded to mourning and melancholia in both (see Lloyd 2007b).
6 This argument is developed in more detail in Lloyd 2007b, ch. 4.
7 This point is also developed by Chambers (2003: 146–48).
8 Recall that one of the strategies of argumentation that Butler deploys in *Gender Trouble*, and elsewhere, is to contend that all notions of the prediscursive are, in fact, constructions of discourse that are posited as prior to discourse. It is not the fact that she is inconsistent that bothers me; it is what consequences follow from this in terms of how she conceptualises the relation between ethics and politics.
9 On the opposition between Derrida and Foucault in relation to Butler, see Nealon (1996).

Part IV
Ethics and sovereignty

8 Change of address

Butler's ethics at sovereignty's deadlock

Jodi Dean[1]

A 26 June 2006 editorial in *The Nation* urged progressives in the United States to recognise that now is the time for conviction, not caution. Judith Butler, in her 2005 book, *Giving an Account of Oneself*, suggests otherwise, opposing conviction to responsibility. Butler reads conviction critically, in terms of an ethics that 'takes the self to be the ground and measure of moral judgment' (2005a: 108). And, even as she acknowledges that there might be times for condemnation and denunciation, her discussion works against these modes of judgement, associating them with a kind of certainty and opacity that disallows connections to another. Whose advice should we heed? Is Left politics fundamentally incompatible with conviction, condemnation, and denunciation?

My concern here is with Left responses to the religious, nationalist, and market fundamentalisms dominating contemporary social and political life. Some critical theorists writing today emphasise generosity and tolerance. Their recommendations for dealing with contemporary fundamentalisms involve micropolitical and ethical practices that work on the self in its immediate relations and responses. Others focus on debate and exchange. They are inclined to look to legal remedies, to guarantees of rights and to regulations concerning the proper extension of religion and the market into political affairs. Still others insist upon more militant approaches anchored in truth and the possibility of a radical act capable of changing the very contours of the political situation. In this chapter, I consider Butler's efforts to work through these questions in her later writings on law, politics, and ethics.

The primary characteristic of this later work is Butler's persistent turning of impossibilities into possibilities, of barriers into if not exactly grounds then opportunities for responsibility, recognition, and resignification (cf. Žižek 2005: 137). Opacity, vulnerability, exposure, and grief become, in Butler's hands, openings to others and to ourselves, resources that might enable us to understand how our human being is necessarily and unavoidably a being together. Yet, Butler's ethical sensitivity is purchased at the cost of politics. Butler presents ethical resources as available only under conditions of the denial of politics. Should we make political choices, or act politically, we will cut ourselves off from the insights and capacities arising out of vulnerability and grief. Thus, she offers a set of responses to contemporary fundamentalisms that eschew condemnation and conviction, that present openness and critique not only as ethically preferable to decisions for or against but as necessarily incompatible with the division necessary for politics.

Butler's ethical turn need not displace politics. Rather, this displacement results from her constrained conception of sovereignty, wherein sovereignty functions less as a political arrangement than as a kind of Master capable not only of holding together diffuse meanings and effects by the force of its word, a word with power to initiate and to end, but also of fully determining the words that it utters and the effects of these words. I show here how Butler's critique of sovereignty misfires, shooting at fantastic returns of a Master rather than attending to the more complex reformatting of sovereignty in globalised communicative capitalism (cf. Dean 2002).

Governmentality and fantasy

I begin with *Excitable Speech* (1997a). Butler presents her exploration of power and agency against the background of Michel Foucault's notion of governmentality. From the eighteenth century on, Foucault argues, state power has formed an ensemble of 'institutions, procedures, analyses and reflections ... calculations and tactics ... which has as its target population, as its principal form of knowledge, political economy, and as its essential technical means apparatuses of security' (1991: 102). For Butler, governmentality means that, rather than 'constrained by the parameters of sovereignty', contemporary power is 'diffused throughout disparate and competing domains of the state apparatus, and through civil society in diffuse forms' (1997a: 78). In contrast to Foucault, who, even as he recognises that the governmentalised state is lacking in unity, individuality, and functionality, asserts nonetheless the continued centrality of the problem of sovereignty, Butler reads governmentality as replacing sovereignty. She writes that 'contemporary power is no longer sovereign in character' (1997a: 74) and that power is 'no longer constrained within the sovereign form of the state' (1997a: 78).

The claim that governmentality has replaced sovereignty is crucial to Butler's critique of critical legal studies arguments in favour of regulating hate speech. She argues that accompanying the dispersion of power characteristic of governmentality is a 'particular historical anxiety' linked to problems in locating injury and finding the origin of specific acts: the historical loss of the sovereign organisation of power appears to occasion the fantasy of its return (1997a: 78). Butler sees evidence of such fantastic returns in idealisations of speech acts as sovereign actions coupled with idealisations of sovereign state power, idealisations she finds underpinning arguments for hate speech codes. Again, these fantasies are said to compensate for a prior loss of sovereign power. The fantasies that in speaking one wields sovereign power and that state speech takes a sovereign form compensate for the absence of such a sovereign.

Although one might do well to note the Nietzschean resonances in Butler's reading of legal theorists, efforts to produce a subject capable of being responsible, such an approach misses the way sovereignty in Butler's account functions as a kind of master signifier capable of holding together an unstable chain of significations. Butler's criticism presumes that holding a person legally accountable for her words requires viewing that person as a sovereign speaker, as an originator of words, a controller of words, a user of words who remains unbound and unconditioned by them. For Butler, hate-speech codes overdetermine 'the scene of utterance' as they reduce racism to a single linguistic site. This reduction, she explains, presupposes the efficacy of the speaker in injuring and subordinating another through the force of her speech. It presupposes, in other words, the fantasy of a *sovereign* speaker, of a speaker capable of consolidating at a single site the structures, practices, and harms of racism.

Butler rightly rejects this fantastic figure of sovereignty. But, why should we accept that such a figure inhabits the writings of critical legal theorists or hate speech codes at all? Two aspects of Butler's own account make her figure of a fantastic sovereign returning to haunt the law unconvincing.

First, given that her focus in *Excitable Speech* is on American law and the place of free speech in American jurisprudence, it is difficult to make sense of the phrase 'no longer' when Butler claims that 'contemporary power is *no longer* sovereign in character'. If the notion of sovereignty she has in mind is one invested in a single sovereign body or locus of authority, then the American framework of separation of powers eludes from the start a simple notion of sovereignty. The innovation of the American constitution was its investment of sovereignty in the people and its provisions for enabling the people to exercise sovereignty not only through laws but through necessarily separated powers (cf. Passavant 2002). The federal system relies on separating and distributing the means of governance, again, so as to insure that the people remain sovereign. If sovereignty in the United States has been thought as a sovereignty of the people, then what could it mean to say that the figure of a unified, powerful, sovereign master returns in legal discourse?

Second, given Butler's reliance on Foucault's notion of governmentality, why should we not consider hate codes and the discourse around hate codes likewise in terms of the decentred structure of the state? Interventions into the constitution and management of a population, regulations on hate speech are typically pursued at campus, local, and state levels rather than as federal laws. We might say, then, that such codes are tools or instruments that the people use in governing themselves, in arranging their interactions with one another. And, we might well recognise that these instruments will be contested, open to interpretation, and implicated in other practices through which the people attempt to change their collective modes of being (cf. Passavant and Dean 2001). Yet Butler treats these legal codes as somehow resistant to interpretation and resignification, insisting instead that they are attempts to isolate accountability in the words of a single sovereign speaker.

Perhaps my reading of governmentality misses what is actually at stake in Butler's emphasis on a 'particular historical anxiety'. She is working against the background of what Lacanian psychoanalysis theorises as a change in the discourse of the Master, the loss of the ability of a Master signifier to hold together a chain of unstable significations and thereby guarantee meaning. Understood against this background, Butler's account of the change in sovereignty appears not simply as an account of legal arrangements of power but also as an account of changes in subjectivity and the character of the social link. The speaking subject is not sovereign. Speech is out of its control. This subject is called into being in and through speech and necessarily remains vulnerable to and dependent upon these linguistic arrangements. Just as sovereignty is not concentrated in a single extra social location but penetrates society as a whole, relying on various state and non-state apparatuses, so does the subject persist in and through language, wielding the very terms that produce and sustain it. Thus, Butler notes that the 'contemporary scene of cultural translation emerges with the presupposition that the utterance does not have the same meaning everywhere, indeed, that the utterance has become a scene of conflict' (1997a: 91).

Slavoj Žižek reads this scene of conflict in terms of the decline of symbolic efficiency (1999: 322). The decline of symbolic efficiency refers to a fundamental uncertainty in our relation to the world, to the absence of a principle of charity that pertains across and through disagreement. We do not know on whom or what to rely, whom or what to trust. Arguments persuasive in one context carry little weight in another (Dean 2006: 40).

One way to understand the difference between Butler's notion of the utterance as a scene of conflict and Žižek's discussion of the decline of symbolic efficiency is in terms of openness. Does the decline usher in opportunities for resignification and new experiences of freedom? Or does it bring with it closure and domination?[2]

In *Excitable Speech*, Butler argues the former, asserting the subversive resignification conflict over an utterance enables even as she treats law as incapable either of such resignification or of providing an opportunity for such resignification (cf. Passavant and Dean 2001). For her, the possibility of new, unanticipated meanings 'offers an unanticipated political future for deconstructive thinking' (Butler 1997a: 161). Butler juxtaposes the willingness to remain open to the futures opened up by the 'insurrectionary effects' of the reappropriation of terms like 'freedom' and 'justice' to a dogmatism that opposes the destabilisation of reality (1997a: 162).

In contrast, Žižek notes the suffocating closure effected by the decline of symbolic norms. The undecideability of basic questions, the ready availability of multiple, conflicting, interpretations, turns decisions into risky gambles. The decline of symbolic efficiency thus results in a combination of impotent interpretations and raw violence. For example, Žižek points to the rise of 'ethical committees' that issue instructions and recommendations, noting that these suggestions are unable to orient the subject in a world. Instead, the subject tends to cling to imaginary spectacles and simulacra, on the one side, while both striving for and being impacted by experiences in the Real, on the other (1999: 369). Left unprotected by symbolic norms, the subject feels threatened by all sorts of imaginary figures, at the mercy of the super-ego injunction to enjoy even as these figure threaten its enjoyment – *why does everyone else seem to be having more fun, wilder sex, cooler vacations, fitter bodies, and better jobs than I?* In sum, the decline of symbolic efficiency introduces new opportunities for guilt and anxiety as well as new attachments to domination as subjects seek relief from the endless injunctions to enjoy – and to do so properly.

I return to these injunctions below. For now, I want to emphasise Butler's account of the conditions of resignification as openings to a political future, openings that the return of the fantastic figure of a sovereign risks closing off.

Sovereignty and resignification

In *Precarious Life* (2004a), Butler confronts the resignifications that followed the attacks on the World Trade Center and the Pentagon on September 11, 2001 ('9/11'). The unanticipated future installed by the insurrectionary effects of this resignification has unfolded as one of preemptive war, indefinite detention, and ever increasing threats to civil liberties. In the name of freedom and democracy, the United States attacked a country that not only had not attacked it but presented no imminent danger. Given that resignification worked to advance militarism, what role does Butler assign it in this later work?

'Assign' is likely the wrong term here. Butler does not speak of resignification. She enacts it, though, as she reworks vulnerability and mourning into opportunities for connecting with others rather than occasions for securing violated borders. Yet, the very sensitivity Butler brings to these moments of vulnerability and mourning exceeds a notion of resignification: after all, she is not saying that mourning means that one has not undergone a loss; rather, she takes awareness of this loss as an opportunity for a deeper appreciation of the way we are given over to others. Vulnerability and loss, as she puts it, might provide new bases for 'reimagining the possibility of community (2004a: 20).[3] So, it is rather inapt to read Butler's method in terms of resignification.

This is particularly true with respect to Butler's argument against former Harvard President Lawrence Summers's charge that criticism of Israel is effectively anti-Semitic. For, rather than resignifying that charge and identity, rather than noting the ways that Summers's speech might misfire, might open up opportunities for insurrection, rather than attending to the repetitions and citations enabling Summers's speech, as one might expect from her arguments in *Excitable Speech*, Butler criticises Summers for identifying Israel with the Jewish people (2004a: 111) and for attempting to stifle critical debate (2004a: 126). I agree with Butler's criticisms. Yet, I am surprised she attributes to Summers's words 'a chilling effect on political discourse' that stokes 'the fear that to criticise Israel during this time is to expose oneself to the charge of anti-Semitism' (2004a: 102). Butler attributes the kind of sovereignty to Summers's speech that she criticises critical legal studies scholars for attributing to hate speech. Her arguments in *Excitable Speech* tell us we should recognise how Summers's words do not have the power to determine the limits of what can and cannot be said.

Butler's move away from resignification unfolds against a refining of her account of the relationship of governmentality and sovereignty. Whereas her concern in *Excitable Speech* is with the encroachment of law as relying on the fantasy of a sovereign power that is attributed to speech, in *Precarious Life* she attends to the way law's suspension itself produces sovereignty. In this later book, sovereignty appears where law is not; it is unbounded by law, 'outside the law' (2004a: 51), in excess of law. Butler continues to assert that governmentality operates through law as a 'set of tactics' (2004a: 52). Yet she focuses on sovereignty's 'resurgence within the field of governmentality' (2004a: 53). She argues that in this new formation, sovereignty is exercised through acts that 'suspend and limit the jurisdiction of law itself' (2004a: 53). So, while *Excitable Speech* analyses the way that a fantasy of sovereign power accompanies extensions of the law, *Precarious Life* confronts situations wherein an anachronistic sovereignty is 'reintroduced in the very acts by which the state suspends law, or contorts law to its own uses' (2004a: 54). In each case, the resurgence of sovereignty is compensatory, compensating for sovereignty's loss (2004a: 56).

The cases differ insofar as resignification is a contestory practice opposed to sovereignty in *Excitable Speech* and an aspect of the very operation of sovereignty in *Precarious Life*. In the earlier book, Butler treats resignification as a practice external to law, a practice she links to the subversion of authority. In the later one, resignification is figured as a means of consolidating authority as sovereign power. Thus, discussing US assertions that it treats the prisoners held in the camp at Guantanamo 'humanely' and in a way consistent with the Geneva Convention, Butler (2004a: 82) writes:

> When the US says, then, that it is treating these prisoners humanely, it uses the word in its own way and for its own purpose, but it does not accept that the Geneva Accords stipulate how the term might legitimately be applied. In effect, it takes the word back from the accords at the very moment that it claims to be acting consistently with the accords. In the moment that it claims to be acting consistently with the

accords, the US effectively maintains that the accords have no power over it.

As it takes the word back and applies it in its own fashion, the US resignifies 'humanely', denying the Geneva Accords the power to determine the condition of the terms' use. In so doing, the US asserts its singular sovereignty over and against international norms.

To be sure, Butler herself does not emphasise resignification here, although she notes that sovereign power extends itself by producing equivocation (2004a: 80). For her, the crucial aspect of this extension is the way it is bound up with the 'extra legal status of these official acts of speech' (2004a: 80). Governmentality extends power throughout the population, using law tactically and instrumentally and relying on various non-state bureaucracies and arrangements. With regard to the indefinite detention of so-called enemy combatants, she argues that decisions to detain 'are already outside the sphere of law' (2004a: 58, 67). She refers repeatedly to the extra-legal status of various decisions, decisions which, precisely because of their externality to the law, animate a resurgent sovereignty. Sovereignty appears as and through the emergence of an unaccountable power dispersed throughout the diffuse operations and tactics of governmentality and concentrated in specific sites of illegitimate decision.

I disagree with Butler's account of the compensatory emergence of a lost sovereignty within the field of governmentality, and I think she misdescribes contemporary changes in the structure of the contemporary state when she finds this sovereignty at work outside of law. Butler, in keeping with the limited view of law she presents in *Excitable Speech*, fails to attend to conflicts and changes *within* law: after all, the Bush administration's policies with regard to trying so-called enemy combatants in special military commissions had to be affirmed by the Supreme Court – which, fortunately, rejected such a grab for power out of hand. When law is itself a site of contestation (as well as a contested site), the very idea of a division between inside and outside makes no sense: the conflict is over the limits, extension, and terrain of law and it persists throughout various legal apparatuses, including the writings and opinions of multiple lawyers and advocates, journalists and politics, and the courts, in the context, in other words, of a governmentalised legal regime.

Butler's constrained account of law, moreover, is linked to her general avoidance of the economy and the ways the non-state bureaucracies and arrangements crucial to governmentality are private-sector, corporate, financial, and market enterprises. The actions of the Bush administration are thus abstracted from the legal and economic contexts that enable them. Paul A. Passavant (2005) attends to these contexts, explicating changes in governance from the Keynesian welfare state to the contemporary post-Fordist state. On one hand, he situates the policies of so-called preventative detention within criminology's 'zero tolerance' approach to crime, imprisonment, and security. He emphasises as well the legal precedents for the US Patriot Act, particularly the Anti-Terrorism and Effective Death Penality Act of 1996. On another hand, he draws out the economic dimensions of the current 'strong neoliberal state', the way that the combination of consumerism and communicative capitalism produce new opportunities for extensions of state power. Describing the emergence of massive commercial databases, the securitisation of places of consumption, and the commodification of security, Passavant concludes:

> Consumer capitalism has made extensive and intensive systems of surveillance, which, through a process of articulation, have vastly extended state surveillance powers. We are also governed by the state through a logic of consumerism whereby the state zones subjects as security risks for differential treatment based on one's consumer profile compiled from commercial data bases. And we are governed by a homeland security regime that is becoming increasingly resistant to change as more and more elements become financially invested in this state's projects and projections.
>
> (Passavant: 2005)

Like Passavant, Saskia Sassen (1996) emphasises the fundamental importance of the global capitalist economy in understanding changes to the institutions and practices of sovereignty. She theorises sovereignty as decentred, its elements 'unbundled' from earlier constellations, displaced from national to international territories and reconstituted for the benefit of financial capital. Both scholars alert us to the emergence of a new legal regime that strengthens the power and reach of the state by securing and protecting corporate, financial, and market interests. For example, contracting for services, outsourcing, and competitive bidding are practices through which public agencies make use of private concerns legally to extend their reach and sidestep the regulations and oversight that typically govern public projects. To describe these developments in terms of the resurgence of sovereignty condenses the larger economic matter into singular loci of decisions, displacing attention from the state's imbrications in the global capitalist economy. Law is not suspended; laws are introduced, changed, and applied in ways that alter and extend state power in some directions (surveillance, detention, military force) rather than others (education, health, social welfare).

If we return to the view of sovereignty as a master that I have suggested underpins Butler's account in *Excitable Speech*, we can reread Butler's notion of the resurgence of sovereignty in the decisions of unaccountable, managerial officials in a way that links to the economy and highlights excessive, lawless power.

As I mention above, Žižek points out that the decline of symbolic efficiency, the disintegration of the discourse of the master, ushers in not new freedoms and possibilities, but new anxieties and experiences of domination. He emphasises the role of capitalism in contributing to this disintegration, its deterritorialising impulses such that 'all that is solid melts into air' (2000: 17). Drawing from the link between Lacan's notion of *jouissance* or surplus enjoyment and the Marxian notion of surplus value, Žižek argues that capitalism relies on the circulation of enjoyment, on an inescapable injunction to enjoy. He writes:

> Because it is focused on the surplus of *objet petit a*, capitalism is no longer the domain of the discourse of the Master. This is where Lacan takes over and paraphrases in his own terms the old Marxian theme, from the *Manifesto*, of how capitalism dissolves all stable links and traditions; how, at its onslaught, 'all that is solid melts into air'. Marx himself made it clear that this 'all that is solid' does not concern only and primarily material products, but also the stability of the symbolic order that provides a definitive identification for subjects.
>
> (Žižek 2000: 40)

The discourse of the Master is replaced in late capitalism by the emergence of nuggets of enjoyment (*objet petit a*) that provide momentary, fleeting sites of attachment. And, rather than providing symbolic identities, capitalism offers multiple, imaginary identities: capitalist subjects are encouraged to remake themselves, to see themselves as projects or works of art available to for remoulding, transformation. They are bombarded with messages telling them that the purchase of a given item will provide them with that extra special something that is missing in their lives. Yet, even as no item ever really has that 'extra something', capitalist subjects continue to shop and strive and capitalism continues to intensify and expand, subjecting ever more aspects of life to its inexorable processes. Žižek thus analyses communicative capitalism in terms of the prevalence of the superego injunction to enjoy. Rather than constrained by a master, contemporary subjects are told that they can have it all, that they must have it all, that something is deeply wrong with them if they do not have it all.

These injunctions are a trap: not only do contemporary subjects know full well that they cannot have it all, they know that actually having it would be completely dangerous. Fully losing oneself in sexual delirium could lead to the transmission of disease; taking fabulous party drugs or drinking large quantities of absinthe could result in death; eating loads of expensive chocolate could lead to obesity and diabetes. All the regulations associated with enjoyment return us to the regulations suggested by experts and ethical committees. These regulations do not provide subjects with symbolic identities grounded in norms. Instead, they provide advice, advice that is ultimately contested and ungroundable and therefore experienced as an illegitimate constraint. The shift away from the discourse of the master, then, does result in the emergence of authorities and regulations, as Butler notes. But these authorities are not signs of a resurgent sovereignty. Instead, they are part of a capitalism's incessant self-revolutionising, its generation of and reliance on excess, wherein supereogistic injunctions to enjoy overlap with contested regulations to suffocate the subject in a situation of unbearable closure (cf. Žižek 2006: 297).

Žižek's emphasis on the superego injunction to enjoy also helps explain the obscene underside of power accompanying public law, thereby accounting for the lawlessness Butler links to sovereignty (cf. Dean 2006: ch. 4). Recall, Butler argues that sovereignty reappears through the suspension of law in an extra-legal operation of power. To call specific practices of the Bush administration resurgences of sovereignty – practices that include the use of signing statements to limit the scope of legislative acts, as well as surveillance activities undertaken with the knowledge of Congressional leaders – mistakenly covers over the split already within law, that is to say, the pervasive criminality already supporting public power. Not only does it treat as something new the lawless irrationality already pervading law as law, but it unnecessarily consolidates and strengthens this lawlessness into the figure of a sovereign.

In a more persuasive account of the irrational violence accompanying law, Žižek argues that law is split between its public letter and its obscene superego supplement (Žižek 2006: 10). At the basis of all law is a violent, irrational element, the tautological force inextricable from law's command, from law's claim that it must be obeyed because it is the law. This violent, irrational, superegoistic side appears as the obscene, nightly or underground, dimension of law sustaining the public ideological edifice, attaching members to a community as it unites them in a shared, dirty secret. For example, the Bush regime continues to deny that it tortures prisoners in Abu Ghraib or any where else. At the same time, it is more than clear from its evasions, from public discussion of the conditions under which torture might be permissible, and from published photographs of victims of torture that, yes, the US is permitting and performing torture. And, far from a new development, this sort of obscene violence has long suffused American prisons and persisted as an aspect of covert US operations abroad. Obscene violence is widespread as the set of officially disavowed transgressions conditioning and staining the law. We might also think of sexual abuse within the Catholic Church and the traditional nuclear family, the everyday harassment of women, sexual, and ethnic minorities, the brutal rituals of fraternities, secret societies, and sports teams, in short, those unmentionable acts the practice of which differentiates members from non-members. As Žižek makes clear, this obscene underside 'forms the necessary supplement to the public values of personal dignity, democracy, and freedom' (2006: 370). To speak, then, of a resurgence of sovereignty ignores the obscene supplement of violence that accompanies law, the split in law between its public letter and the unacknowledged practices that must be disavowed for law to remain, as it were, in force.

Nonetheless, Butler speaks of sovereignty, of the resurgence of arbitrary, exploitative, and instrumental power through the suspension of law. Governmentality enables this resurgence, this state power that is not of the state, this legal power that is, paradoxically, outside the law. To focus on a sovereignty that operates through the tactics of governmentality might suggest a variety of sites from which to intervene politically (Butler 2004a: 98). As Butler points out, one advantage comes from the possibility of recognising and focusing on the stateless. I would add that any such advantage is lost to the extent that it is not tied to a critical politicisation of globalised neoliberal capitalism. Yet Butler, albeit rightly attuned to the complexities of rights claims in international law, not only forgoes the opportunity to condemn US militarism and imperialism as a specific set of governmental tactics, but also moves to the question of the 'human'. That is, she takes a key benefit of the notion of governmentality to be the way it opens up 'those discourses that shape and deform what we mean by "the human"' (2004a: 99).

I am not convinced that the (religious, imperialist, militarist) terms of the so-called war on terror or, more specifically, indefinite detention, call into question the human status of either the enemy or the imprisoned (*contra* Butler 2004a: 89). George W. Bush, Dick Cheney, and their conservative supporters are explicit about their entitlement to take human life. Their self-understanding of their power is premised on precisely this entitlement: they are the ones who know which *humans* can be killed – they do not need to exclude some from the category. Additionally, it may well be that the ethical command is towards not just the human but the *inhuman*, towards those that I cannot see as like me in any way, who remain monstrous to me, completely different, completely other. Thus Žižek, criticising Butler for ignoring the status of the inhuman in Kant's ethics, argues that the inhuman marks 'a terrifying excess which, although it negates what we understand as "humanity", is inherent to being human' (2005: 159–60). A key exemplar of such an inhuman, Žižek notes, is 'the terrifying figure of the *Muselmann*, the "living dead" in the concentration camps' (2005: 160).

Butler's discussions of governmentality seem to back her into a corner. Resignification under conditions of governmentality is not simply a progressive, democratic, or liberating practice available to those unbound by law; it is also available to those in power, to those using law instrumentally, to those who have led the country into the horrifying future of indefinite and pre-emptive war. Likewise, sovereign power, a power to effect a closure, to cut off, to decide, operates both as law and lawlessly, through law and through law's suspension. Perhaps Butler moves to ethics so as to escape this deadlock.

A passage in *Precarious Life* suggests this might be the case. Butler describes participating in a discussion about the current situation of the humanities. She notes a confusion in the discussion, an uncertainty regarding whether people were willing to stand by their words, 'whether anyone really was willing to own a view' (2004a: 129). She acknowledges that her work has tried to 'cut the tether' of author to words, an effort that I understand as linked to her critique of sovereign speech. She acknowledges as well that it would be a 'paradox' were she now to try to tether discourse to authors. To avoid this paradox, she offers another move, 'a consideration of the structure of address itself' (2004a: 129). As she explains:

> The structure of address is important for understanding how moral authority is introduced and sustained if we accept not just that we address others when we speak, but that in some way we come to exist, as it were, in the moment of being addressed, and something about our existence proves precarious when that address fails. More emphatically, however, what binds us morally has to do with how we are addressed by others in ways that we cannot avert or avoid; this impingement by the other's address constitutes us first and foremost against our will or, perhaps put more appropriately, prior to the formation of our will. So if we think that moral authority is about finding one's will and standing by it, stamping one's name upon one's will, it may be that we miss the very mode by which moral demands are relayed.
>
> (Butler 2004a: 130)

Morality, then, is less a matter of a will than of relations prior to that will, relations that Butler considers in terms of the structure of address. We come to exist by being addressed; this address, and consequently our own existence, can fail or misfire. Hence, we need to attend to this structure. If we move too quickly to willing, Butler suggests, we may fail, harm, or do violence to our relation to the other who addresses us, a relation on which we depend.

Address and condemnation

Butler's sustained consideration of the scene of address appears in *Giving An Account of Oneself* (2005a). She takes up the limits that condition our ability to give an account of ourselves, limits that include exposure, or our condition of corporeality before others (as opposed to pure interiority, say), normativity, or the way that we come into being within a set of norms that precedes us and remains indifferent to us, and, the structure of address in which any account of ourselves takes place. She elaborates, moreover, the way our very foreignness to ourselves is the source of our ethical connections to others (2005a: 84). And, she offers a conception of ethics 'based on our shared, and invariable, partial blindnesses about ourselves. The recognition that one is, at every turn, not quite the same as how one presents oneself in the available discourse might imply, in turn, a certain patience with others that would suspend the demand that they be self-same at every moment' (2005a: 42–43). Insofar as we remain opaque to ourselves, we cannot demand an impossible transparent or self-knowledge from the other. The lack in what we can know about ourselves thus might be understood as the lack in what others know about themselves. And, although I may often be tempted to fill in this gap with an always impossible certainty, my ability to cultivate an awareness of this lack could enable me to be more forgiving of others and perhaps even of myself. Allowing for openness, not demanding an impossible accounting from another, thus provides for Butler a necessary emendation to theories of recognition, insofar as it attends to an underlying desire to persist (2005a: 44).

The exposure and normativity conditioning us also condition the other. Our relation to each other, the mutual dependence through which we impinge upon one other, condenses into a kind of irreducible, enigmatic stress, an excessive unknowability which addresses us and which we cannot avoid. Describing this 'signifying stress' immanent to our relations with others, Eric Santner writes:

> To use a Heideggerian locution, our *thrownness* into the world does not simply mean that we always find ourselves in the midst of a social formation that we did not choose ... it means, more importantly, that this social formation in which we find ourselves immersed is itself permeated by inconsistency and incompleteness, is itself haunted by a lack by which we are, in some peculiar way, addressed, 'excited', to which we are in some fashion answerable ... reality is never fully identical with itself, is fissured by lack.
>
> (2006: 86–87)

Santner thus adds to Butler's account of the conditions of address an emphasis on how a certain lack within these very conditions addresses us as well. Our conditions are inconsistent and incomplete, exposed to potentials unfulfilled, harms unrecognised and unredressed.

For Butler, living as a subject split between the norms through which we emerge and the corporeal, finite life that we lead means we must become critical. She develops this idea as she rethinks responsibility, arguing that insofar as we remain strangers to ourselves responsibility cannot rest on a myth of transparency but must instead be understood as dependent on the unknowable, the limit, the trauma within and necessary to me. In making this argument, she draws from Adorno's account of the inhuman as necessary for the human, as well as from Foucault's telling the truth about himself. Crucial to each account is a limit that conditions the becoming of subjects and reminds us how ethical norms not only guide conduct but decide who and what is human. Persisting in a poorly arranged world poses ethical dilemmas: our own desires to persist have consequences for others. Although we do not choose the norms through which we emerge, insofar as we speak within them, or recognise another in the way that they frame, we transmit these norms and thus bear a responsibility for their consequences.

To this extent, an ethics that does not involve critique, that does not call into question these norms and their consequences, is itself unethical, culpable, unresponsive as it disavows the relations of power on which it depends.

The ethical disposition Butler finds in the context of address may arise. Or, it may not. It may well be the case that sometimes something more is called for – judgement or perhaps even condemnation. Butler allows for this when she observes that judgment does not 'exhaust the sphere of ethics' and when she says that judgments are necessary for political life (2005a: 45). Yet Butler holds back, refusing to condemn those persons and practices, those norms and desires upon which our poorly arranged world depends. She writes:

> Condemnation, denunciation, and excoriation work as quick ways to posit an ontological difference between judge and judged, even to purge oneself of another. Condemnation becomes the way in which we establish the other as nonrecognizable or jettison some aspect of ourselves that we lodge in the other, whom we then condemn. In this sense, condemnation can work against self-knowledge, inasmuch as it moralizes a self by disavowing commonality with the judged. Although self-knowledge is surely limited, that is not a reason to turn against it as a project. Condemnation tends to do precisely this, to purge and externalize one's own opacity. In this sense, judgment can be a way to fail to own one's limitations and thus provides no felicitous basis for a reciprocal recognition of human beings as opaque to themselves, partially blind, constitutively limited.
>
> (Butler 2005a: 46)

That condemnation *can* work against self-knowledge does not mean that condemnation everywhere and always *does* so. Condemnation does not always moralise a self through disavowal, seeking to purge and externalise opacity and necessarily failing to own its limitations. Can we not imagine a condemnation capable of acknowledging its own limits? Can we not imagine a condemnation born of past failures, indeed, a condemnation indebted and responsible to failure? Butler, in opposing condemnation to connection and the acknowledgement of opacity, blocks from the view the political possibility of drawing a line, of saying 'this, not that' and in so doing transforming our connections, to which condemnation may very well give rise.

If I condemn racism, homophobia, or cruelty in another, I am not necessarily disavowing racism, homophobia, or cruelty in myself. I may be addressing it in myself as I confront these tendencies in another. More importantly, I may be calling into question, condemning, practices in which I, too, am implicated such that I recognise this condemnation as a self-condemnation, a condemnation of us and of our practices. Such condemnation, then, may well be my ethical as well as political responsibility insofar as I seek to transform the set of norms in which I find myself, thereby changing the contexts in which others are addressed.

If I condemn someone for pursuing preventive war, or for defending a notion of preventive war, I need not base this condemnation on a sense that my knowledge is more certain. I can base it on the sense that the pursuer of preventive war aims to produce a future I reject, or even if these are not his aims, that I fear will arise in the course of its pursuit. My condemnation, again, may be a way of grappling with, of confronting, additional elements of the contexts of address, elements that involve power, hierarchy, and responsibility for other futures, other contexts, other beings. Failure to condemn, then, risks disavowing relations of power and confronting one's complicity in them. Rather than indicating an ethical responsiveness, such failure retreats from the political demand to refuse to remain within a certain structure of address and to challenge its terms, to acknowledge the way these terms block from view those who remain incapable of addressing us at all. Refusing the address, denouncing the presumption of relations an address may endeavour to reinforce, could well be necessary if we are to attend to the peculiar lack that addresses us and to which we are responsible. As Santner argues, responsibility to the excluded and for opportunities missed in the past may require radical acts that *suspend* the social bond (2005a: 89).

Butler does not always avoid condemnation. Important to my argument is the fact that her ethics need not preclude condemnation and that it can and should be sharpened so as to account for such divisive, political moments. Yet, it is striking that when Butler does condemn, it is as if she finds herself in that moment trapped within a discourse she rejects, to which she can only gain access through a condemnation. In *Precarious Life*, she condemns 'on several bases the violence done against the United States and do[es] not see it as "just punishment" for prior sins' (2004a: 40). Butler seems to find herself compelled to condemn those who attacked the United States on September 11, 2001 *before* she criticises the US government, as if this condemnation gives her permission to argue. Yet, in her analyses of US policies of indefinite detention in Guantanamo Bay, US violence against Afghanistan, the 'shock and awe' attacks on Iraq, and the Bush administration's hegemonisation of political discourse after September 11, 2001 in terms of its own position as victim, she does not condemn. Rather, she analyses, explains, contextualises, interprets, interrogates, and, in so doing, critiques. This raises the question of Butler's separation of condemnation and critique and the political place and function of each.

Butler presumes that condemnation involves closure and that closure entails finality and disconnection. That is, she treats condemnation as an act of sovereignty bent on effacing its own supporting conditions, its own vulnerability and dependence. So even as she recognises judging as a mode of address and thus premised on the context of address that 'can and should provide a sustaining condition of ethical deliberation, judgment, and conduct', she reads condemnation as violently eroding 'the capacity of the subject addressed for both self-reflection and social-recognition' and denunciation as working to 'paralyze and deratify the critical capacities of the subject to whom it is addressed' (2004a: 49). If the one who is condemned and denounced is already positioned in a prior relation of subordination such erosion and paralysis may result. But not necessarily. The condemned may reject the bases, the terms, of condemnation – 'I am not who you say I am' or 'Because I am who you say I am, you are the one who ultimately suffers, who is left shattered and bereft in condemning me'. The denounced may accept the words of the denunciation, but challenge the suppositions supporting these words, the suppositions that give it an ethical valence beyond a mere statement of fact – 'Yes, I am a godless communist, so?'

Condemnation and denunciation may not succeed. Their effects on the addressee as well as their relation to other acts and interpretations cannot be determined in advance. If the condemned is powerful, at the head of a mighty military machine, then associating condemnation with paralysis and deratification surely overstates the power of the address. One could wish that condemnation had such effects, and with respect to Bush's unconscionable, immoral, unjustified, illegal, and imperialist war against Iraq, I certainly do. Bush's persistence in his pre-emptive war against Iraq in the face of the condemnation of millions throughout the world, however, points to the weakness and inefficacy of condemnation unbacked by force.

At the same time, condemnation may work in a different direction. Weakness in one respect may enable another sort of strength, a capacity to form new alliances and connections, to open a space wherein to imagine the possibility of another world. So condemnation and denunciation may produce new links. When I condemn, I may do so in the context of addressing another, one whom I am not condemning. If in a political gathering I condemn the President of the United States, I will be addressing others, attempting to politicise and change the scene in which we find ourselves. Such politicisation, moreover, may well be called for by the very inconsistency and lack in this scene that calls out to and excites us, as Santner suggests.

Condemnation is not as powerful and efficacious as Butler implies. And, insofar as it occurs within a context of address, condemnation is citational, relying for its efficacy on a set of prior norms that it reiterates, a set of prior practices and values to which it connects. Condemnation does not occur *ex nihilo* but is based on something, something shared, something that will be unavoidable incomplete and fissured. As with other utterances, condemnation is 'uncontrollable, appropriable, and able to signify otherwise and in excess of its animating intentions' (Butler 1997a: 98). To condemn, then, is to appeal to a prior set of connections at its basis and thereby to open up this basis for critique and politicisation. It is also, and more importantly, to be excited by the lacks fissuring our social formation and to take responsibility for the past harms and omissions that enable it.

Conclusion

Butler argues for an ethics that stems from an irresolvable unknowability, a trauma that limits and makes possible our need and capacity for response. Attunement to this unknowingness, this limit within each of us, calls up the ways we are each given over to another.

She rejects moralising responses to vulnerability, trauma, and opacity that seek to shield the subject from pain through appeals to self-defence and recourse to violence. Yet her rejection remains *ethical*. That is to say, she offers an alternative response to vulnerability, one that emphasises our common place, our common risks, our common limits.

What can be said about a *political* response to those who reject this ethics? What about those who prioritise preservation of a narrowly conceived self and nation over acknowledgement of common vulnerability? Should they not be condemned, denounced, opposed? Butler's account of the context of address seems to presume an other who shares this context or who can and will accept her account of it, as if the other answers the call to give an account in necessarily the same way, without a fundamentally different ethics of his own. If the subject's self-crafting takes place in relation to the norms in which he finds himself, then differing sets of norms will condition senses of oneself and others and differing ways of conceiving this relation.

Moreover, in light of the decline of symbolic efficiency, one, and the inconsistency of any formation, two, the risks to which we find ourselves vulnerable, the experiences of embodiment inflecting our senses of exposure, will necessarily be *uncommon*: for you, to be in my presence as a menstruating woman may risk defilement; for me, to confront your *jouissance* may be unbearable. Once we emphasise these fundamental gaps, such conflicts and antagonisms, politics cannot be avoided. Not only are we called by inconsistencies in our social formations, by the past harms and omissions that make them what they are, but we are responsible for the arrangements of power in which we encounter each other. In the face of these inconsistencies and responsibilities, we make decisions, political decisions for and against, decisions of which we may remain unaware (insofar as we fail to attend to how in our daily practices we repeat and reinforce given arrangements) but which are no less political for this unawareness. Butler, however, displaces attention from the political matter of decision as she presents an ethics animated by an appreciation for the opacity and unknowingness rupturing any expectation to complete coherence or fully transparent self-identity.

If unknowingness conditions ethics then it necessarily conditions politics as well. Our political choices to condemn and denounce, the connections we pursue through what we exclude, take place under traumatic conditions of unknowability and unpredictability. Our decision for this rather than that will necessarily involve a kind of violence, a foreclosure of the possibility of the future that would have resulted had we decided otherwise. When we intervene politically, we act within situations not of our own making, often in terms of representations and practices we might otherwise trouble or critique. Through our actions, we affect these representations and practices, changing them and ourselves in ways we cannot predict.

Associating condemnation and denunciation with sovereignty, Butler eschews a politics of conviction as necessarily incompatible with the ethical conditions sustaining the scene of address. Yet, condemnation and denunciation need not be associated with a notion of mastery or unconditionality. Instead, they can be necessary and proper political responses to the violence that informs the scenes in which we find ourselves and the inconsistencies that attempt to cover over past omissions and harms, responses necessary for emboldening Left politics. As I mention above, despite the way she opposes conviction to responsibility, Butler also condemns: she condemns the attacks made on the US on September 11, 2001. She does so as a way to enter into a certain conversation, enacting thereby the way that condemnation may provide not closure and detachment, but an opportunity for openness and connection. Condemnation of one may be the way that we address another, answering the lack that excites us, and forming a new, militant, connection.

Notes

1 I am grateful for discussions with Matthew Calarco and Paul Passavant that helped me get this essay off the ground. I also want to thank Sam Chambers, Paul Passavant, and Lee Quinby for their careful, critical readings of an initial draft.
2 I should note here that Žižek does not view this closure as final; rather, throughout his work he emphasises possibilities for rupture, as in, for example, the radical act that changes the coordinates of a situation, in Lacan's feminine formulae for sexuation that present a logic of the non-all, and in the gaps and ruptures inherent in the material structures in which we find ourselves. In what follows, I draw from Eric Santer's specific figuring of these gaps as stresses that call to and excite the subject.
3 I am not sure how new these bases are. Judith Shkar (1984), for example, theorises liberalism by prioritising a fundamental hatred of cruelty.

9 Sovereignty and suffering

Towards an ethics of grief in a post-9/11 world

David S. Gutterman and Sara L. Rushing

I have walked among the desperate, rejected, and angry young men, I have told them that Molotov cocktails and rifles would not solve their problems. I have tried to offer them my deepest compassion while maintaining my conviction that social change comes most meaningfully through nonviolent action. But they ask – and rightly so – what about Vietnam? They ask if our own nation wasn't using massive doses of violence to solve its problems, to bring about the changes it wanted. Their questions hit home, and I knew that I could never again raise my voice against the violence of the oppressed in the ghettos without having first spoken clearly to the greatest purveyor of violence in the world today – my own government. For the sake of those boys, for the sake of this government, for the sake of the hundreds of thousands trembling under our violence, I cannot be silent.

(King 1986: 233)

In April 1967, at a time of escalating violence both at home and abroad, Dr Martin Luther King, Jnr spoke from the pulpit at Riverside Church in New York City. King was focused not only on the violence suffered by African Americans in conditions of racial injustice, nor only on the violence suffered by soldiers and peasants in Vietnam. He was also gravely concerned with the commands of soldiers to inflict violence on others and on the growing inclination of African Americans and other citizens to turn to violence in the struggle for justice in the United States. Invoking his responsibility as a Nobel laureate, as a Christian minister, and as a citizen, with anguish and despair in his voice King offered the harrowing conclusion that his nation, his United States, was 'the greatest purveyor of violence in the world today'. Breaking his silence – a silence born of fear, dismay, shame, pride, and disbelief – King challenged himself and his listeners to consider what the nation had become, what worlds it was destroying, what world it was creating, and what other possibilities might be pursued. Such reflections, King suggested, ought to begin by listening to the voices of those who had been made to suffer at home in the United States and in Vietnam, to listen to their grief, to acknowledge their sorrow and their longing.

King's concern with how suffering violence is used to authorise inflicting violence, or how mere life rather than a just or moral life somehow becomes an ultimate aim, is in many ways a timeless one. In this essay we examine how Socrates and Judith Butler, two thinkers spanning the historical spectrum, share this concern about the causes and effects of violence. Like King, both Socrates and Butler share a concern with ending 'the cycle' of violence – the cycle of revenge and retribution commonly justified as a response to suffering and a desperate longing for self-preservation. Indeed, much of Butler's recent work, particularly *Precarious Life* and *Giving an Account of Oneself*, addresses precisely those questions posed by the Greek tragedians and philosophers regarding the seductive appeal of vengeance and the dehumanising effect of violence, issues that resonate loudly in the United States today. Butler puts the problem bluntly when she writes, 'Tragically, it seems that the US seeks to preempt violence against itself by waging violence first, but the violence it fears is the violence it engenders' (Butler 2004a: 149). The cycle cannot be violently broken, and it can never be morally justified – if there is a point uniting Butler and Socrates it is this one.

Although the strong connection between Socrates and Butler is not one often highlighted, both are distinctly concerned about the all too human capacity to treat others inhumanely. For Socrates, this is a question about the health of our souls and the pursuit of justice. For Butler, this is a question about how our conduct works either to safeguard or foreclose the possibility of undertaking the collective project of 'becoming human'. Moreover, for both Socrates and Butler, the fear driving their analysis is the role that fear itself plays in justifying actions that do violence to our humanity by doing violence to others. Finally, for both, the solution (albeit partial and contingent) to this tendency is akin to the resistance to easy gratification and the preservation of mere life. Socrates describes this resistance in terms of happiness and self-control; Butler describes this resistance in terms of identification with suffering itself. And both, significantly, describe this resistance as an act of courage in the face of certain conventional notions of power. In the face of violence, Socrates and Butler strive to help us think about how we might respond to a heightened awareness of our own vulnerability, and to the dispossession we experience in loss and grief, in ways other than by more violence in the name of retribution, security, or solace. Accordingly, this chapter examines a gnawing problem: how we ought to respond to conditions of loss, grief, suffering, and the painful testimony to our own human vulnerability.

Suffering and violence, fear and vengeance

The attacks of September 11, 2001 were a terrible shock to the United States, shattering a common myth of American superiority and invulnerability – what Butler calls our 'grandiose fantasy of self-mastery'. In the wake of

September 11, the physical and psychic suffering of the United States was widely acknowledged. In nations across the world, people marched in solidarity and sympathy. The front page of *Le Monde* captured this spirit, declaring: 'Nous Sommes Tous Américains' ('We Are All Americans'). This identification with the suffering of Americans amounted to a declaration that despite the powerful story of 'American exceptionalism', Americans are just like everyone else because they are vulnerable, because they suffer, because they grieve. Such identification was not a proclamation that all people are vulnerable to the same degree nor that all people face the same threats, but simply that all people can be made to suffer, and that this vulnerability is vital to what makes us human. This post-9/11 moment of identification represented an opportunity for reconceiving the political order around what Butler might call an 'ethics of grief'. In her post-9/11 writing Butler has explored the opportunities and challenges grief presents for responding to the violent rupture of personal and political order. Butler's analysis is situated in a context in which the United States has chosen a violent response beholden to an illusory idea of strength that denies its vulnerability, that seeks to transcend its susceptibility to suffering, and that denies this opportunity for a humanising ethics of grief.

As is by now all too familiar, instead of seizing the opportunity to find solidarity with others on the basis of the undeniable fact of our shared vulnerability, the United States responded to the attacks by trying to re-establish or reassert its power by striking back. As Butler asserted in an interview in the days following the beginning of the current war in Iraq: 'The US ... is acting out of vengeance. It seeks to revenge the injustice done to it on 9/11 and it doesn't care if those whom it destroys were not responsible for that particular injustice. It felt itself to be humiliated by those events, and now it seeks to "shock and awe" in order to "restore" its damaged sense of impermeability and supremacy' (Butler 2003a: para. 5). 'Shock and Awe' was aptly named: the use of the awful power of the United States' military was supposed to not simply re-establish (and expand) the asymmetrical power enjoyed by the 'American empire', it was also intended to stun Islamic militants into submission and provide opportunities for Western-influenced democratisation to take hold in the Middle East. As Vice President Dick Cheney proclaimed in a speech before the Veterans of Foreign Wars on 26 August 2002, 'Extremists in the region would have to rethink their strategy of jihad ... Moderates throughout the region would take heart, and our ability to advance the Israeli-Palestinian peace process would be enhanced' (Butler 2003a: para. 46). To say that these goals have not been met is something of an understatement.

The War on Terror in Afghanistan and Iraq has resulted in the deaths of more than 3,000 United States military personnel and the injury – often severe – of thousands of other soldiers. The Iraqi government recently released a report that 150,000 Iraqi civilians have died as a result of the war that began with the United States invasion in 2003. A recent *Lancet*/Johns

Hopkins study has attributed approximately 650,000 Iraqi deaths to the War on Terror.[1] Of course, there have also been further deleterious health effects as well as expectations for further health crises. In addition much of Iraq's infrastructure has been destroyed and, according to Congressional reports, the United States is currently spending two billion dollars a week on the war in Iraq and reconstruction.[2] To date electricity and oil output still remain at levels below what was present prior to the United States invasion and the reconstruction efforts have been marked by enormous waste and little tangible success. In short, as much of the world has recognised for years, and as the American electorate apparently recognised belatedly but finally in the elections of November 2006, there is a general consensus that the United States' efforts in Iraq have been devastating, grossly expensive, and neither made the United States safer nor sparked the 'democratisation of freedom loving people' in the region. Indeed, as the United States' National Intelligence Estimate concluded in fall 2006, the war in Iraq has helped increase the ranks of militant extremists and the violence in Iraq continues unabated.[3]

The violence of the War on Terror, the violence born of fear and the desire to maintain a fantasy of security and self-mastery, has taken many forms, but none perhaps has been as poignant as the authorisation of the use of torture. The images are stark: a hooded man standing on a box with wires dangling from his body, a pile of naked men on the floor of a prison, a terrified man kneeling before a snarling dog, a man with women's under-wear over his face and his arms stretched up and backwards handcuffed to a bed frame, a dead man with a disfigured face packed in ice. And more: images of the United States military personnel who were conducting the torture and abuse of prisoners, smiling, giving the thumbs up sign over dead and broken people, and generally going about their business as if the abuse was a regular occurrence. The pictures of the abuse at Abu Ghraib are certainly the most visual, but hardly the only, evidence of the torture, cruelty and mistreatment of the prisoners held by the United States. Further evidence abounds, much of it (including Administration memos and reports about the torture scandals from the Department of Defense) collected by Mark Danner (2004) in *Torture and Truth*, and by Karen J. Greenberg and Joshua L. Dratel in *The Torture Papers*.

Torture is but one illustration in this crisis, but it is paradigmatic as a 'world-destroying act' (Scarry 1985: 29). Torture is often the product of the unsettling of relations of power, of the revelation of the fragility of the torturers' own status or identity. Torture, though often accompanied by interrogation that 'masquerades as the motive' for acts of cruelty, is what Elaine Scarry calls a 'grotesque piece of compensatory drama' (Scarry 1985: 28).[4] That is, torture is an act of compensating for threat to or loss of one's identity by seeking to destroy the world of another; it is an act of proclaiming one's power by seeking to render others less than human.

If torture is a compensatory drama, it says much more about the identity of the torturer than it does about the tortured, and it is with this issue – and with the more general questions about responses to suffering raised by the debates about torture – that we are primarily concerned here. In every age, and certainly in our own violent era, we are at risk, we are vulnerable. The question remains: what does our vulnerability legitimate or authorise? Torture is typically justified in terms of self-preservation, as necessary to save our lives. And self-preservation is cast as the bottom line, indeed, as common sense. In the ticking-time-bomb scenario – a hypothetical scenario in which a suspect has information about a bomb that will go off and kill civilians – who would not justify torture to save innocent lives? And, in the War on Terror, where ticking time bombs are exploding with great frequency and anyone might be the source – or the target – who would hesitate to 'take the gloves off' (Serrano 2004, quoted in Danner 2004: 36) to humiliate and break the bodies and the wills of the imprisoned, to prepare them for interrogation, in the effort to preserve life?

Both Socrates and Butler question this basic premise that it is common sense to respond with violence when vulnerable to violence, and that even the threat of loss of life makes such violence justifiable. Each argues for the persistence of ethical obligations to others who may threaten our lives. Our human fragility, they insist, does not cancel out our ethical obligations. Indeed, both Socrates and Butler suggest that the ethical ground for politics should develop *from* an acknowledgement of our fragility and limitations. Socrates offers what we might think of as a hopeful, aspirational vision of the human capacity to act nobly despite vulnerability. It is a demanding vision, one that seeks to cultivate the courageous ability to, if not quite transcend limitations, then to live virtuously in resistance to human frailties.

Butler, in contrast, provides a less aspirational, a less noble, but a perhaps no less challenging, vision for dealing with human limitations. Whereas Socrates counsels the pursuit of knowledge of the self and the pursuit (despite the impossibility of attainment) of self-mastery, Butler grounds her ethics in the very unknowability of the self, in our vulnerability, and our distance from one another. Despite the human impulse towards violence and this distance from others, Butler wants to draw from her ethics a politics of resistance to the seduction of vengeance. In short, in response to violence and with appreciation of human limitations, Socrates and Butler want to sustain ethical obligations that engender the resistance to violent reactions. Their respective efforts raise two fundamental questions: If human fragility does not cancel out our ethical obligations, then how are we to conceive ethics in times of crisis, siege, and threat? What are the resources that Socrates and Butler offer for reconceiving ethical obligations to not do violence when one is vulnerable, threatened, or violated?

Socrates on committing and suffering injustice

In Plato's *Gorgias*, the issue of human suffering and vulnerability provides the motivation and the tension for Socrates' exploration of justice and the limits of philosophy. The heart of the dialogue is Socrates' claim that 'to commit injustice [is] worse than to suffer it' (Plato 1952: 36). Polus, a young rhetorician, finds this claim patently absurd and responds:

> If a man is caught red-handed in a criminal plot to make himself tyrant and is arrested and tortured and castrated and his eyes are burnt out; and, after he has suffered all manner of torments of the worst sort, is forced to watch his wife and children being tortured; and at last is crucified or tarred and burned alive, this fellow will be happier than if he were to escape and become a tyrant and ruler in his state and continue throughout life doing whatever he liked, envied and congratulated by both citizens and foreigners? Is it this that you say is impossible to refute?
>
> (Plato 1952: 37)

With this hyperbolic utterance (after all, how can someone whose eyes have been burned out watch his loved ones be ravaged?), Polus threatens Socrates and seeks to frighten him into an appreciation of a certain notion of power. Socrates, of course, refuses to succumb – 'Bosh, my dear Polus! You're trying to give me a scare, not a refutation' (Plato 1952: 37) – and throughout the ensuing discussion with Polus and then Callicles on the question of how one ought to live, Socrates returns repeatedly to the claim that it is 'worse to do injustice, than to suffer injustice'.

It is significant that Socrates' argument about how one ought to live begins with this claim about suffering. The focus on suffering, on what Butler would call our 'injurability', remains at the heart of the dialogue as Callicles, the exemplary representative of politics, enters the discussion, challenging the philosopher Socrates' manhood, accusing him (and by extension philosophy more generally) of 'lisping and prattling' like a child, and threatening to 'strike [Socrates] hard' (Plato 1952: 53). Confronted by this verbal assault, Socrates does not seek quick recourse to self-protection or respond in kind, but rather welcomes Callicles, ultimately celebrating him for his 'knowledge, good will, and candor' (Plato 1952: 55).

In fact, Socrates seizes the hostility and threatening posture of Callicles as an opportunity to try to establish a bridge between the two realms they represent – politics and philosophy. This bridge is to be built on the mutual recognition of their common vulnerability. The very first words Socrates directs towards Callicles begin by highlighting the need for humans to 'have certain feelings in common' and then identify the ways in which both Callicles and Socrates are subject to the whims and desires of their respective loves (Plato 1952: 49). As a politician, Callicles is compelled to abide by the opinions of the Athenian demos, while Socrates is compelled to follow his love, philosophy, which, although less capricious than the demos, can also be notably hard to live with. One difference between Socrates and Callicles lies in their attitude toward self-mastery and vulnerability. Whereas Socrates does strive for self-mastery, this endeavour is distinguished by his recognition of its impossibility and his capacity to transcend the fear of his essential fragility. Callicles, however, denies the impossibility of self-mastery and fears the revelation of his fragility. As Socrates works through the argument that it is 'worse to do injustice, than to suffer injustice' with Callicles, Socrates ultimately recognises that not only is Callicles unconvinced, but that his scepticism is understandably a product of the fears of his own vulnerability. Socrates, accordingly, raises the question on Callicles' mind:

> With what, then, shall a man provide himself to secure this double advantage: insurance from doing wrong and suffering it? Is it power that he needs, or willpower? What I mean is this: can a man escape from being wronged merely by willing to escape it, or may he escape it by acquiring power to prevent it?
>
> (Plato 1952: 85)

Callicles maintains that it is worse to suffer wrong and the way to avoid such suffering is by acquiring power. Socrates, however, demonstrates that Callicles cannot answer the question of how one avoids doing wrong. Indeed, Socrates argues that if one focuses on avoiding suffering, one will do so by toadying up to those who have more power and might inflict pain, even or especially if those who have power are unwisely attracted to pleasure and gratification rather than improvement.

In contrast, Socrates argues that it is worse to do wrong and the way to avoid such wrongful acts is by cultivating virtue – chief among the virtues is a resistance to gratification. Socrates argues that if one focuses on avoiding doing wrong, then, unlike Callicles, one will seek wisdom and not public approval or power. However, Socrates is unable to provide ready 'insurance' for Callicles' fear of being harmed. He is unable to persuade him not to succumb to the fear of his own injurability. The only recourse Socrates has, the only answer he offers to address Callicles' fears of suffering, is the 'true art of politics': 'persuading and coercing fellow citizens to the point of self-improvement ... this and this alone is the task of the truly good citizen', Socrates says (Plato 1952: 95). And given Plato's portrayal of the trial and death of Socrates, which serves as the implicit backdrop to this exchange, the 'true art of politics' provides no insurance at all of avoiding unjust suffering. Indeed, in this sense, politics is not about providing security, but about risking ourselves and our security to seek common betterment despite the temptation to pursue individual gratification.

Socrates' exchange with Callicles tells us a bit about his hopes for his fellow Athenian citizens, and a lot about his concerns. The problem exemplified by Callicles is that humans lack the dedication and conviction necessary to pursue the good life rather than settling for immediate pleasures and the avoidance of pain – mere life. A good life in pursuit of justice requires 'fleeing from profligacy' and the embrace of hard lessons or bitter medicine when one goes astray (Plato 1952: 83). The pursuit of power to overcome our vulnerability is not an answer, and the reliance on 'willpower' in the face of temptation, fear, and suffering does not bode well on the individual level, let alone at the collective level of politics. In fact, the very willingness to engage in the 'true art of politics' and to strive to improve, rather than gratify, our fellow citizens or other sources of political power, increases the likelihood of provoking unjust suffering.

There is, as suggested, a basic acknowledgement of human fragility here. Socrates is convinced that absent conviction about the relative merits of the good life, and thus the cultivation of the capacity to wilfully pursue this life, we will succumb to the sacrifice of both principles and other people in order to secure our mere life. Indeed, Callicles essentially articulates precisely this argument as the natural state of human existence: it is the rule of the stronger, with strength defined as the capacity and willingness to act to preserve life. As Socrates explains, placing primary value on the preservation of mere life is the first step on the road not simply to unethical behaviour, but the devastation of friendship and the polis: 'Wise men say, Callicles, that heaven and earth, gods and men, are held together by the principles of sharing, by friendship and order, by self-control and justice' (Plato 1952: 82). It is for this reason that Socrates begins with and returns to the claim that it is 'worse to do wrong than suffer wrong'. Socrates is concerned about the weakness of our bodies, and our capacity to be subjected to the violent injustice of others – but neither of these human limitations speaks to the condition of our soul or our capacity to corrupt our friends, or our city. Our very fragility leaves us far too willing to commit injustice either for the purposes of gratification or to secure the preservation of our mere life. Only when we are willing to sacrifice mere life in the pursuit of the good life are we able to reconcile the quest for justice and virtue with the frailty of our bodies and human mortality. It is only when we refuse to be cowed by Polus' talk of miserable suffering, when we can face the ignominious slaps of Callicles, that we accept the conclusion that it is worse to do wrong than suffer wrong. Unfortunately, as Socrates' failure to persuade Polus and Callicles indicates, it is exceedingly hard to convince people to embrace their vulnerability when they are strong. It is perhaps even more difficult to convince people to do so when, while they were once perceived to be invulnerable, they have been exposed as weak and permeable.

Injurability and 9/11: Butler, ethics and vulnerability

The attacks of 9/11 did nothing if not expose the weakness and permeability of the United States. In a move reminiscent of Callicles' arguments, the United States acted out a theory of power as force in an effort to demonstrate to itself and the rest of the world that its invulnerability could be 'restored'. Like Socrates, Butler seeks to develop an account about why such a response is not tenable; an account that would be compelling to an audience defined by both great might and great fear. Like Socrates, she aims to 'situate individual responsibility in light of its collective conditions', and regards these collective conditions as ones of mutual risk and vulnerability to each other (Butler 2004a: 15). Like Socrates, who argues that despite our natural aggression the best line of self-defence is to act justly, Butler grounds moving 'beyond the current cycle of revenge' on an ethics of non-violence in the face of our very human 'murderous impulses'. For both Butler and Socrates, self-preservation cannot be the highest goal. Rather, each posits something higher as that which is worth striving for as we shape our collective world. In Butler's language this value is described not in terms of virtue or healthy souls, but in terms of our chances of what she might call living 'livable lives'[5] and 'becoming human', which is an ongoing project – something that is always 'in the making' – and which can be safeguarded or foreclosed by our conduct (Butler 2004a: 89). To ensure the health of our souls or safeguard the possibility of 'becoming human', then, both Socrates and Butler argue for the importance of resistance to a certain gratification.

Socrates makes a rational case for an ethics of self-restraint as a foundation for justice. If he fails to convince Callicles and Polus it is partly because the content of his argument does not move them: his answer to the question of what a man might provide himself with as insurance against doing and suffering injustice ultimately falls on deaf (or fearful and pleasure-seeking) ears. But it is also because his method of argumentation fails. Socrates appeals to his interlocutors at the level of reason and discipline, and on the basis of an ideal of commonality, knowledge, and recognition of each other. For example, in the *Gorgias* he begins many of his arguments with some variation on the theme 'if you are the sort of person I am' (Plato 1952: 17), or if 'you are a friend of mine' (Plato 1952: 36). The rhetorical nature of this question is as much a concession to the limits of commonality as it is a tacit longing for that commonality despite its likely impossibility. What the breakdown of the dialogue here suggests is that Polus and Callicles (and so many of Socrates' interlocutors) are not like him, are not willing to accept vulnerability for the sake of the argument or the pursuit of wisdom. Indeed, Socrates himself is not always able to sustain such a temperament, as his willingness to occasionally embarrass, ridicule, and demean his interlocutors indicates.[6] Yet he remains committed to the true art of politics, the infinite task of rationally persuading his fellow citizens towards self-improvement, self-mastery, and good and just living.

Here is where Butler and Socrates part ways: while Butler advocates resistance to gratification (casting peace as the 'active and difficult resistance' to the 'terrible satisfactions of war'), her appeal hinges on the acceptance of the limits of recognition, on a hope for responsiveness to other human beings and 'the conditions of life itself', and on what have been described as certain 'dispositional supplements' (Butler 2003a: 5; Butler 2000c: para. 33). Instead of urging us to transcend our fear of vulnerability and to embrace virtue and a higher good, Butler's account of ethical obligations is conspicuous for the way it takes failures of recognition and limits to knowability as its ground, not its foil.

If the traditional question of ethics is 'Who are you and how should I treat you?' then the failure fully to account for oneself – to answer the first part of the question satisfactorily – amounts to the failure of ethics. And in so far as anyone's account of herself is necessarily incomplete, because there are 'limits of knowability in oneself and others', and because narrative coherence always breaks down in any attempt to give an account of oneself, this ethical failure seems guaranteed (Butler 2005a: 63). Furthermore, while recognition can be a way of humanising an other, acknowledging them as a human worthy of being recognised, it is also a 'site of power' that determines who qualifies as human and who does not (Butler 2004b: 2). Thus the very scene of address that has traditionally figured recognition can be used to deny or 'undo' the person by withholding recognition. The possibility of responsible politics can thus not be tied to the ethical demand to give a full, narrativisable account of oneself so as to make oneself recognisable to an other who will necessarily heed you.

The War on Terror continually raises the question of our ethical obligations to those we do not know (like the people of Iraq), those we know only as inhuman (like bin Laden), and those we refuse to know (like the torture victims who have been rendered utterly 'other' to us, masked, both literally and figuratively). If the condition for having ethical obligations to these others is some impossible ideal of recognition grounded on firm epistemological and communicative foundations, then it seems we are at an impasse unless there are other ethical resources to be found. Butler seeks these resources in the very failure of recognition that would seem to void ethical obligations. Thus she counsels that, 'it will be important that we do not expect an answer [to who the other is] that will ever satisfy. And by not pursuing satisfaction, we let the other live, offering a recognition that is not based on knowledge, but its limits' (Butler 2000c: para. 10). Another word for this sense of recognition is responsiveness, as an awareness of the constitutive conditions of life that form us all: opacity and vulnerability. If full recognition is the demand that traditionally precedes and grounds ethics, and yet is a demand we can never meet, then responsiveness, understood as being awake to the world we are affected by and affect, is a way of responding to this failure.

For Butler, ethical relations cannot hinge on ideals of commonality and recognition like those that Socrates discusses. In contrast, she seeks to predicate ethical relations on 'humility about one's constitutive limitations' and generosity as 'a disposition toward the limits of others' (Butler 2005a: 80). These dispositional supplements – humility and generosity, as well as patience and restraint – are Butler's answer to the question, 'With what, then, shall a man provide himself to secure this double advantage: insurance from doing wrong and suffering it?' Furthermore, in contrast to Socrates, Butler argues that ethical responsibility cannot be a matter of reason and will, for she worries that 'if we locate notions of political responsibility in a willful subject, then we become preoccupied with our own willfulness and our own calculations ... ' (Butler 2003a: 5). Socrates might look at Callicles and Polus and agree, and yet would continue to try to convince them to strive for self-mastery. For Butler, though, making responsibility a matter of individual will affirms what she sees as the fantasy of self-mastery. When we figure responsibility as a matter of will, Butler fears that 'we are not necessarily responding to what is outside of ourselves and understanding that outside – the world – as essential to who we are' (Butler 2003a: 5).

And the world is essential to who we are, 'grandiose fantasies' of first-world entitlement and sovereignty notwithstanding (Butler 2004a: 40). To be sure, we have a certain agency within these conditions of essential interdependence. We have a kind of freedom. But it is not the kind of freedom we promised ourselves in the classical liberal story. It is not Autonomy or Sovereignty, or any kind of thorough-going self-determination, for this freedom is possible only within the context of our being political beings, which means in and of, conditioned and constrained by, the world. For Butler, agency can be understood simply as 'struggle within the unchosen conditions of one's life' (Butler 2005a: 19). Against this backdrop, the surge in claims of (an albeit convoluted) sovereignty by the United States – the rejection of the International Criminal Court, the repudiation of the Kyoto Accords, the withdrawal from the Anti-Ballistic Missile Treaty and the Nuclear Non-Proliferation Treaty – can be read as an attempt to trump these conditions at the very moment when the attacks of 9/11 made their 'unchosenness' indisputable.[7] Sovereignty appears as a means to fortify a myth of self-determination even as it is coming undone; it stakes a claim of being above domestic and international law – of being above the world.

Such sovereignty is impossible to sustain; it is a fantasy of independence, an unstable vision of freedom redolent of Polus' posturing and Callicles' manly bravado. Butler makes this point quite bluntly. 'Let's face it', she writes, 'We're undone by each other' (Butler 2004: 23). We are 'dispossessed by our relations to each other' (Butler 2004a: 24). We are constituted by this relationality, which means by a fundamental susceptibility to others that is simply not a matter of choice or will. This is what it means to be human, to be a political animal. In this vein, when asked in an interview whether 'politics is about making citizens feel secure', Butler responded, 'Well, security is the banner right now. But is politics what makes us feel secure or is politics what places us mutually at risk?' (Butler 2003a: 4). Like Socrates, Butler believes it is the latter. Unlike Socrates, Butler provides what can only be described as an affective account of how we might orient ourselves toward each other in a just and responsible way. That is, she attempts to answer the question of what limited, fearful, vulnerable people might provide themselves with, what dispositions they might cultivate, 'to insure against doing and suffering wrong'. The qualities Butler has in mind – generosity, humility and patience – are seemingly modest ones in contrast to the virtue and discipline Socrates extols. Furthermore, these are qualities that she suggests might be cultivated not through force of will or mental and physical gymnastics, but simply by working to 'develop a point of identification with suffering itself', or by working to 'heed the claim of precarious life' (Butler 2004a: 30, xix, respectively).

Butler figures the precariousness of life – the fact that 'we can be injured, that others can be injured, that we are subject to death at the whim of another' – as a constitutive condition of existence (Butler 2004a: xii). If we share anything, if there is a human community, it is predicated on this 'general state of fragility and physical vulnerability' (Butler 2003a: 4). To accept this fact, and to come to identify with suffering, loss, and pain instead of claiming some sort of exemption from such raw corporeality, could be politically revolutionary. Rather than scrambling to consolidate some imagined identity of 'first world privilege' in the aftermath of the attack on our first world soil, the United States could have opened itself to the opportunity of experiencing solidarity with untold friends around the world. This did not happen. The claim of precarious life, needless to say, was not heeded. The demand of ethics, namely 'to risk ourselves precisely at moments of unknowingness, when what forms us diverges from what lies before us, when our willingness to become undone in relation to others constitutes our chance of becoming human' – this demand was squarely rebuked (Butler 2005a: 136). Instead, injury was taken to authorise injury, go-it-alone 'cowboy diplomacy' was pitched as justice (or at least justifiable), and the 'dry grief of an endless political rage' continues (Butler 2004a: xix).

The precariousness of life is something we readily spurn. In so doing we foreclose the potentially transformative encounter with the other. As Butler reminds us, 'A vulnerability must be perceived and recognized in order to come into play in an ethical encounter, *and there is no guarantee that this will happen*' (Butler 2004a: 43, our emphasis). Tragically, more often than not the denial of vulnerability and the fantasy of mastery triumph, perpetuating a world in which the vengeance persists. This is a familiar world in which 'I could put an end to my fear of my own death by obliterating the other, although I would have to keep obliterating … ' (Butler 2004a: 134). Like Socrates, Butler hopes for something beyond this sickly gratifying cycle, and she imagines that 'an entirely different kind of politics would emerge if a community could learn to abide with its losses and its vulnerability' (Butler 2003a: 4). However, where Socrates continues to hope for something like communicative rationality, the transcendence of fear and desire, and the pursuit of virtue, Butler entertains no such hopes. It is only abiding our losses, grieving them – going through them, not rising above them – that Butler thinks might enable us to accept our own fragility.

In stark contrast to Socrates, Butler considers whether 'nonviolence may well follow from living the persistent challenge to egoic mastery that our obligations to others induce and require' (Butler 2005a: 64). There is nothing particularly glorious about this vision. Socrates may betray a realisation that the likes of Callicles and Polus, indeed, even his friend Crito, might never surpass their fear and desire, but Butler utterly foregrounds this realisation: we are 'only human' – vulnerable, fragile, precarious and capable of exploiting this very permeability of others. But out of that realisation new political resources emerge, first and foremost among them the possibility that flows from 'tarrying with grief', staying with it when it seems unbearable, remaining in what she calls the 'sphere of dispossession' where one 'undergoes something outside one's control and finds that one is beside oneself' (Butler 2004a: 28). Grief robs us of our sense of control, and this is finally what it is to be human: without final control, disposed to others, othered from our self, susceptible. We are all able to recognise this disorderly power of grief on a personal level and its disruptive capacity is typically what politics seeks to overcome.

'Let's face it': grief and risk post 9/11

Can grief – with its visceral reminder of our human fragility and interdependence or relationality – serve as an ethical and political resource? For the crucial task, as Butler suggests, is to move from an awareness of the grievable, injurable nature of human being to the cultivation of an ethical disposition of generosity, humility, and patience in the face of our own and others' vulnerability. These dispositions, she suggests, can make possible a politics that actively refuses to pursue the immediate gratification of obliterating, and instead stays attuned to the other by staying attuned to the other in ourselves that grief enables us to know. Such attunement, Butler writes, 'could only make us more humane' (Butler 2003a: 4). Such humanity, she hopes, could enable us to 'imagine and practice another future, one that will move beyond the current cycle of revenge' (Butler 2004a: 10).

Grief is thus cast as a resource, and one abundantly available to us right now for affecting a shift from a tenuously maintained politics of mastery to a politics of mutual vulnerability. And yet as President George W. Bush made perfectly clear, in declaring the time for grieving to be over a mere ten days after 9/11, grief can figure within American political discourse as nothing but weakness and inaction. The sign of our strength, in Bush's opinion, is that 'Our grief has turned to anger and anger to resolution' (Bush 2001: para. 6). It is this rapid conversion – this quick hardening and turning away from grief – that Butler laments. For grieving humanises us, it humanises others. Furthermore, insofar as none of us is above the reality that all human life can be instantaneously annulled, regardless of class, race, ideology, or nationality, 'grief equalizes us' (Butler 2003a: 7). Or at least, grief has the potential to equalise us, if we can recognise both the *inequality* of our vulnerability and the *equality* of our grievability. Here, then, is the political and ethical test Butler places before us.

The actions of the US in the past years – the waging of pre-emptive war, the authorisation of torture, extraordinary rendition, and indefinite detention – can be read as a resounding rejection of the hand of solidarity extended by the world after 9/11. If there was an opportunity to heed the precariousness of life and to break the cycle of revenge – by identifying with others and with suffering itself, by grieving our losses, becoming undone by them – it was rapidly and decisively shut down. This opportunity was not merely a casualty of war. Bush Administration policies after 9/11 can be read precisely as an attempt to effect that foreclosure, and as a rejection and/or failure of Butler's test.

Butler's inclination to find in vulnerability and suffering the possibility of an ethics of grief offers an ironically hopeful glimpse in these dark times. The process of grieving tears at all the ways we protect ourselves, reveals us as permeable, unable to secure ourselves from the dislocating force of loss and the recognition that we may – we will – lose still more. Butler suggests that if we abide in grief, if we allow ourselves the space to acknowledge not just our own grief but the grief of others, dispositions informed by generosity, humility, and patience can develop. Such dispositions – which amount to an identification with suffering instead of the pursuit of an identity as sovereign – present perhaps a more viable foundation for ethics than the lofty recognition, discipline, and virtue that Socrates champions. That is, Butler invites us to come to terms with ourselves, she does not ask us to overcome ourselves. But is this 'improvement' on Socrates enough? Socrates could not convince Polus and Callicles to accept, let alone embrace, their vulnerability. Could Butler do any better? In the face of fear, can philosophers who refuse to resort to scare tactics or a utilitarian calculus of self-preservation triumph over politicians who do not? Can we be moved to abide in grief, and grieved to an abiding peace, instead of turning, again and again, to violence?

Characteristically, Butler does not offer us a promise, a blueprint, or a resolution to such challenges. She confronts us with vital and demanding questions about how we might become human otherwise and about the worlds we might create (or at least not foreclose) together. But she does not suggest that resisting the foreclosure of certain futures will be easy. Nor is she particularly optimistic herself; she seems largely to expect that the cycle of revenge will persist. Yet she is genuinely hopeful that we might allow the losses attendant to 9/11 and the War on Terror to present an opportune crisis, a 'risky moment in politics', where we resist perpetuating the old and open ourselves, avail ourselves, put ourselves at the mercy of each other and a new and ultimately more responsible way of being together in an uncertain and always potentially destructive world. 'So how does one live in that risk?' she asks (Butler 2003a: 19). It is up to us, it seems, to answer.

Notes

1 See Burnham 2006.
2 See Bender 2006.
3 See Mazetti 2006.
4 Scarry's point about masquerade, one made by many scholars of torture includ-ing notably Darius Rejali, is that while torture is commonly justified in political rhetoric and the public imagination as an unfortunate but necessary means of information extraction, the information extracted is not just legally illegitimate, it is fundamentally suspect. 'No one has figured out a precise, reliable way to break human beings or any adequate method to evaluate whether what prisoners say when the do talk is true' (Rejali 2004: para. 6). The use of torture as a means of asserting one's authority rather than interrogation is illustrated of course by the abuse of prisoners in Iraq, Afghanistan, and Guantanamo Bay who can offer little if any in the way of 'actionable intelligence', especially (as in the case of Guantanamo Bay), after being held in prison for years.
5 Variations on the term 'livable life' are found throughout Butler's *Precarious Life* (2004a) and *Undoing Gender* (2004b) in particular, to the extent that 'Livability' is an entry in the index of the latter.
6 See, for example, Socrates throwing Callicles' taunts back in his face at the con-clusion of *Gorgias*; compare line 485–86, Plato 1952: 53–55 with line 527, Plato 1952: 106.
7 For Butler's discussion of the notion of 'sovereignty' and of the influential work of Giorgio Agamben, see her essay 'Indefinite Detention' in Butler 2004a.

Part V
Law and rights

10 Butler and life

Law, sovereignty, power

Elena Loizidou

'Life' is a consistent theme in Butler's work. In *Subjects of Desire* (1999b) she offers a reading of desire that is inextricably linked to life. In *Gender Trouble* (1990) life takes the form of gendered life, as in *Bodies that Matter* (1993) and *Undoing Gender* (2004b). *Excitable Speech* (1997a) reflects upon injuries inflicted on lives by speech acts. In more recent work, *Antigone's Claim* (2000a), *Giving an Account of Oneself* (2003c; 2005) and *Precarious Life* (2004a), she complicates claims made upon life by the ethical, political and legal sphere and unveils their discursive and material limitations. Nevertheless, despite the attachment to the concept of 'life', Butler makes no ontological claims regarding 'life' but rather articulates the practices involved in draining, restraining, or even destroying 'life'. And she analyses the possible ways in which we may resist restrictions imposed upon us by state apparatuses (such as governmental officials and legislative limitations), disciplinary regimes, and norms – all so as to make possible liveable lives.

As is well known, Butler is suspicious of the juridical order and its ability to create better life conditions for subjects. Thus, some readers may be surprised to read, in *Precarious Life*, Butler's call for a robust juridical intervention to curb the growing executive powers exercised by the George W. Bush administration. However, as I explain below, Butler's polemical approach there proves consistent with her overreaching philosophical thesis. That is, Butler's concern for how we may create better conditions for life entails an agonistic relationship between the various spheres of life, and this, in turn, requires the law. Thus, the demand for a more robust law in *Precarious Life* gestures towards the creation of vital conditions that may not only ensure survival but also reinvigorate the conditions for what Butler calls 'a livable life'.

When the US government issued a de facto state of emergency after the September 11, 2001 ('9/11') attacks in New York, Butler suggests that a new, synthetic modality of power emerged. The 'decree' (neither a piece of legislation nor an executive order, but a disciplinary and discursive production) not only suspended the laws but also did away with the separation of powers considered to be the pillars of the US constitution. This essay explains how this disciplinary production was managed, how it is still sustained and what its effects are. Ultimately, I argue that these effects are produced through the re-emergence of a new type of sovereignty – one that *uses governmentality as technique.*[1]

Governmentality and law

Governmentality, Foucault writes, is a practice of government emerging in the sixteenth century but reaching its apex in the eighteenth century (2002a: 212). While sovereignty had as its end the preservation of the sovereign and its territoriality, governmentality's end is the management of populations. Foucault links its emergence with the coming into being of an administrative apparatus, the police, mercantilism and statistics. Foucault's reception of the concept of government comes from La Perrière's *Miroir Politique* and is defined 'as a right manner of disposing things so as to lead not to the form of the common good, as the jurists' text would have said, but to an end that is "convenient" for each of the things that are governed' (2002a: 212). A good governor, who above everything has to be patient (unlike the sovereign), will use tactics (even laws *as* tactics) to secure maximum security for their own population. This modality of power, as Foucault suggests, allows the state to survive (2002a: 221).

While Foucault provides us with a chronological understanding of the emergence of sovereign and governmental power, Butler, following Agamben, reminds us that both sovereign power and governmentality are *contemporary* forms. Further, she shows that they hold an inverse relation to the rule of law (Butler 2004a: 60).[2] For just this reason, it proves highly significant, when, just two pages into 'Indefinite Detention', Butler proposes the following regarding the US treatment of detainees in Guantánamo and the use of power:

> I would like to suggest that the current configuration of power, in relation both to the management of populations (the hallmark of governmentality) and the exercise of sovereignty in the acts that suspend and limit the jurisdiction of law itself, are reconfigured in terms of the new war prison.
>
> (Butler 2004a: 53)

From the very start of the well-known essay, first published as a newspaper editorial, Butler separates modalities of power and law. Governmentality and sovereignty are read from the start as forces that act upon jurisdiction, the 'territory'[3] of law. At first blush, the proposition (and its consequences) creates an aporia, at least to those who are familiar with Foucault's modalities of power, the very modalities that Butler is invoking in this essay. In *Discipline and Punish* (1991a), Foucault hardly differentiates between the sovereign and the law: both fall under the category of juridical power. Nevertheless, I want to emphasise that Foucault does not *equate* the sovereign with the law; rather, he vests the sovereign with the 'force of law'. Foucault recognises that there is a jurisdiction that is legal. This jurisdiction, through the instrument of the *trial*, decides upon the 'truth' of the alleged event, and through the instrument of *punishment*, publicises the 'truth'. In this context, Foucault writes, '[t]he body, several times tortured, provides the synthesis of the reality of the deeds and the truth of the investigation, of the documents of the case and the statements of the criminal, of the crime and the punishment' (1991a: 47). For Foucault, the juridical order entertains itself with the trying of the accused (1991a: 44–48), but the king or prince, engages in distinct practices with distinct effects. In the sovereign is vested the power of deciding life or death.

Therefore the sovereign's power falls under the name 'force of law'. This power, as Foucault explains, is a power of vengeance:

> Besides its immediate victim, the crime attacks the sovereign: it attacks him personally, since the law represents the will of the sovereign; it attacks him physically since the force of law is the force of the prince ... The intervention of the sovereign is not, therefore, an arbitration between two adversaries; it is much more, even, than an action to enforce the respect of the rights of the individual; it is a direct reply to the person who has offended him.
>
> (Foucault 1991a: 47–48)

This passage makes clear that under the juridical model of power, the law is the instrument of the will of the sovereign. And Foucault sustains this position in *Society Must be Defended* where he shows that the juridical system serves the demands of, and benefits, royal power (2003c: 25). Moreover, he explains that even when the juridical system concerns itself with the *limits* of sovereign power it never ceased to be *about* royal power. Nevertheless, this proximity between the juridical order and the sovereign cannot allow us to conclude that the sovereign *is* the law. In establishing a juridical order precisely for the *exercise* of his power, the king demonstrates that his interests reside in preserving himself and his territory. The interests of the juridical order itself thus *include* the preservation of sovereign power. The *telos* of the juridical order, on the other hand, lies in the production of 'truth' (no matter how fictitious this might be). However, and most importantly, when the sovereign decides over the life or death of subjects, what is being reproduced is not the truth but the sovereign's *will*, i.e. power backed by the 'force of law'. It is this distinction between the juridical order's production of truth and the sovereign's expression of force and will through that order which informs Butler's analysis of the contemporary political situation in the US.

New modalities of power

Sorting out the relation between sovereignty, law, disciplinary power and governmentality proves to be a highly fraught, yet extremely worthwhile endeavour: fraught because no one seems to map the relations in quite the same way; worthwhile since the stakes of such mapping prove very high indeed. Agamben, Foucault and Butler all provide essential contributions to this effort to grasp the relation of these modalities of power, but each comes at the problematic from a distinct angle, and sometimes those angles are irreconcilable with each other. Nevertheless, as much as the overlaps in their accounts help to clarify the concepts under discussion, the differences in those accounts show how high the political stakes may be.

Agamben suggests that sovereign and governmental powers' antithetical relation to the rule of law emerges at the moment when the norm is suspended, or when the law is withdrawn. Law, as Butler explains, ' ... withdraws from the usual domain of its jurisdiction; this domain becomes opened to both governmentality (understood as an extra-legal field of policy, discourse, that may make law into a tactic) and sovereignty (understood as an extra-legal authority that may well institute and enforce law of its own making)' (2004a: 60). For his part, Foucault also describes the withdrawal or ineffectiveness of law when new powers emerge. Disciplinary power, he says, often operates with the human sciences rather than law as its reference point (2003). Foucault thereby confirms that normalisation is not intrinsic to law, but rather to concrete disciplinary practices like policing, schooling, psychoanalysis and psychiatry. From Foucault's (or Butler's) perspective we might say that Agamben conflates the norm with the law and effectively makes the law the epitome of normalisation.

Butler, however, uses Agamben's exposition of contemporary modalities of power to provide us with an analysis of power relevant to our current context. She builds upon Agamben's understanding to propose her own version of sovereignty. Sovereignty, she writes,

> [is] ... produced at the moment of this withdrawal, [therefore, we must] consider the act of suspending the law as a performative one which brings a contemporary configuration of sovereignty into being, or more precisely, reanimates a spectral sovereignty within the field of governmentality.
>
> (Butler 2004a: 61)

This is a distinct and powerful (if not unproblematic) understanding of sovereignty. Agamben has proposed that the sovereign declarative utterance of a state of emergency activates the suspension of the law and constitutes the new modality of sovereign governmentality. This proposition implies that the sovereign pre-exists the utterance. And it may imply that Agamben himself knows who the sovereign is (e.g. the President of the United States, the Roman Emperor, etc.). For Butler, on the other hand, it is precisely the utterance of the state of emergency, or extraordinary conditions, that forms this sovereign governmentality. In other words, there is no sovereign before the declaration. *The declaration brings about the sovereign power.* Her reading refuses any naturalisation of power, in the sense that there would be an originary holder of such power. And her interpretation resists any foundationalist account of power, even if she proposes, as we shall see, that this type of power has the characteristics of a totalitarian regime.

Thus, one might say that Butler holds to the general 'structure' of power proposed by Foucault – power as multifaceted dynamic, shifting *relations*. Her account creates multiple sites for sovereign governmentality and, simultaneously, creates multiple sites for resistance. Butler proposes that the withdrawal from law shares the characteristics of a performative act, in the sense that it brings into being what we would normally take to be already there, but at the same time it transplants this modality of power onto governmental practices (e.g. the management of detainees, the decisions of military tribunals). These governmental practices that would otherwise have been part of some legal apparatus – such as prison codes of practice or laws of evidence – now act as 'sovereign' satellites without any legal foundation. Moreover, these very practices become endowed with the 'sovereign' power to make decisions over the right to life or death of these detainees (2004a: 94–95). Governmentality, generally associated with the practice of managing populations, becomes revitalised as new modality of power that takes on the very 'rights' previously reserved for the sovereign.

Performativity and the dangerous detainee

This new coalition between governmental and sovereign power, as Butler suggests earlier in the same essay, has as its aim the augmentation and proliferation of state power (2004a: 58). This is achieved in two ways: first, by establishing military tribunals, whereby trials can come to 'independent' conclusions that nevertheless can be reversed by the executive; and second, by detaining the prisoners in Guantánamo Bay indefinitely. As the essay covertly suggests, there is a clear interrelation between the two practices: each of them presupposed the other for its successful operation. More explicitly, they are both produced performatively.

Butler argues that this new form of sovereign power comes into being at the moment when it withdraws the applicability of law. The withdrawal correlates to the performative act that brings this new type of power into being and inaugurates a series of performative speech acts not *founded* in law but *justified* by the 'force of law'. In relation to the establishment of military tribunals, Butler explains the operation of performative speech acts by citing an example. She analyses the justification provided by a Department of Defense (DOD) representative when asked by a reporter why the DOD did not use the already existing military courts to try the detainees. The DOD representative justifies the establishment of these tribunals by saying that the circumstances needed another 'instrument' (2004a: 83). As Butler writes, 'the law is not that to which the state is subject nor that which distinguishes between lawful state action and unlawful, but is now expressly understood as an instrument, an instrumentality of power, one that can be applied and suspended at will' (2004a: 83). Thus, the utterance itself, the DOD representative's response, brings into being the coincidence of these two models of power. Law is withdrawn, due to the 'special circumstances' that the state finds itself in, replaced by sovereign power that uses law as a technique of governmentality. Withdrawal of law achieves the best management of the detainees. Moreover, by delegating the power to decide over the future of the detainees to a tribunal, power is transferred to the President to decide on the life of these detainees. While the tribunal can decide whether it could apply the death penalty, for example, the President has the power to decide whether or not to overrule their decisions. Butler's essay also tracks the response to journalists' questions put to William Haynes (DOD General Counsel). What would happen to the detainees if the military tribunal found them not guilty? Haynes's reply: even under these conditions, detainees would not be released unless the state was satisfied that they were not dangerous (2004a: 74–75). Once more we witness a speech act that suspends the law. The place of law is taken up by sovereign power that could at any point withdraw its applicability for the so-called better protection of US citizens. At the moment of legal withdrawal we can see the efficacy of sovereign power and governmentality.

Haynes's statement is also telling in other ways since, as Butler observes, the detainees are not considered by the US administration to be common criminals but something more – *dangerous individuals*.[4] The alleged 'dangerousness of the detainees' – cited as reason for the withdrawal of the rule of law – is also integral to a series of answers given by US Secretary of Defense Donald Rumsfeld regarding indefinite detention. When asked why the US administration was holding these detainees indefinitely, Rumsfeld answered that if they were not restrained they would kill (2004a: 73). Rumsfeld uses clear ends-justify-means logic here, but he also contends that such means have a legal foundation. Rumsfeld suggests that the US administration is acting within the parameters of international and national law, even citing the example of Britain and the case in which 'European human rights courts ... allowed the British authorities to detain Irish Catholic and Protestant militants for long periods of time, if they "were deemed dangerous, but not necessarily convicted of a crime"' (2004a: 71). And in relation to domestic legislation, the US administration cites the restraining and hospitalisation of mentally ill people that takes place without the invocation of a criminal charge (2004a: 73). In both cases, while one sees the detainees linked to the category of 'the dangerous individual' one sees little explanation or justification of this categorisation.

The invocation of the 'dangerous individual' allows the state once more to use law as a technique of sovereign power. This tactic further suspends the norm of the rule of law, but at the same time it transforms the exception to the norm into the norm itself (2004a: 67). As Butler suggests, the performative speech acts justifies both the indefinite detention of the detainees while it simultaneously sustains, and renders coherent, the constitution of special military tribunals. The invocation of danger and the dangerous individual creates a space from which extra-legal power can be exercised indefinitely. According to Butler, the release of images of the detainees, both through television and photographs, aims to strengthen the effect of this performative act: 'there is a reduction of these human beings to animal status, where the animal is figured as out of control, in need of total restraint' (2004a: 78).

If we consider in their totality the effects of this series of performative acts, we can clearly see that they reduce the detainees to bare life, to sub-jects that are outside *'bios politicos'* (2004a: 67–68). Butler agrees with Agamben on this point, but she does not hesitate to problematise this con-clusion. Agamben does not explain why only certain citizens are reduced to bare life (2004a: 67–68). In her attempt to grasp the problem of who or what counts as 'bare life', Butler turns to the equivalence that the US administration draws between the Guantánamo Bay detainees, on the one hand, and the mentally ill (as dangerous individuals) on the other. 'Bare life' includes those who are dead but not sacrificed; it captures a category of human being *not* equated with danger, animality, incivility, and madness. Thus, one sees a certain type of life, one deemed unliveable and unviable, read as a threat to those lives that are worth something.[5]

Liveable lives

Butler's central concern lies with the very possibility of a liveable life. Butler indicates that this new form of power (sovereign-governmentality) produces unliveable and unviable lives, and she thereby forces us to think about whether it is possible, given the conditions that govern us, to produce liveable and viable lives. Would law be such a space? Throughout the essay Butler appears to want the detainees to be put through the process of a proper trial, within the parameters of the rules of evidence, but towards the end she clari-fies her account and contends that she is *not* interested in merely upholding the rule of law. We can interpret this to mean that she is not interested in rule-based trials if rule-based trials will be in the hands of sovereign-governmentality. We might say that in Butler's case a rule-based trial will still produce the unbearable effects for detainees if the rules and the practice of trying them remain instruments of governmental sovereignty. Nevertheless, she is cur-ious to see whether law can have a ' … place … in the articulation of an international conception of rights and obligations that limit and conditions claims of state sovereignty' (2004a: 98).

Butler clearly recognises the limitations of international law; the Geneva Conventions, for example, only provide protection for the states that are signatories to it (2004a: 86). States described as 'rogue', displaced stateless people and citizens of emerging states – none of these can be protected by the conventions. In and of itself, the law cannot provide sufficient conditions

152   *Elena Loizidou*

for a liveable and viable life. Still, throughout the essay, she stubbornly and consistently calls for the detainees to be tried through the criminal or military courts. Why does she do so? If we are to understand her paradoxical position, we must look not only to this essay but to her other work where she either explicitly or inexplicitly invokes the law. If we are to give a more meaningful understanding to her call to put detainees on trial than merely saying that Butler is a left liberal who upholds a faith in law, we need to grasp more fully the architecture of her thought.

To do so, I suggest a return to *Excitable Speech* (1997a), a place where Butler writes explicitly that the subject comes into being through language. We are named at birth. This is a type of proto-violence, since a subject's ability to answer to that given name, may *enable* rather than avert future violence. At the moment of responding to our name, we gain a certain agency, but we also come under the force of an undeniable power. This process of agency and injury goes on throughout one's life; life itself depends upon this endless process of 'speaking back'.[6] *Excitable Speech* invokes the possibility of creating vitality through the modality of agonism – a sort of warring with the conditions that bring us into being.

In significant and subtle ways, this agonism resembles the process of the trial. Butler's invocation of the trial[7] in 'Indefinite Detention' might thereby be read as a call to sustain this agonistic spirit, to sustain it *through the law.* If law's central characteristic is agonism then law may itself cultivate the conditions under which a liveable life becomes possible. Thinking the law in this way makes it powerfully clear why Butler would insist on a trial for the detainees: it is only in the first place through the law that they might struggle for the conditions for a bearable, liveable life. Unlike Agamben, who thinks that law has no connection with the production of life, Butler can see the role that law can play in this production. At the same time, like Agamben, she is aware that for this production to come about we need to transform the conditions of political action, so as to reconsider what it means to be human. Human rights, she argues, have failed so far to wrestle with the meaning of the human. The trial as a model creates the space for such consideration to take place. Nonetheless, the meaning of 'human' will remain open, contested:

[t]o be human implies many things, one of which is that we are the kinds of beings who must live in a world where clashes of value do and will occur, and these clashes are a sign of what a human community is. How we handle those conflicts will also be a sign of our humanness, one that is, importantly, in the making.

(Butler 2004a: 89)

Butler not only emphasises the *concept* of humanness but also, and more importantly, she focuses on the way we *negotiate* conflicting understandings of the human. It is precisely our handling of such an issue that will (or will not) produce our humanness. Butler, as I am reading her here, makes a powerful suggestion: that law can have a meaningful and important role to play in this process. Of course, negotiations with the human must transpire in many other spheres as well, and the political domain will be central to this endeavour.

Butler wonders what type of power would be able to limit, alter, or utterly transform the dehumanising effects of the current status quo (2004a: 98–99). Indeed, what type of power could provide such an opening? If our lives are totalised by a sovereign power that uses governmentality as its strategy for re-territorialising itself, then what type of power can put a stop to the production of this death machine? If law is impotent because it cannot allow subjects to answer back, then what type of power could reverse this decay? In response to questions such as these, Agamben calls for pure violence, in the spirit of Walter Benjamin. Reflecting upon both 'Indefinite detention' and Butler's broader body of work leads to me the conclusion that she would consistently refuse to invoke the modality of pure violence. Indeed, in recent public lectures Butler has stated that she is searching for possible answers within philosophies of peace (2004e) and that she is committed to a type of violence that does not kill (2004d). Butler gives violence new requirements: not to kill but rather to revitalise life. I explain below that this search returns her to a combination of disciplinary and governmental power, whereby the very materiality of bodies and the conditions that they find themselves in can be re-addressed through practices of resistance.

Disciplinary power and resistance through the law

In *Discipline and Punish* (1991a) and *History of Sexuality*, vol. 1 (1990), Foucault explains how the subject is produced through disciplinary power. For Foucault, disciplinary power is a different type of law, an infra-law: a type of law that is ahead of the juridical, that permeates the social, cultural and political body, and produces subjects precisely through the exercise of a series of disciplinary practices, including those of surveillance. As Brown and Hartley (2002: 11) remind us, disciplinary power does not lie with the state but rather with culture and society. To this extent Foucault imagines disciplines fighting against the juridical order (Foucault, 1991a: 222). This argument promotes an understanding of the norm, engendered by a series of practices, as located not within the law but rather within the social and cultural body – a part of its various institutions and discursive practices. The law is no longer perceived as the sole producer of the norm.

In *Gender Trouble*, Butler uses disciplinary power to offer an understanding of how certain genders become intelligible, and how others are foreclosed from the visible spectrum. Intelligible genders are the ones that can maintain a certain stability and continuity between gender, sexuality, sex and desire (1990: 18). Any sexual practices or desires that derogate, destabilise and break the above unity are foreclosed. But Butler also shows that there is no ground lying behind these practices that would somehow 'pronounce' certain genders to be intelligible (or not). Rather it is the practices themselves, and the norms that they both (re)constitute and instantiate, that produces intelligibility as such. The idea of gender performativity serves to reveal these practices as constitutive of gender norms. Butler argues that the practice of *gendering* proves always to be a performative practice. At the same time these practices enable the very agency of the always *gendered* subject to become agentic. And this agency makes possible a certain resistance to the very norm that formed it. Resistance emerges as a critical genealogy (1990: 5), one that is embedded in legitimising practices but not confined to them.

Therefore, Butler can be said to use disciplinary power as a weapon for challenging juridical law, in the sense of encountering and countering law's claim to universality and demonstrating that its very existence relies on those foreclosures that it brings about. Disciplinary power is also used to show that the normative does not always coincide with the law; the normative is *not* the law. This means precisely that norms are not static; they can be transformed by the subjects that are to be formed by them. To be called a woman, for example, relies on a cultural understanding of what a woman 'is' that, in turn, is based on the differentiation between man and woman. But when a woman becomes a man through reassignment, for example, we can see that the trans-sexual person both destabilises the normative understanding of what 'is' a woman (gender, sexuality, sex and desire), unconceals the very phantasmatic grounds of the norm, and simultaneously shows that norms are not static.[8]

Similarly, when a young man runs away from the police who are shouting at him, he resists the interpellative call that somehow names him as a criminal. His running away enables us to see that the normative understanding of who is a criminal is based precisely on discursive practices that produce the category of 'the criminal'. So, to put it another way, disciplinary practices, as Foucault would have it, create counter-disciplines that produce different narratives of the normative, and these different narratives may allow for the subject's survival. This was not the case with Jean-Charles Menezes, who was mistakenly shot by the Metropolitan Police in London, but our survivability as citizens of or visitors to the UK relies precisely on possibilities opening up, no matter how minimal they may be, that can allow us to undo normative hegemony. Consider, for example, Butler's own understanding of the norm from 'Competing Universalities':

> [n]orms are not only embodied, as Bourdieu has argued, but embodiment is itself a mode of interpretation, not always conscious, which subjects normativity to an iterable temporality. Norms are not static entities, but incorporated and interpreted features of existence that are sustained by the idealizations furnished by fantasy.
>
> (Butler, 2000d: 152)

The re-interpretation of the norm, through resistance to it, creates the conditions for one's survivability. Moreover, such resistance reconfigures the plateau of intelligibility. In *Excitable Speech*, Butler calls for the avoidance of any form of censorship that could do away with the constant reconfiguration and survival of subjects, even if and when their interpellation into being is an injurious one.

At the heart of Butler's understanding of how we can sustain liveable lives lies the structure of agonism. When norms do not become the law – when, in other words, the state and the sovereign do not totalise the sphere of intelligibility, either by using the law as a governmental instrument or by using disciplinary practices like surveillance to govern every aspect of our lives – then we can resist the cultural norms that bring us into being. Moreover, if we engage with this struggle then we may attain something more than our survival, our viability.

However, and this is I think what explains Butler's recent quest for a different role for the juridical law, *when the law and norms become one* then the possibility for survival as humans becomes delimited. That is, when President George W. Bush presents the law and norms as unitary then only a very small space for resistance remains, since every form of dissent is rendered not only unintelligible but also dangerous, a threat to national security and cohesion. Under these conditions, law becomes for Butler the only vehicle for resistance, and, specifically, through the practice of the trial, the only force for dissent. Crucially, in order for law to become such a force for resistance it must, as Benjamin and Agamben suggest, do away with its interest in its own preservation. How could this become possible? As Butler suggests in 'Competing Universalities', borrowing from Spivak's work,[9] the practice of translation may enable the agonism between competing universalities, competing concepts of the human. Such a practice will entail working with precisely the differences between competing notions without reducing the one into the other. Law perhaps can take up the task of the translator. But, nevertheless, the task of the translator necessitates, despite any logical incompatibilities between competing universalities, that there might be some common grounds for 'social and political aims' (2000d: 167). So perhaps the law could become that space whereby the illogical incompatibilities – or at least the illogical incompatibilities between those that are said to perpetuate the global terrorism and those that fight it – could meet. And perhaps a translation of what it is to be human, without the confinements of justice, the ends of law, can become the means for such discussion, if human survival and vitality can still be entertained. For, as Butler writes, life is precarious (some lives more than others), always an ambivalent concept, but as things now stand it risks losing its ambivalence if we continue to support the sovereign's contention that what it is to be human and what life means are neutral terms.

Notes

1 This position still holds true of the time of this writing, even after the cases heard by the Supreme Court of the US relating to grant of a writ of *habeas corpus* to certain detainees in Guantánamo Bay; see Motha (2005).

2 It is also important to note that Foucault is relatively clear in *Society Must be Defended* that neither sovereign power nor disciplinary power disappears once governmental power emerges; rather, 'society' is permeated by this new form of power called governmentality (Foucault 2003: 241).

3 'Territory' designates not only spatial boundaries, but also the custodian status of a detainee. For more in relation to a case of detainees in Guantánamo Bay and their *habeas corpus* challenges brought before the Supreme Court of the US, see Motha (2005).

4 Her observation invokes subtly Foucault's essay 'About the Concept of the "Dangerous Individual" in Nineteenth-century Legal Psychiatry' (Foucault 2002b: 176–200). In this essay Foucault writes of the institutionalisation of individuals who committed motiveless crimes. The dangerous individual, who was in some respects insane, was the one whose crime was without motive or reason. The dangerous individual was to be assessed via the concept of risk. When an individual cannot account for, or take responsibility for, their act, judicial practice is rendered impotent.

5 However, when Butler problematises the correspondence of terrorist detainees with the mad she appears – unintentionally, I would suppose – to suggest that the mad are totally unintelligible, dangerous, etc. That is, she implies that the equivalence or correspondence of mad–terrorist is *truly* catachrestic. This move runs the risk of presenting the insane as unintelligible, unmotivated and uncivilised. Foucault, of course, alerted readers to the clinicians' *invention* of insanity and, moreover, alerted us to precisely the construction of the insane as based on instrumentalisation. In *Madness and Civilization* (1991b) he suggests that the separation of madness from reason coincides with the birth of the profession of psychiatry and this specialised knowledge. The perception of insane acts as unintelligible, bereft of will and uncivilised is clearly a historical production, and Foucault's historical accounting of this epistemic shift serves, in its own peculiar way, to render the category of 'madness' more intelligible. I have no intention here of dismissing Butler's position, but rather I am suggesting that there are ways in which one could use this precise metonymic practice to the advantage of those who are deemed 'bare life'. We can, for example, challenge in its totality the construction of the dangerous individual and its various configurations that has permeated both the legal and the political discourse.

6 All of this explains why the regulation of injurious language (hate speech, pornography, etc) *may curtail* the possibility for the subject to stay alive, to be recognised and recognisable (1997a: 5).

7 In *State of Exception* (2005), Agamben argues that in the case of juridical law, the concrete case always entails a 'trial' of which the end is to pronounce a sentence guaranteed by other institutions of the state (39–40). Amongst other things this observation suggests that the operability of law necessitates the practice of trial, otherwise we would clearly see the decay of law.

8 I am by no means suggesting, nor is Butler herself, that this is uncomplicated, nor that it can occur outside of processes and practices of surveillance.

9 See Spivak (2003: 162) and Benjamin (2004: 253–63).

11 Rights and the politics of performativity

Karen Zivi

Strategies devised on the part of progressive legal and social movements ... run the risk of being turned against those very movements by virtue of extending state power, specifically legal power, over the issues in question ... [S]uch strategies tend to enhance state regulation over the issues in question, potentially empowering the state to invoke such precedents against the very social movements that pushed for their acceptance as legal doctrine.

(Butler 1997a: 23–24)

[E]ssential to so many political movements is the claim of bodily integrity and self-determination. It is important to claim that our bodies are in a sense *our own* and that we are entitled to claim rights of autonomy over our bodies ... It is difficult, if not impossible, to make these claims without recourse to autonomy. I am not suggesting that we cease to make these claims. We have to, we must. I also do not wish to imply that we have to make these claims reluctantly or strategically.

(Butler 2004a: 25)

To say that Judith Butler's theory of performativity has had an important influence on contemporary understandings of gender identity is to make a fairly uncontroversial statement. To say that her theory of performativity makes a valuable contribution to progressive democratic politics is, however, to make a claim likely to elicit puzzled looks. Given Butler's critique of traditional social-movement strategies and her call for the somewhat unusual political practices of drag, parody, and insurrectionary speech, it is not surprising that she has failed to win over many who see themselves as committed to progressive politics. Indeed, her theory of performativity has been charged with positively undermining emancipatory politics, with threatening the theoretical and strategic resources essential to responding to and transforming relations of inequality and injustice (for example, Nussbaum 1999). But what then are we to do with Butler's avowed commitment to and her continual engagement in democratic politics? Is performativity really antithetical to or at odds with progressive politics? Is a 'politics of the performative' an oxymoron at best? Or might a theory of performativity actually contribute to or advance a theory and practice of politics?[1]

To answer these questions requires a more careful consideration of the relationship between performativity and politics. In this essay, I take a closer look at the political dimensions and implications of Butler's work by focusing on the insights she offers about rights throughout the body of her work. I suggest that traditional criticisms of Butler overlook important political dimensions of performativity that are actually manifest in the practice of making rights claims. Critiques of Butler, particularly those concerned about the lack of gravity associated with, and the potential determinism of, performativity, fail to give adequate attention to the important theory of language on which Butler's argument rests. Appreciating the linguistic dimensions of a theory of performativity reveals a very different conception of politics at the heart of Butler's work, a conception of politics that entails the 'double movement' of invocation and critical self-reflection. In the second half of this essay, I suggest that the practice of making rights claims aptly illustrates the politics of double movement demanded by a theory of performativity and offers insights into Butler's conception of democracy. Rights-claiming, as we will see, is never wholly state-directed nor can it guarantee particular political outcomes. What it signals, instead, is the open future that Butler associates with the promise and practice of democracy.

In reconciling Butler's various critiques of rights claiming with her embrace of it, we come to see how and why it is that, even in the face of devastating critiques and disappointing outcomes, rights-claiming can remain an important part of a democratic politics. Moreover, we gain insights into what makes performativity political and into what makes a political practice like rights-claiming performative.

Doing and thinking politics

What is to be done about inequality and injustice? How are they to be fought? What kind of political practices and strategies should be used to make things better for marginalised individuals? These questions are not new to theorists or activists interested in advancing progressive political goals. In recent years, however, concern has arisen that questions of identity and subjectivity have eclipsed questions of political practice and action, leaving progressive social movements with few resources with which to combat the pressing injustices faced by individuals around the globe.[2] Perhaps no one's work has been more routinely challenged for contributing to this problem than Judith Butler's. Since the publication of *Gender Trouble* (1990) more than a decade ago, and the widespread embrace of its theory of gender as performatively constituted, questions about the 'political' implications of a theory of performativity have haunted her work. Questions persist despite Butler's stated commitment to a project of radical democracy, despite her active engagement in social-movement politics, and even despite a book explicitly subtitled 'A Politics of the Performative' (Butler 1997a). Though Butler has reworked her theory of performativity in response to criticism and misunderstanding, considered the applicability of performativity beyond the realm of gender, and even proffered examples of alternative forms of politics such as drag and insurrectionary speech, Butler's critics remain unsatisfied. They contend that the theory she advances and the 'political' alternatives she offers fail to bear out her commitment to expanding democracy (for example, Fraser 1998; Nussbaum 1999; Kruks 2001).[3] While Butler's work may actually contribute to such concerns, as I suggest below, her work also offers an important response to these charges, one that requires taking seriously the linguistic dimensions of subjectivity and political agency.

As her critics charge, Butler's work would seem to position performativity as somewhat at odds with politics. For example, in *Excitable Speech* (1997a), the book most explicitly addressed to exploring the relationship between performativity and politics, Butler criticises traditional practices of contemporary social movements. She questions the wisdom of continuing to turn to the state and to use the law and rights discourse to respond to injustice, particularly in the context of fighting hate speech. According to Butler, fighting hate speech with rights claims and the law – demanding the right to be free from 'words that wound' and crafting hate speech codes – may actually do less to enhance individual freedom than to increase state power. This is due, in part, to the fact that hate-speech codes, designed to censor injurious speech and further progressive ends, are actually premised on a set of beliefs that work to enable the disciplinary power of the state. Hate-speech codes, that is, assume that words have specific and unwaveringly harmful effects on individuals and that the state has the power to protect individuals and groups from such assaults and should do so. Unfortunately, in asking the state for protection as a way to be free from harm, we fail to appreciate the instability of language and actually increase the control that the state has over our lives. Hate-speech codes, Butler argues, often backfire because they 'tend to enhance state regulation over the issues in question, potentially empowering the state to invoke such precedents against the very social movements that pushed for their acceptance as legal doctrine' (1997a: 23–24).

Butler raises similar concerns with regard to the fight for same-sex marriage rights. The 'relentless search for legal remedy' to the problem of gay and lesbian inequality contributes to state regulation: 'Those who seek marriage identify not only with those who have gained the blessing of the state, but with the state itself. Thus the petition not only augments state power, but accepts the state as the necessary venue for democratisation itself' (Butler 2000d: 176). For example, same-sex marriage rights would make the distinction between married and non-married all the more explicit, legitimating only certain forms of intimate association. Legalising same-sex marriage, Butler argues, enhances the state's power to sanction relations of sexuality.

From Butler's perspective, a turn to the law, the state, and the discourse of rights is likely to be problematic, if not self-defeating. Such strategies 'run the risk of being turned against those very movements' that invoke them (Butler 1997a: 23), but not simply by virtue of extending state power. According to Butler, a reliance on traditional political practices (such as turning to the law and the state) also diminishes the vibrancy and demo-cratic potential of progressive politics. We have become a bit lazy, she sug-gests, relying on familiar tactics, no longer engaging in creative and innovative practices of democratic contestation, no longer engaging in 'nonstate-centered forms of agency and resistance' or 'nonjuridical forms of opposition' that occur outside the realm of the courts (Butler 1997a: 19, 23–24). Rather than continuing to rely on courts and traditional forms of legal redress, Butler encourages such 'non-juridical' political strategies as drag and insurrectionary speech. But what do such practices look like and why might some find them lacking?

Perhaps Butler's most familiar example of a nonjuridical form of political engagement is drag. Drag – the performance of one gender by a person whose anatomical sex would suggest they are a different gender reveals a radical contingency between sex and gender – reveals the ontology of the sovereign gendered subject to be a 'normative injunction' (Butler 1990: 148). Drag is a form of parody, and as such, reveals the gap between anatomical sex and gender identity challenging the naturalness of both gender and sex. But drag does more than simply illuminate the way in which the perfor-mance of gender norms 'creates the illusion of' a gendered essence. It also functions as a political practice with subversive potential. If gender identity is not a given reality, but rather a construct that can be adopted or par-odied, embraced or contested, then the norms associated with putative nat-ural sex and gender can be challenged. From Butler's perspective, drag, because it reveals the contingency of identity, gives rise to or takes the form of a hopeful politics: 'If identities were no longer fixed as the premises of a political syllogism, and politics no longer understood as a set of practices derived from the alleged interests that belong to a set of ready-made sub-jects, a new configuration of politics would surely emerge from the ruins of the old' (1990: 149).

Unfortunately, whether it is drag, parody, or insurrectionary speech that Butler calls for, such practices seem unfamiliar if not incomprehensible given our traditional conceptions of politics. Moreover, whether it is because of our common associations of parody with a kind of silliness or because we think of speaking as distinct from doing, the political practices Butler urges seem to lack the seriousness and potency associated with more traditional forms of legal or institutional change. Critics of Butler's work argue that drag or parody fails to address serious material concerns of the world and reduces political activity to superficialities, to play and appearance, failing to recognise that politics entails the difficult work of addressing real inequality (for example, Fraser 1998; Nussbaum 1999; Kruks 2001). This concern, of course, assumes that there is a considerable chasm between the theatrical and the political, between performance and materiality. While we may acknowledge that performances can have political overtones or implications, the common intuition is that performance is distinct from the 'real' politics of public policy making or institutional and material change. Performances are fictional representations of the real, but not the real itself; actors merely adopt a persona, take on a role that they can take up or leave behind at the stage door. At the same time, of course, performers appear to be at the mercy of and constrained, if not determined, by external factors such as scripts and directors. The performer seems unlikely to coincide with our common conception of the political agent.

Traditionally, when we think of emancipatory political action we have in mind activities that have a gravity and seriousness to them, that are directed at making clear and lasting change. Such purposeful politics presupposes a vision of the political agent as a 'sovereign subject', as an individual with a will and intention, an agency, of his or her own whose goal it is to oppose or radically alter existing power relations. The interest this subject has in challenging relations of power is presumed to be linked to, if not derived from, some essential aspect of his or her identity (for example, gender, sexuality, race, class). Moreover, the political actor is assumed to have a measure of control over the intended outcome of the language and strategies used to challenge relations of power. He or she takes a particular action, whether it is juridical or legislative, for example, with the expectation that a particular end will result. Political agents, when engaging in emancipatory and transformative political activities, are presumed to have an identity that exists prior to language and to have an instrumental relationship to language as well, 'the ability and power to exercise speech in a straightforward way' (Butler 1997a: 84).

Butler's theory of performativity, however, challenges this vision of political agency. Her work calls into question not simply the political *practices* of progressive social movements, but also the basic epistemological and ontological *intuitions* upon which they rest. For example, if we follow Butler in understanding identity as performative, a repetition of norms for which there is no original, then we can no longer assume that political activity emanates from a fixed identity or reflects a particular perspective associated with a supposedly stable identity. Instead of a sovereign subject, Butler offers us a notion of the performative subject; instead of a subject with command over language, Butler describes a subject produced through language. In other words, Butler suggests that we are not sovereign subjects who use language as a tool, but, rather, we are beings who come into existence through language. Drawing inspiration from the work of J.L. Austin, Butler explains that we must recognise that 'Language is a name for our doing: both "what" we do (the name of the action that we characteristically perform) and that which we effect, the act and its consequences' (Butler 1997a: 8). For example, when I name a ship or make a bet (Austin's examples), I am not describing actions that I have already taken, for it is in the process of speaking that I do the act: 'to utter the sentence is not to *describe* my doing of what I should be said in so uttering to be doing or to state that I am doing it; it is to do it' (Austin 1975: 6). And one of the things that we do through language is create rather than simply describe our personhood.

As Butler explains, via Althusser, it is through language we come into being. This complicated process of interpellation reveals that 'by being called a name, one is ... given a certain possibility for social existence' (Butler 1997a:2). Linguistic recognition, in other words, makes possible rather than simply reflects social existence and humanisation:

> [T]o be addressed is not merely to be recognized for what one already is, but to have the very term conferred by which the recognition of existence becomes possible ... One 'exists' not only by virtue of being recognized, but, in a prior sense, by being *recognizable*.
>
> (Butler 1997a: 5)

Hailing, calling one a name, is constitutive rather than merely descriptive; it is 'inaugurative' to the extent that it confers social existence on the individual. If we come into being through such hailing, through being recognised linguistically, then there is no sovereign subject who precedes the calling. I, the I who speaks and presumes my own sovereignty, is, actually, 'an effect in discourse, there is first a discourse which precedes and enables that "I" and forms in language the constraining trajectory of its will' (Butler 1993: 225).

The process of interpellation is not simply a process of being called a name by an other. It requires that we act in ways that correspond to the name we are being called. Butler describes this as a form of *ritualised repetition*. For example, if I am hailed as a woman or a man, I am required to act in ways that correspond to femaleness or maleness. It is not that some gendered essence gives rise to my activities or to the name I am called. But rather I come to be both an 'I' and a woman through the repetition of gender norms that correspond to that which I am being called. The stakes of this repetition are extremely high. My very intelligibility depends upon reiterating already understood norms. As Derrida explains, a performative utterance – whether it is a saying or a doing – only makes sense, is intelligible, if it repeats a "coded" or iterable utterance'. For 'if the formula I pronounce in order to open a meeting, launch a ship or a marriage were not identifiable as *conforming* with an iterable model, if it were not then identifiable in some way as a "citation"', how could my claim make sense? (Derrida 1988: 18).

This theory of performativity as a theory of subjectivity has important consequences for how we understand politics. According to traditional conceptions of politics, our identity (e.g. femaleness, blackness) is not only presumed to be natural, but is also presumed to give rise to our political activities, to motivate and direct our political goals and aspirations. From Butler's perspective, however, the very identity that is posited as prior to and motivating political activity is actually the effect, rather than the cause, of a set of actions or performances. The implication is that instead of thinking of feminists as a group whose political interests stem from some common and essential identity as women, we recognise that their political agency, their being political agents, is actually constituted through the performances in which they engage.

Several ideas are important here. First the stakes of performativity are very high. Performativity is not mere play. Parodic performances, like drag, may be voluntary, adopted or shed as one would a role on stage, but the enactment of gender, for example, is compulsory. We cannot opt in or out of repeating gender norms without extremely serious consequences. The performance of gender identity is, Butler argues, absolutely essential to an individual's ability to be intelligible, recognisable as a speaking subject. We have 'to do gender' in order to be taken seriously as subjects, our very personhood (physical as well as psychic) requires that we enact gender norms. Unlike a role we may play or not play, we are compelled to repeat social norms of gender intelligibility, or we risk a kind of death, whether social or physical.

Moreover, it is not something we do once and have completed. Creating the illusion of a core gendered self is not the result of one discrete act, but rather the very fragile and temporary result of repetition of acts, 'incessant activity', the sedimentation or effect of repeated rituals. In fact, there are serious consequences for failing to perform or act in accordance with the discourse through which one is hailed: 'those who fail to do their gender right' are punished (Butler 1990: 140). This punishment could range from beating to death of a gay man or transsexual, refusing to allow same-sex couples to marry, adopt, or share health benefits, or simply ignoring someone who is different. The point here is that gender performance, or acting in accordance with any other kind of hailing, is not purely voluntary. Hailing, interpellation, entails norms that shape and constrain our very ability to be taken seriously as persons.

Of course, this raises the question of political agency: if we are compelled to enact gender or some other norm in order to be recognised as persons, how then can we challenge or contest such norms? If discourse 'seeks to produce a lawful subject', what room is left for agency (Butler 1993: 122)? If we *must* enact gender norms, and gender norms exist prior to us and constrain us individuals, has Butler left us with a determined subject? For Butler, the repetition of norms is not a simple replication; being 'conditioned' by discourse is not the same as being determined by it. Indeed, from her perspective, there is a great distance between that which conditions or compels and that which determines, and this is because language is never perfectly instrumental or seamless; there is always excess. As Butler explains, 'language refers to an open system of signs by which intelligibility is insistently created and contested' (1990: 145). Language should be understood as a 'sign-chain' in which continuity is accompanied by innovation: 'the entire history of a "thing", an organ, a custom can be a continuous sign-chain of ever new interpretations and adaptations whose causes do not even have to be related to one another but, on the contrary, in some cases succeed and alternate with one another in a purely chance fashion' (1993: 224). Thus the interpellative call of gender norms, for example, may seek to produce a subject that conforms to these norms, but it always also produces the unexpected, the new, what Butler describes as excess. Butler draws some of her insights into the excessive quality of language from Derrida who suggests that we recognise the gaps that exist between intention and outcome, between intended and actual effects, not as Austinian failures of language, but rather as part of the grammar of language itself. In other words, a written or spoken sign is 'a mark that subsists ... does not exhaust itself in the moment of its inscription and ... can give rise to an iteration in the absence and beyond the presence of the empirically determined subject who, in a given context, has emitted or produced it' (Derrida 1988: 9). And such excess has the capacity to undermine the disciplinary power of the state and the law (Butler 1993: 122).

A written or spoken sign, even a bodily gesture, that seems to be a copy of some original is never exactly the same as the original. Repetition is not exact replication. Signs can be misheard or misinterpreted by those to whom they are directed. They may also be deployed in new ways and at new sites and in ways that break with context, displacing the original meaning of a word or norm, denaturalising the concept, changing the way we think or act, even engendering new forms of the culturally intelligible. For example, the performance of gender identity through drag, if understood not as a simple replication of an original, but rather as 'a de-formity, or a parodic repetition', calls into question the solidity and naturalness of gender identity, revealing it to be a norm rather than an essence. In 'expos[ing] the phantasmatic effect of abiding identity as a politically tenuous construction', drag may make it possible to think and do femininity and masculinity in new or different ways (Butler 1990: 141). Repetition that breaks with context might look like reappropriating the terms 'queer' or 'chick' to signify something empowering rather than demeaning. It could also entail using terms or enacting norms in new contexts, such as using the language of rights outside the realm of the court or describing something not usually thought of as rights-bearing (for example, trees, animals, etc). To use a word such as marriage, for example, to refer to a relationship not sanctioned by the state may also dislodge common ways of thinking and acting such that new forms of being and doing are opened up. In these cases the signs or utterances may be a repetition of an authorised discourse, but only to a certain extent, enough so that the claim is intelligible, and yet allowing for the expropriation or misappropriation of an authorised discourse (1990:

145, 157). The result is that we are speaking in ways 'that have never yet been legitimated ... hence producing legitimation in new and future forms' (Butler 1997a: 41).[4]

Of course, not all forms of repetition are necessarily progressive. Subversive repetition can be practised by those with troubling political agendas. One could use individual rights claims to demand access for men to classes designed only for women, or, as Butler notes, reappropriate civil-rights discourse to oppose affirmative action in California. But even here, new ways of thinking and doing come into being. What is opened up, then, is a gap between speech or norms and outcomes or effects, 'between the originating context or intention by which an utterance is animated and the effects it produces' (Butler 1997a: 14). According to Butler, therein lies the possibility for political agency. By dislodging a speech act from its original context, we may be able to resignify the meaning of a word or a practice: 'Untethering the speech act from the sovereign subject founds an alternative notion of agency and, ultimately, of responsibility, one that more fully acknowledges the way in which the subject is constituted in language, how what it creates is also what it derives from elsewhere' (Butler 1997a: 15–16).

Rights claiming as a politics of the performative:

What might it mean to apply a theory of performativity to the politics of rights? Would it only lead to a concern about increasing the regulatory power of the state as Butler's criticism of traditional methods of legal redress suggests? As I will suggest in this section, rights-claiming need not be seen as antithetical to the kind of performative politics at which Butler hints. Quite to the contrary, rights-claiming may be best understood as performative, as the reiteratation of norms and repetition of already authorised discourses. Of course, as with other forms of performative politics, this means that rights-claiming is neither perfectly subversive in its effects nor an exact replication of existing regulatory norms. Instead, what Butler helps us see about rights claiming is that, as a performative practice, it must involve two moves: invocation and critique.

To think of rights-claiming as a performative activity may seem, at first, counterintutitive. We often consider rights to be 'things' such as universal and ahistorical truths or legal artifacts. On this understanding, to make a rights claim would be to describe something that already exists, to represent the real. Accordingly, to say that I have a right or that women have rights would be to refer to something that exists prior to my saying it. My speech, in this case, is simply representational or descriptive, and I orient my claims to the state, seeking recognition or confirmation of my description.

And yet, our traditional understandings of rights also entail a recognition of their performativity. Think of the arguments that making claims for rights reinforces masculine notions of personhood or reinforces decidedly liberal norms of individualism and antagonism or even the common notion that rights 'trump' other concerns. Here we find intuitions about the performative dimensions of rights claiming. Such arguments suggest that in saying 'I have a right' I am not simply describing an already existing reality, but bringing into being a set of relationships or ways of being that may not have existed prior to my speaking. I am not simply representing a reality, but actively doing something in the process of making the claim, and doing something more than just making the claim itself. For example, if 'I have a right' is understood to reinforce liberal individualism, then what I do through making the claim is to bring into being a particular understanding of myself and my relations with others based upon and reinforcing norms of separation and autonomy, perhaps.

As the examples above suggest, the recognition of the performativity of rights is often connected to a critique of the practice. For example, feminists may reject rights-claiming as a political practice because of its harmful effects on women, communitarians may worry about the destructive effects rights have on our sense of responsibility and connection to other, or someone like Butler may worry about the regulatory and constraining effects of a turn to rights. Despite their differences, these critiques serve to remind us that rights-claiming reiterates already existing norms, whether these have to do with liberal ontology or state–citizen relationships. This should come as no surprise for, as Derrida reminds us, the intelligibility of an utterance, in this case a rights claim, *requires* that it repeat an already existing coded iteration. The intelligibility of the statement – indeed my intelligibility as a person who is making an understandable remark and my intelligibility as, in this case, a rights-bearing subject – rests on the fact that my utterances (and my doings) bear some comprehensible relationship to our common intuitions and norms about rights-bearing subjects. When I make a rights claim, that is, I may have to explain why I think I have that right or I might have to contextualise my claim to rights. I cannot simply say I have a right, whether it is to bread or to a mobile phone, and expect that it is understandable. Nor can I say something like 'Cheese needs space' and assume that you will understand my utterance as a claim to a right to privacy. I may also have to enact or perform certain forms of victimhood or rationality or capability in my attempt to be rendered intelligible, or, as Butler puts it, to 'establish [my] legitimacy within a legal framework ensconced in liberal versions of human ontology' (Butler 2004a: 24–25).

But as important as it is to recognise that intelligibility requires the replication of norms, and thereby reinforces existing relations of power, we should not lose sight of Butler's other insight about performativity: performativity is much more than a simple replication. Performativity, indeed language itself, always entails an excess that holds out the promise of transformation. As Butler explains, 'speaking is not a simple assimilation to an existing norm' (Butler 1997a: 91), in fact, reiterating norms or concepts associated with an established or authorized discourse may actually be 'the act of "making a new claim"' (Butler 2000e: 41). Take the example of claiming rights for gays and lesbians as human rights or the notion of women's human rights. In these cases, though we use a familiar author-itative discourse like human rights, we never simply reiterate the norms of liberalism, the discourse most commonly associated with human rights. Why not? Because the very norms that we cite are premised on the exclusion of those who cite the norm (Butler 1997a: 91). If the 'human' of human rights traditionally excludes lesbians, gays and women, if the 'human' is defined through the very exclusion of these groups, then, when using the language of rights, such groups are not simply suggesting that they are human in the way that we usually conceive of the human. They are, instead, challenging us to rethink the meaning of the human, 'expos[ing] the con-ventional limitations of the human' (2000e: 39) while challenging its uni-versality.

In this way, rights-claiming functions as a *perverse reiteration*. The per-verse reiteration is an 'unconventional' formulation of the universal that not only reveals the universal to be 'limited and exclusionary' but also 'mobi-lize(s) a new set of demands' (2000e: 39–40). By calling myself a name that I am not usually called, indeed expected *not* to be called, I make a claim that is new and yet intelligible, both unfamiliar and familiar at the same time. My claiming is not a simple assimilation of the norm but rather a claim in which 'we are confronted with a strange neighboring of the universal and the particular which neither synthesizes the two, nor keeps them apart' (Butler 2000e: 39). In calling myself human when human is premised upon my exclusion, I both highlight that exclusion and suggest that 'human' can be understood in more inclusive ways. I thus challenge traditional under-standings of the intelligible, helping to shape and expand possible ways of thinking and being (Butler 1997a).

As a perverse reiteration, rights-claiming entails double-movement; it is never simply a citation of liberal norms, but it is also their transformation. And for Butler, this transformation is something to take very seriously for it entails nothing less than the 'remaking [of] reality' and the expansion of the livable (Butler 2004b: 30). For example, when gays and lesbians make claims to human rights, whether that is the right to love freely or to be protected from violence, such rights-claims both reinforce and a reshape the meaning of humanness. Rights-claiming thus reflects not the traditional liberal practice of 'struggling for rights that attach to my person' when my per-sonhood is assumed to be already constituted, but rather the practice of constituting personhood, the practice of 'struggling *to be conceived as per-sons*' (2004b: 32). Such rights-claiming, according to Butler, transforms traditional meanings and makes space for alternative ways of living. 'The assertion of rights', she argues, 'becomes a way of intervening into the social and political process by which the human is articulated.' To make interna-tional human rights claims on behalf of gays and lesbians, or any other group previously excluded from traditional definitions of humanness, actu-ally 'rewrites the human and rearticulates the human' (2004b: 33).

Of course, the process of transformation and rearticulation is not fool-proof. Just because I say that those who have been traditionally excluded from human rights are actually rights-bearing subjects does not mean that my claim will be understood. Such claims can certainly go unheard or be rejected. Indeed, as Butler acknowledges, the excessive character of lan-guage means that a doing or a saying that seems to replicate existing norms may be deemed unintelligible or incomprehensible at times. There is no guarantee, in other words, that my utterance, even if it does cite already existing norms, will be acknowledged or accepted as a repetition. Nor is there any guarantee that my utterance, even if intelligible, will engender subversive or progressive outcomes. A politics of the performative must remain, then, a politics of double movement. If we take performativity ser-iously, we must also engage in practices of critical self-reflection that call into question the presuppositions, expectations, and even outcomes of our practices. And Butler certainly does this, illuminating the risks associated with rights-claiming or some other traditional political practice.

However, Butler is also quite clear that critical scrutiny is not about rejecting problematic practices altogether. Critical scrutiny is a process of freeing a concept or practice 'from its metaphysical lodgings in order to understand what political interests were secured in and by that metaphysical placing'. This is not the same as doing away with the term or practice. In fact, it is to open up the space for the term or practice 'to occupy and to serve very different political aims' (Butler 1993: 30). As I suggested above, even as Butler is highly critical of hate-speech codes and same-sex marriage rights, she does not give up on rights (see Chambers 2004). She argues that 'It is important to claim that our bodies are in a sense *our own* and that we are entitled to claim rights of autonomy over our bodies. ... I am not sug-gesting that we cease to make these claims. We have to, we must. I also do not wish to imply that we have to make these claims reluctantly or strategically ... ' (Butler 2004a: 25).

Performativity as a politics of hope

According to a theory of performativity, terms and norms can be invoked and cited in ways that exceed and help shift dominant ways of thinking, being, and doing. This makes a performative politics a hopeful politics. The potential of performative politics lies with the fact that unconventional repetitions can expand the thinkable. As Butler explains, we are 'con-strained by not only what is difficult to imagine, but what remains radically unthinkable'. In making claims for human rights, gays and lesbians expose and challenge those constraints, potentially expanding the domain of the thinkable to include, for example, disavowed forms of desire or the lack of heterosexual desire (Butler 1993: 94).

And yet, throughout her work, Butler engages in the very double moves she encourages. In her writings on rights we see her efforts to balance the hopefulness of a politics of performativity with a recognition of the limitations and constraints of language and power. As she explains in *Bodies That Matter*, even when reiterations are perverse, 'Neither power nor discourse are rendered anew at every moment; they are not as weightless as the utopics of radical resignification might imply' (Butler 1993: 224). A politics of performativity, in other words, may recognise political agency and transformation, but it continues to acknowledge its implication in sustaining and reinforcing existing relations of power.

> Performativity describes this relation of being implicated in that which one opposes, this turning of power against itself to produce alternative modalities of power, to establish a kind of political contestation that is not a 'pure' opposition, a 'transcendence' of contemporary relations of power, but a difficult labor of forging a future from resources inevitably impure.
>
> (Butler 1993: 241)

Though difficult, though offering only an uncertain future, this work is, for Butler, the very practice and promise of democratic politics.

Notes

1 My efforts to ask and answer these questions would not have been possible without the advice and encouragement of Terrell Carver and Sam Chambers, as well as the ongoing and always provocative discussions had with Michaele Ferguson, Patchen Markell, and Laurie Naranch.
2 I explore and respond to some of these debates in Zivi (2004) and Zivi (2005).
3 Zerilli (2005) is also sceptical about the political dimensions of Butler's theory of performativity. Her critique, however, positions performativity not as antithetical to politics but as engendering a problematic politics, one that fails to adequately address the role of the spectator and fully to understand freedom as an intersubjective practice.
4 In her review of Butler's work, Disch (1999) offers a wonderfully helpful example drawing on Holloway Sparks's work on Rosa Parks to illustrate what it might look like to cite 'a term anew, to break with its customary associations and challenge the relations of power they serve to naturalize' (555).

Part VI
Humanity and vulnerability

12 This species which is not one

Identity practices in *Star Trek: Deep Space Nine*

Kathy E. Ferguson

In the 1999 preface to the second edition of *Gender Trouble,* Judith Butler asks:

> what will and will not constitute an intelligible life, and how do pre-sumptions about normative gender and sexuality determine in advance what will qualify as the 'human' and the 'livable'? In other words, how do normative gender presumptions work to delimit the very field of description that we have for the human? What is the means by which we come to see this delimiting power, and what are the means by which we transform it?
>
> (Butler 1999a: xxii)

This chapter looks to science fiction, specifically *Star Trek: Deep Space Nine*, for ways to bring into view the delimiting power of our practices of intelligibility concerning the politics of sex and gender identities, set within the larger political context of assumptions concerning the humanly liveable life.[1] The genre of science fiction contains unique possibilities for calling the human into question, not least because 'human', in such a context, is not what everyone aspires to be. Science fiction enhances our capacity to see beyond the familiar by imagining compelling stories and characters based in ways of living that defy the categories readers/viewers bring to them. By thinking differently about what is possible, the genre can bring to visibility 'certain habitual and violent presumptions' that haunt established patterns of intelligibility (Butler 1999a: viii). Politically robust science fiction can recruit us into an imaginary universe in which we are invited to refuse nor-malising violence by extending legitimacy to bodies and identities otherwise considered 'false, unreal, and unintelligible' (Butler 1999a: xxiii). Yet science fiction, particularly in the form of a popular prime-time TV series, also stays in business and cultivates corporate sponsorship by confirming some of the cherished expectations held by readers/viewers. So there are both centripetal and centrifugal energies within the genre: it is in the play of resistance to and reauthorisation of the normative practices of sex, gender, and humanity that science fiction plays out some of its feminist possibilities and limitations.

Deep space heterotopia

Deep Space Nine takes place on a space station of the same name, strategically located near the planet Bajor and at the mouth of a phenomenon known as a worm hole, a powerful transitional space housing Bajor's gods, the Prophets. The station was built by the Cardassians, a militaristic species who until recently ruled Bajor with an iron fist. After a successful independence struggle, Bajor overthrew Cardassian rule and entered an alliance with the Federation, a scientific and military coalition of planets led by Earth. The Federation sent Commander Benjamin Sisko to run the station in conjunction with the new Bajoran leadership.

The station can be viewed as an example of Foucault's idea of a heterotopia, a potentially disruptive space that 'simultaneously represented, contested, and inverted' the other more stable spaces from which people move to and from the station (Foucault 1986: 23). Exiles and deviants both come to the station and are produced by the station: Garrack, the exiled Cardassian ex-spy who became the station's tailor; Gul Dukat's half-Cardassian, half-Bajoran daughter, a mixed-species child whose only possible home is the liminal space of the station; Quark, the Ferengi bartender who both upholds and subverts his species' fanatical pursuit of profit; Sisko, an officer in the secular Federation who has been picked by the Prophets to be their sacred Emissary; Odo, the orphaned changeling who combines a longing to rejoin his murderous species with an unflagging loyalty to 'solids' (species which cannot change shape); Worf, the Klingon raised by humans; Dax, the symbiotic being called a Trill who has lived nine lifetimes. These beings are all 'in-betweens', their liminality enabled by the station's heterotopic ability to be both linked to other spaces – the homeworlds of human, Ferengi, Cardassians, changelings, Bajorans, Klingons, and Trill; the home political institutions of the Federation, the Klingon and Cardassian empires; the guerrilla army of the Maqui – and to contradict them, to loosen their demands for membership. The threshold space of the station can both 'designate, mirror or reflect' these other, more stable spaces, while at the same time allowing participants 'to suspect, neutralise, or invert' the relations they represent (Foucault 1986: 24). The space station combines Foucault's two categories of heterotopias: the crisis heterotopias, those that 'are privileged or sacred or forbidden places, reserved for individuals who are, in relation to society and to the human environment in which they live, in a state of crisis' (Foucault 1986: 24), and the heterotopias of deviation, housing 'those individuals whose behavior is deviant in relation to the required mean or norm' (Foucault 1986: 25). Deep Space Nine hosts both kinds of outsiders. Garrack, for example, is in temporary crisis, his exile commuted at the end of the series by the revolution he helps to lead on Cardassia. Similarly, for Odo the station is a crisis heterotopia, the site of confrontations through which the shapeshifter eventually resolves his in-betweenness by returning to the changelings' home planet, sharing his affection for solids with his paranoid fellow changelings through the Great Link. Dukat's daughter, in contrast, is a permanent deviation, a mixing of two races across seemingly unbreachable chasms of resentment and contempt. Heterotopias juxtapose incommensurate sites, hosting contradictions that can remain unresolved because the space can both isolate itself from and allow penetration by other spaces.

Foucault connects heterotopias with imagination and motion, suggesting they are spaces of both illusion and perfection. He ends his consideration of heterotopias with these words: 'The ship is the heterotopia *par excellence*. In civilisations without boats, dreams dry up, espionage takes the place of adventure, and the police take the place of pirates' (Foucault 1986: 27). This lovely image is rather ironic for my argument, since *Deep Space Nine* is the only *Star Trek* series that is not based on a ship. It is also the darkest, least pure, most ethically challenged *Star Trek* setting: the good guys are not always good, and the bad guys are fascinatingly complex. It is in part this greater complexity of characters that produces the fluctuating liminality of the station, while the more rigorous policing of heroes and villains in the other series undermines the heterotopic possibilities their ships might otherwise have offered. Deep Space Nine is more like a frontier town, placed on the border between civilisation (Bajor, the Federation) and wilderness (the haunted worm hole and the unknown quadrant beyond). It functions as both a border and a threshold, both marking the differences among contrasting spaces and inviting the traveller to journey from one space to another.

A sound locked in movement

Among the mobile subjectivities and compromised coherencies inhabiting Deep Space Nine is the liminal being known as Dax. Lieutenant Commander Jadzia Dax is a Trill, a humanoid species that attains its fullest realisation in symbiotic connection with a species of large, long-lived slugs called symbionts. A trill is also a musical articulation created, with an instrument, by the rapid alternation of two tones, either a whole or a half tone apart, or, with a voice, by the rapid vibration of one speech organ against another (Webster 2002). A trill, then, is a singular musical motif created by the contiguous motion of two distinct notes or organs. It is simultaneously mobile and arrested, present and absent, 'a sound locked in movement'.[2] Likewise the Trill, in their fullest realisation, are a plural species, two distinct organs creating a unique and fluid singularity. The constant transformation between the two voices/organisms constitutes the fragile yet durable continuity of the t/Trill. Attending to the modulation between the two beings, the tensions and enhancements within the two-in-oneness, occupies the primary discursive energies and institutional investments of Trill political life.

Both Trill and symbionts are born unjoined, their reproductive processes unspecified. At her death Jadzia Dax was pregnant, having successfully mated with Worf. The innuendo surrounding their energetic sexual encounters suggests that, for all its violent frenzy, Klingon-Trill reproduction is not dissimilar to that of humans. The symbionts live and breed in milky, interlinked, underground pools on the Trill homeworld. They are tended by the Guardians, eccentric unjoined Trill whose subterranean engagements have fostered an exasperated intimacy with the symbionts. The slugs evidently communicate with each other and the Guardians by way of energy discharges within the pools ('Equilibrium'). The joining is highly valued by the Trill; it brings an enhancement, an inspired confidence, an accumulated wisdom. Since the symbiont carries with it the memories, desires, and abilities of its previous hosts, each new host is both enriched and burdened by the concentrated legacy of experiences and ways of living carried by the symbiont. 'It's a joining, a total sharing, a blending', proclaims a Trill representative ('Dax'). The Guardians are able to assess the degree of harmony infusing the host/symbiont relation, pronouncing that 'the balance is off' when unincorporated disturbances threaten the modulated integrity of the many-in-one ('Equilibrium').

In order to become joined, a young Trill must be selected through a highly competitive process in which only the best and the brightest can prevail. Numerous tests of knowledge and character are required, and it is considered a great honour to be chosen ('Dax'). Every year over 5000 Trill qualify, but only 30 symbionts are available ('Playing God'). In 'Invasive Procedures', Dax states that 1 in 10 Trill are chosen for joining. This would make the process more common than it is generally held to be in other episodes. Each initiate must serve a three-year training period with the Symbiosis Commission. The successful initiate is prepared for joining through a complex process of self-discovery and preparation for otherness. As the name of the episode 'Equilibrium' suggests, the key to the relationship is balance. Extensive resources are invested in supervising the competition and eliminating the unworthy; as Dax scolds the young initiate, Arjun, 'The opportunity is too rare and too important to waste on the wrong candidate' ('Playing God'). Once the joining is accomplished, both beings are biologically interdependent, and neither can survive without the other ('Dax'). When a renegade Trill named Verad tries to steal the Dax symbiont, Jadzia implores Verad to understand that 'an improper joining can cause permanent psychological damage to both the symbiont and the host' ('Invasive Procedures'). Several episodes reaffirm the primacy of the host's moral commitment to the symbiont: 'Sometimes the host is sacrificed to save the symbiont' ('Equilibrium'). 'For a joined Trill, nothing is more important than to protect the life of the symbiont' ('Rejoined'). 'Each host is only a link in the chain' ('Rejoined').

In 'Playing God', Jadzia serves as field supervisor for the young and overly eager Arjun. Addressing the relation between symbiont and host, she

(I use the pronoun that corresponds to the gender of the host *du jour*) counsels: 'The symbiont's influence is very strong, Arjun, but *you're* the host. You've got to be strong enough to balance that influence with your own instincts. If you can't, the symbiont will overwhelm your personality.' While as a species the Trill are known for their calm confidence, often bordering on arrogance, this equanimity is an achievement that requires an active wrestling with turbulence. When Arjun comments to Jadzia, 'You're nothing like I expected', Jadzia retorts: 'I'm nothing like *I* expected. Life after life with each new personality stampeding around in your head ... you get desires that scare you, dreams that used to belong to someone else' ('Playing God'). Without years of training, a young Trill can be overwhelmed by the multiple voices, as is Ezri Dax when she unexpectedly receives the Dax symbiont after Jadzia's murder ('After Image'). Yet the knowledge cacophony is essential; Jadzia comments, 'If you want to know who you are, it's important to know who you've been' ('Equilibrium').

Joining is achieved surgically. The optimal time of joining is when the host is in her/his early to mid-20s. The slug slides into the host's abdomen and establishes connections. The official position of the Symbiosis Commission is that relatively few Trill are suitable for joining, although the episode 'Equilibrium' reveals the Commission's role in both excluding otherwise suitable hosts and in selecting hosts who prove disastrous. An unsuitable host would be rejected by the symbiont within three to four days, although it is not clear what traits make for an unsuitable host. The Symbiosis Commission requires a reincorporation ritual called a Jentara to be held for each host, so that the current host can 'meet' the distinct individualities of previous hosts by projecting them temporarily into the bodies of living, unjoined beings ('Facets'). Through the Jentara the current host is encouraged to sort out her/his inherited gifts, burdens, and desires, to identify and come to terms with specific legacies of prior hosts. Terias, in the body of Dr. Julian Bashir, voiced the sentiments of a well-adjusted (dead) Trill host when he said, 'We're part of something bigger than any one of us. I just feel lucky to have been chosen' ('Facets').

One is not born, but rather becomes a Trill[3]

The Dax chain extends back a total of nine host lifetimes, totalling nearly 400 years: Leela, Tobin, Emeny, Audrid, Terias, Joran, Curzon, Jadzia, Ezri. Like the musical trill, the sequence of linked Trill 'flow[s] in a small stream or in drops rapidly succeeding each other' (Webster 2002). Both kinds of t/ Trill manifest a grace that comes from careful coordination of contrasting moments; they craft difference by both maintaining distinctness and turning in relation. Each is a unique voice that incorporates a living echo of previous voices, a rapid vibration of speech organs against one another.

The Dax symbiont came to Jadzia when Curzon died at a ripe old age. Curzon, as both Jadzia and Commander Sisko frequently remark, was not your ordinary, law-abiding Trill. He was impulsive, passionate, undisciplined; he gambled; he drank more than was wise; he had an eye for the ladies. He was blood brother to a boisterous, carousing crowd of Klingon warriors and mentor to the then-young Ensign Sisko, launching a friendship that followed the Dax symbiont through three lifetimes. Recalling his old friend, whom he calls 'Old Man', regardless of the sexed body that temporarily hosts the symbiont, Commander Sisko remarks 'Curzon Dax tended to be a little cavalier about life, even about his personal responsibilities from time to time ... he had more faults than the usual socially acceptable Trill' ('Dax'). Other previous Dax hosts had their idiosyncrasies and pathologies as well: Tobin, the brilliant mathematician, was excessively nervous and shy; Terias was an impulsive risk-taker; Joran, the renegade, was a murderer.

While humans can find ample discursive resources for projecting univocity onto our own subject positions, and attributing our embodied normalisations to 'nature', it is difficult not to notice that, for the Trill, 'the body is a situation' (Beauvoir, quoted in Butler 1999a: 12). Dax does not have a univocal sex. Leila, Emeny, Audred, Jadzia, and Ezri were female hosts; Tobin, Terias, Joran and Curzon were male. Each of the hosts, and sometimes their friends as well, plays with the gender slippage of their embodied situation. 'It always takes me longer to get ready as a female' Jadzia calls out flippantly to the young and befuddled Trill initiate Arjun ('Playing God'). Ezri, confiding to Sisko that the formidable Klingon Worf is intimidated by his captain, underscores her knowledge by claiming, confidently, 'I've been a man; I know' ('After Image'). Dax has been both a father and a mother, many times over, and Jadzia calls readily on both sources of experience to offer advice on parenting to Sisko. Commander Sisko, barely containing his fury at Jadzia for refusing to defend herself against murder charges made against a prior host, takes an aborted swing at her and cries, 'Dammit! If you were still a man!' ('Dax'). Ezri's tribulations are more extreme because she lacked the years of training as an initiate, receiving the symbiont after Jadzia's sudden death when there were no trained Trill available. Trying to come to terms with the unexpected rotating identities of prior hosts, Ezri exclaims, with exasperation, 'These pronouns are going to drive me crazy!' ('After Image'). Describing her struggles with joining to her uncomprehending family, Ezri explains, 'There are times when the computer asks me to identify myself, and I have to think about what to say. Or worse yet, there are days when I wake up, and I don't even know if I'm a man or a woman until I pull back the covers' ('Prodigal Daughter').

Interestingly, with the single exception of the Trill diplomat who fell in love with Dr Beverly Crusher in *The Next Generation* episode 'The Host', all the interesting Trill characters developed in *Star Trek* have been female. That is, they are recognisable as women within the prevailing gender economy. Perhaps some explanation for this parallel can be found in Luce Irigaray's

(1985a, 1985b) analysis of the unrepresentability of the feminine vis-à-vis masculine economies of binary exclusivity. The Trill, in the imagined discursive economies of *Star Trek*, are 'like women' in the hegemonic discursive economies of the viewers. Women's encoded manness, in relation to the singular stability of the phallocentric One, parallels the Trill manness in relation to the assumed self-identity of humans. In this sense Trill are the excess in the human economy of signification in the same way that women are the excess in the codes of men. Perhaps the imaginations of the *Star Trek* writers stumbled over the challenges of representing manness in conjunction with masculinity, while finding a more amenable metaphorical terrain in the bodies and life worlds of women.

In some ways this stabilisation of the Trill host body around the figure of the heterosexual female, even though it is temporary, recoups the radical uncertainty of the Trills' embodied situation. Jadzia Dax falls in love with men (with one intriguing exception, explored below), has sex with men, marries a (Klingon) man, becomes pregnant, and is referred to as 'she'. Ezri Dax, similarly, falls in love with and has sex with men and is interpellated in the third person, singular, feminine. Trill male characters are relatively undeveloped. Curzon, present only in memory, is called 'he' and evidently fell in love only, and often, with women; his boundary-blurring behaviour disrupts the sedate Trill image but is readily recognisable as both a 'womanizer' and a 'man's man'. Yet these re-stabilisations of gender difference do not fully undo the radical relationality of Trill identity. Trill identity is clearly an *effect* of prior significations. While a certain stabilisation, grounded in a persistent heterosexual matrix, marks the body-texts of each particular host, the overall mobility of Trill identity irrevocably haunts all its manifestations. Dax disrupts; while the physical appearance of each host is categorisable within the gender binary, the overall subject position proliferates outside of those terms, suggesting possibilities of recirculation and displacement.

Responsibility and reassociation

Two pivotal episodes of *Deep Space Nine* establish some key parameters and paradoxes of the Dax character. 'Dax' in the first season and 'Rejoined' in the fourth engage the specific host histories of the Dax symbiont, sketching the 'drops rapidly succeeding each other' (Webster 2002) that constitute the t/Trill manness-in-one. 'Dax' features a trademark setting for *Star Trek* identity battles: the courtroom. The question before the Bajoran extradition hearing is: 'Is a Trill responsible for the conduct of its antecedent hosts?' Specifically, is Jadzia Dax responsible for crimes committed 30 years earlier by Curzon Dax? Commander Sisko opposes the extradition by appealing to the gender binary, arguing that the warrant is for Curzon Dax, a male, not Jadzia, a female. The young man pushing for extradition, the son of the man Dax is accused of killing, finds gender difference irrelevant, claiming that the beings are the same because each host can recall the details and feel the emotions of previous hosts' lives. Tellingly, Sisko and his opponent make use of the same body of evidence to draw their opposing conclusions. Each is stuck in the mirrored terms of the opposition that Joan Scott and others have analysed as the identity/difference debates within feminist theory. Sisko, trying to save his friend, argues for absolute difference; he focuses on the unique life experiences of Jadzia prior to joining, and on the (for him) obvious, 'common sense' distinction between an old man and a young woman. The prosecutor, eager to avenge his father, emphasises the (for him) real sameness hidden inside the superficial differences, finding a coherent unity also based in 'common sense'. The arbiter, an elderly Bajoran woman with a caustic tongue, begins to figure things out:

> Lieutenant Dax, you are either 200 years older than I am, or you're about the same age as my great granddaughter. At first I wondered which of those you were, and now I am bothered by the likelihood that you may be both.

Dax's manyness is unintelligible to Sisko because he insists on a unified gendered individual who is absolutely distinct from other unified gendered individuals. Sisko is stuck in difference (that is, difference *between* subjects). Dax's identity terrain is similarly unintelligible to the prosecutor because he expects absolute sameness, resting on complete opposition between appearance (host, outside) and reality (symbiont, inside). Both men reside within the mutually constitutive entrapments of the metaphysics of substance, 'trapped within illusions of "Being" and "Substance" that are fostered by the belief that the grammatical formulation of subject and predicate reflects the prior ontological reality of substance and attribute' (Butler 1999a: 27). For Sisko, the 'prior ontological reality' is the stable sexed body, the truth of sex; for the prosecutor it is the fixed symbiont 'inside' rather than the changeable host 'outside'. Neither man finds any liveable coherency in the continuity-within-difference of the t/Trill.

Dax remains mysteriously silent throughout the proceedings, and is saved from the need to address or resolve the contradiction by another well-worn *Star Trek* narrative convention: the nick-of-time rescue. Jadzia Dax's rescuer is the widow of the dead man and Curzon Dax's former lover. Jadzia's subsequent conversation with this ghost of Curzon's past confirms the Nietzschean suspicions held by the judge and ironically disqualifies both versions of the metaphysics of presence, that held by her friend and that held by her enemy. 'There's much of Curzon that's still a part of me', she says quietly to the elderly woman whose caresses retain some command on the young woman. 'I can't tell you which part of Curzon Dax couldn't stop himself from acting shamefully with another man's wife', she confesses later to Sisko, 'but I can tell you, he did love her.' 'He' did love her; not 'I'. Yet

30 years later Jadzia felt compelled, even at the expense of her own life, to keep Curzon's promise and remain silent about their prior relationship.

In contrast, in the third-season episode 'Meridian', it is Jadzia's difference from Curzon that is foregrounded. Jadzia falls in love with a man from a planet caught in an elongated cycle of time; if she stays with her beloved, she will share his disembodied shift into pure consciousness for many decades before returning with him to an embodied state for a time in the material world. Jadzia chooses her love. Her conversation with Sisko, as she explains her choice, re-marks the relations of many-to-one of the t/Trill:

> Sisko: 'If Curzon had told me he wanted to go off with some woman he just met, I would have tried to talk him out of it too.'
> Jadzia: 'And you would have been right. He fell in love with someone new every other week! But I'm not Curzon.'
> Sisko: 'No, and I've never seen Jadzia do anything without thinking it through first.'

Here the terms of the identity negotiations are fairly clear: judgments about sameness and difference are made in particular contexts, weighing detectable patterns of behaviour and felt priorities of love and loss. In her self-representations Jadzia both 'is' and 'is not' Curzon, and the modulation between the two is not presented as inconsistent or confused, but as a dense, rich, and sometimes unpredictable articulation of proximity and distance. Trill identities persist through time with an internal coherence requiring constant mediation; but these identities are not unified, not the same, not fully coinciding with one another.

Jadzia Dax, and the arbiter who confronts her, face the same dilemma in 'Dax' that Joan Scott describes for feminist lawyer Alice Kessler-Harris in the famous Sears EEOC case. Neither can adequately represent their complexities within the signifying economy of the courtroom (although Kessler-Harris would no doubt have been grateful for a judge with the nuanced sensibilities of the Bajoran arbiter whom Dax confronts). Neither can find a way to respond to the yes/no formulation of the legal setting because their responses would require modest generalisations, extensive histories, and scrupulous attention to context: 'well, it all depends', or 'to some extent', or 'under certain conditions' are not valid currency in the discursive economies of the court. The difference, of course, is that Kessler-Harris lost her case, and was found 'contradictory and confusing' by the judge (Scott 1988a: 42), while in *Star Trek* it is the advocates of the metaphysics of presence who lose, who are revealed as inadequate to the task of apprehending the 'sound locked in movement' of the t/Trill. 'The sex [species] which is not one, then, provides a point of departure for a criticism of hegemonic Western representation and of the metaphysics of substance that structures the very notion of the subject' (Butler 1999a: 14). Like Irigaray's construction of the female, which 'cannot be represented in the signifying economy in which the masculine constitutes the closed circle of signifier and signified', the t/Trill cannot be represented in the signifying economy of the courtroom (Butler 1999a: 15). The episode positions the viewer as a critic of the law's requirements and validates Dax's, and thus perhaps our own, mobile subjectivity vis-à-vis the familiar demand to tell the truth of identity, the truth of sex.

Past and present

In 'Rejoined' Trill subjectivity-in-relation is explored with regard to past connections that are prohibited, rather than respected, by Trill society. A Trill female named Lenara Kann comes to the station: after their dramatic first meeting, Jadzia says to Kira, 'She used to be my wife.' The previous Dax host Terias had been married, prior to his sudden death in a shuttle craft accident, to Nilani Kann, the earlier host of the Kann symbiont in Lenara. Recognition between them takes place instantly, intensely, on the level of the symbionts. Jadzia says to Lenara: 'I'm looking at a different face, hearing a different voice, but somehow it's still *you*.' 'I' and 'you' here slide around furiously between current and past hosts, between host and symbiont. Recalling the impulsive, ill-considered decision that led to Terias's death, Jadzia declares fiercely, 'The shuttle was not ready for a full impulse test, but Terias had to do it anyway, and he was wrong. And whatever part of me is still Terias is very sorry, and wishes he'd listened to you.' Jadzia's heartfelt apology for Terias's careless endangering of his life, and their marriage, is delivered in the third person, but addressed to Lenara in the second: 'wishes he'd listened to *you*'. A later dialogue interdigitates 'he', 'I', and 'you' even more vigorously: Jadzia declares passionately to Lenara, 'I don't want to do anything to hurt you. *I* did that before. *I* climbed into that shuttlecraft. *I* made you a widow.' The first 'I' is the current Jadzia Dax; the last three are the former Terias Dax. The first 'you' is the current Lenara Kann; the last 'you' is the former Nilani Kann. The grammar of intelligibility does its work by performing the needed furtive and fertile slides among persons and tenses, allowing needed transitions and valued ambiguities to flourish while enabling a recognisable coherence.

The meeting of Lenara and Jadzia quickly becomes the talk of the station. In a discussion in Quark's bar, Jadzia's friends try to figure things out:

> Kira: 'The one thing I don't understand is why Dax and Lenara can't just pick up where they left off. I mean, if they're still in love with each other.'
> Julian: 'Ah, now there's the rub. Even if they do harbour feelings for each other, it's strictly against the rules of Trill society for them to acknowledge it in any way.'
> Kira: 'Rules?'
> Julian: 'Well, it's more of a taboo, really. Having a relationship with a lover from a past life is called a reassociation. And the Trill feel very strongly that it's *unnatural*.'

Kira: 'Unnatural? How can it be unnatural for a married couple to resume their marriage?'

Julian: 'Well, the whole point of joining is for the symbiont to accumulate experiences from the span of many lifetimes. In order to move on from host to host, the symbiont has to learn to let go of the past, let go of parents, siblings, children, even spouses.'

Kira: 'I don't understand that; two people who have fallen in love and made a life together can be forced to walk away from each other just because of a taboo? There must be some Trill who have reassociated with people from their past lives.'

Julian: 'I asked Dax that same question. It seems that there have been a few.'

Kira: 'And what happened?'

Julian: 'They were exiled from the Trill homeworld.'

Kira: 'That means the symbionts would never be joined to a new host.'

Julian: 'Exactly. So when the hosts die, the symbionts die with them. So you see, even if Dax does harbour feelings for Lenara, she can't take that risk. For a joined Trill, nothing is more important than to protect the life of the symbiont. Nothing.'

On one level this episode is a lesbian parable, making use of a classic science-fiction narrative device to question hegemonic authority by situating the strange within the familiar and the familiar within the strange. Because Jadzia and Lenara are both identifiably female, the taboo around their relationship both suggests and contests the heterosexual paradigm familiar to *Star Trek*'s writers and viewers. In *Alternate Channels*, Steven Capsuto argues that the steamy on-screen kiss between Jadzia and Lenara was not 'really' a lesbian kiss because the two symbionts had been a heterosexual married couple in their prior lives. While Capsuto's concern about *Star Trek's* unwillingness to portray gay and lesbian relationships is well-founded, in this case he is missing the point: the interesting element is not whether the kiss was 'really' lesbian or 'really' straight, but that it is 'really' t/ Trill, and Trill normativity is not bounded by the heterosexual matrix. The disapproval of the other Trill on the station, especially of Lenara's younger brother, taps available narratives of illicit love: the other Trill cast furtive, disapproving glances at the couple, then avert their eyes, lower their voices, move away. 'People are starting to notice', the two women murmur to one another. When Lenara's brother confronts her and suggests that 'something is going on', Lenara responds with the classic denial: 'I told him you and I are just friends.' As their passion for one another grows, they try to come to terms with the punishing terms Trill society sets for their love. Jadzia is willing to pay the price: 'In the end all that matters is how we feel and what we do about it.' Lenara, in the end, is not: 'I don't think that I can do this ... ' The weight of family rejection and the contempt of Trill society outweighs Lenara's passion.

Muted butch/femme codes make some appearance in the story: Lenara's filmy dresses and vulnerability, Jadzia's Star Fleet uniforms and heroism. But for the most part the writers forgo lesbian stereotypes and portray two intelligent, accomplished women collaborating on an important scientific project and bonding as kindred spirits. After an evening in Quark's, one of the women remarks, 'You and I have much more in common than Terias and Nilani ever did.' The viewers are encouraged to root for Jadzia's 'love conquers all' courage and to be disappointed with Lenara's timidity. More radically, viewers are invited to approve of passionate erotic love between two women, and to disapprove of Trill society's efforts to control how people can love one another. As their love rekindles, the station serves as a crisis heterotopia for the two lovers, contesting and inverting the demands of Trill society, against which they have been thrown into sudden and unanticipated opposition. Had Lelani agreed to stay on the station, the space would have become a heterotopia of deviation, housing individuals in permanent rebellion against their social order. While the sympathetic portrayal of love between two women challenges heterosexual normativity, Lelani's unwillingness to endure exile, to face the disapproval of friends and family, and to subordinate the interests of the symbiont to her own desires, tames the potential heterotopic practices and re-establishes the hegemonic Trill norms of intelligibility.

Norms and compulsion

And what, exactly, are these norms? While this episode makes clear that Trill subjects are not subjected to compulsory heterosexuality, some equally punishing and seemingly arbitrary set of compulsions are at work. 'Reassociation' is tricky terrain. In different forms, it is both forbidden and valued. Dax can maintain her friendship with Sisko across three lifetimes, and this is apparently admirable. The continuity of the friendships with the Klingon warriors, also moving across three lifetimes, is equally valued, as is Jadzia's loyalty to Curzon's former lover. Evidently, it is exclusive and intimate relations that are monitored, those with children, parents, and spouses. Jadzia can legitimately retain her loyalty to the old woman, acknowledge it as still a part of her; she can recall the love, even act on the recalled love, but not rekindle the love. In much the same way that our society polices the boundary between homosocial and homosexual, Trill society regulates the relations between past, present, and future loves.

If, following Foucault, we understand that to be a subject is to be subjected, then to what regime of normativity are Trill subjected? The axes of power relations constituting identity in Trill society are those around joined and not-joined, with the Symbiosis Commission evidently playing the part of both church and state. The apparatus for production of identity is that surrounding the practices of joining. Dax's reality is the experience of changing from male to female and back again; even though the categories of male and female, with regard to the host bodies, remain fixed, their relative unimportance and ready mobility recedes their significance. Dax's sorting process, in figuring out her identity and her desires, is not primarily biological or ontological but temporal. That is, Trill prohibitions do not centre on distinguishing male from female, nor real from unreal, but the current from the former. It is not between types of people (male, female) or conditions of being (appearance, reality) but between moments in a temporal process. 'I've never let my past lives interfere with my job', Jadzia pronounces firmly before the arrival of Lenara; it turns out that much more than her job is at stake. Both Jadzia and Lenara comment on the trouble they have sorting out their own feelings from those of past hosts, and Lenara remarks tartly about the 'dangers of getting lost in the past'. Explaining her loyalty to promises made to Curzon's former lover, and her refusal to abdicate the responsibilities such promises entailed, Jadzia says, 'When one of my kind stumbles, Benjamin, it is a mistake that is there forever' ('Dax'). In a more comic mode, young Ezri Dax has trouble figuring out what she wants to eat or drink, how she wants to sit or stand, whether she is male or female, whether she is still attracted to Jadzia's husband, Worf. Interestingly, in contrast to Jadzia's and Lenara's forbidden love, Ezri's slipping around in time is not surrounded by restrictions. Evidently Ezri's temporal slippage does not threaten the reassociation taboo. Perhaps this is because there are no other Trill around to invoke their society's normativity. Jadzia's and Lenara's story suggests that, were other Trill to get wind of Ezri's temporarily renewed relationship with Worf, there would be hell to pay.

Perhaps the Trill heavily regulate joining because they are policing the margins of their society in much the same way that humans do. Mary Douglas argues that the margins of social systems are vulnerable to disorder and therefore considered dangerous. Building on Douglas, as well as Julia Kristeva and Iris Marion Young, Butler suggests: 'If the body is synecdochal for the social system *per se* or a site in which open systems converge, then any kind of unregulated permeability constitutes a site of pollution and endangerment' (Butler 1999a: 168). While Trill identity practices blur the boundaries between male and female, inner and outer, the prohibition on reassociation re-polices: 'The boundary of the body as well as the distinction between internal and external is established through the ejection and transvaluation of something originally part of identity into a defiling Otherness' (Butler 1999a: 170). Trill, it seems, expel the desire for the previously beloved person and become repulsed by it. Like our more familiar repudiation of bodies on the grounds of their sex, sexuality, and/or colour, the Trill 'found and consolidate culturally hegemonic identities along ... [in this case, temporal] axes of differentiation'. Repulsion works to consolidate identities by instituting an 'Other' 'through exclusion and domination' (Butler 1999a: 170). In this case the ejected Other is quite literally the self, in the form of the previous host/symbiont relation, and the Trill quite readily recognise it as such. The exclusion is not based on denial of the initial connection. Yet, once a joining's time has passed, its eros is expelled, and any lingering desires become repulsive, 'unnatural'. With human ejection/repulsion of the abject other, the ineluctable porosity of the body suggests that the danger is still there, the 'inside' and 'outside' still entertain commerce between them. Similarly with the Trill, the memories, desires, and abilities of the previous hosts are still part of the current host, so the boundaries remain porous. The memories themselves are cherished, but acting on them, bringing a past host's relationships back to life, is taboo. Like humans, Trill turn out to organise fantasies, fears, and desires around 'a mediating boundary that strives for stability' (Butler 1999a: 170). They too achieve a hegemonic coherence by bringing identity to order around a distinction ('then' versus 'now') that 'stabilises and consolidates the coherent subject' (Butler 1999a: 171).

And they too experience the erosion of that coherency by its inevitably unstable boundaries and porous thresholds. In the Jentara ceremony in 'Facets', Jadzia meets Curzon in the form of the former host's memories joined with the shape-shifter's body. Curzon confesses that he was in love with Jadzia when she was a young initiate and he was her field instructor, a relation in which erotic attraction was evidently inappropriate. He was very hard on her so she wouldn't know the truth; but he was racked with guilt after he dismissed her from the programme to hide his love, and was grateful when she reapplied and was accepted. After struggling briefly to stay in Odo's body, Curzon agrees to reincorporation within Dax. Jadzia now contains Curzon's memories of being a changeling, while Odo enjoys Curzon's memories of human pleasures – eating, drinking, carousing, loving. The t/Trill manyness has turned on itself: Jadzia now remembers, has taken into herself, Curzon's forbidden love of herself, Jadzia. In this case the temporal slippage among current and former hosts is valued, not reviled. When Odo, referring to Curzon, says 'He must have been a remarkable man', Dax answers, 'Yes, he is'.

Vacillation and violence

In the end, then, it is not that the t/Trill entirely lack a stable ground for identity, nor are they free from the pain of social regulation by which identities are policed; it is, rather, that the terms by which their identity practices do their work, by virtue of their familiarity-within-strangeness, encourage humans to attend to different possibilities within ourselves. While in some ways this imagined ground of t/Trill subjectivity is simply constraining in a different way, in other ways it is enormously liberating for human viewers; it encourages us to participate in a subject position that, somewhat like the intersexed people our culture disqualifies from humanness, suggests that 'the vacillation between the categories itself constitutes the experience of the body in question' (Butler 1999a: xxiii). Our 'naturalised knowledge of gender' is displaced by arrangements that show ours to be 'a changeable and revisable reality' (Butler 1999a: xxiii). By making visible the normalising violence behind Trill identity practices, *Star Trek* encourages us to attend to the parallel normalising violence within our own. Jadzia's calm acceptance of her manyness suggests that we human viewers might also accept the multiple voices within us. Ezri's young confusion about her relations with past selves encourages us also to entertain confusion, to lighten the hand of mastery on the demands for identity. The t/Trill attention to the temporality of identity practices, their acceptance of themselves as a 'culturally sustained temporal duration' can help human viewers to understand ourselves as such as well (Butler 1999a: xv).

The popular circulation of images of a gender-bending doubled creature who is living a compelling and interesting life, one who is, simultaneously, attractively strange and strangely familiar, might contribute to the denaturalisation of the prevailing and violent norms about bodies and identities. Dax redraws 'the ontological field in which bodies may be given legitimate expression' and thus encourages us to do so as well (Butler 1999a: xxiii).

Notes

1 My thanks to Jeannette Koijane for her companionable insights into several *DS-9* episodes.

2 My thanks for this felicitous phrase, and for her shared reflections on *Star Trek* and on the musical connotations of a trill, to Dr Dina Smith, Department of Women's Studies, University of South Florida.

3 Simone de Beauvoir writes, 'one is not born a woman, but rather becomes a woman' (Beauvoir 1989: 269).

13 Vulnerability, vengeance, and community

Butler's political thought and Eastwood's *Mystic River*

Robert E. Watkins

[I]t is characteristic of political philosophers that they take a somber view of the human situation: they deal in darkness. Human life in their writings appears generally not as a feast or even as a journey, but as a predicament ... [T]he human predicament is a universal appearing everywhere as a particular.

(Oakeshott 1991: 225)

For Judith Butler, the particular events of September 11, 2001 ('9/11') suggest a universal human predicament that challenges Hobbes's construction of political society in opposition to insecurity. Butler sees in these events a reminder of the reality of persistent insecurity rooted in a constitutive and persistent vulnerability. Specifically, she refers to this vulnerability as 'a collective condition, characterizing us all equally' (2005a: 35), a condition of 'exposure to violence' and 'vulnerability to loss' that we 'cannot will away' (2004a: 19, 29). This exposed vulnerability is, to be sure, a contingent universal in Butler's view, yet nevertheless, as a universal it is a constitutive feature of our social and political ontology that 'we cannot easily argue against; or, rather, we can argue against it, but we would be denying something fundamental about the social conditions of our very formation' (2004a: 22–23). Given the fact of 'our fundamental dependency' and the tendency of acts of vengeance to generate cycles of violence, Butler interprets violent vengeance as both a denial of vulnerability and a threat to rather than guarantor of security, sounding 'an ethical caution against enthusiasms that might make one impervious to the precariousness of life' (2005a: 33, 75). The precariousness of life, in Butler's felicitous phrase, suggests the ambiguity – both promise and precipice – entailed in the very predicament of vulnerability as the ontological condition of possibility for subjectivity.

This chapter explores the political limitations and possibilities this condition of precariousness or vulnerability entails, through a juxtaposition of two particulars illuminating the universal: Butler's thoughts on vulnerability and (non-)violence, and Clint Eastwood's cinematic critique of revenge, *Mystic River* (2003). Both Butler and Eastwood examine the ties (chosen and unchosen) that bind us together and explore the consequences of violent loss. In the eyes of Butler and Eastwood, loss reveals the condition of common vulnerability and challenges us to keep our rage from overwhelming our common humanity. Their works share the sense that we are not autonomous subjects, but rather dependent upon, yet vulnerable to, each other. Butler summarises the political question that loss amidst vulnerability forces upon us:

> That we can be injured, that others can be injured, that we are subject to death at the whim of another, are all reasons for both fear and grief. What is less certain, however, is whether the experiences of vulnerability and loss have to lead straightaway to military violence and retribution ... If we are interested in arresting cycles of violence to produce less violent outcomes, it is no doubt important to ask what, politically, might be made of grief besides a cry for war.
>
> (Butler 2004a: xii)

Butler's theoretical reflections on the ambivalence of vulnerability and the dangerous seductions of vengeance parallel the dramatisation in *Mystic River* of both the consequences of a violent response to grief and the opportunities for peaceful resolution. Sharing and illustrating the view that socially situated subjects are dependent upon yet different from and vulnerable to others, these two sombre views of the human situation suggest a need to rethink both our use of violence and our understanding of community in light of vulnerability and difference.

Vulnerability as the ontological condition of possibility for subjectivity

In her post-9/11 writings, Butler has taken a dark and revealing view of the human situation as she wrestles with the political consequences of violence and loss and tries to elucidate our common condition of vulnerability. The touchstone for her political theory of vulnerability is the essay 'Violence, Mourning, Politics' from *Precarious Life*, which presents a suggestive new agenda for her readers in political theory. Preserving and extending her critique of the sovereign, autonomous subject, Butler begins the work of 'reimagining the possibility of community on the basis of vulnerability and loss' (2004a: 20). It not only resonates with insights from her earlier work on the sociality and materiality of bodies in *Bodies that Matter* (1993), on subjection and vulnerability in *The Psychic Life of Power* (1997b), and on grief in *Antigone's Claim* (2000), but also presages ideas on ethical responsibility and violence presented in *Giving an Account of Oneself* (2005a). Perhaps most interestingly for the discourse of political theory, Butler's interest in reimagining community in light of vulnerability, loss, and, difference signals an effort to complement the struggles of identity politics with another struggle for what might be called a non-communitarian idea of community. In that vein, she offers this provocative political question to readers familiar with her work on identity and resistance:

> If I am struggling for autonomy, do I not need to be struggling for something else as well, a conception of myself as invariably in community, impressed upon by others, impinging upon them as well, and in ways that are not fully in my control or clearly predictable?
>
> (2004a: 27)

This section explores the sense in which the turn towards vulnerability and community that marks Butler's recent thought simultaneously preserves her interest in power and the ways in which subjects are authored by what precedes and exceeds them, and also shifts focus to the social realm of bodies where the inescapable facts of interdependence and vulnerability might (or might not) be recognised in the service of working towards a less violent political life.

In 'Violence, Mourning, Politics', Butler starts from the fact of the 9/11 tragedy and the feelings of loss it generated and proceeds to reflect on what she calls 'the problem of a primary vulnerability to others, one that one cannot will away without ceasing to be human' (2004a: xiv). The common experience or spectacle of such a traumatic violation of security serves for Butler as a terrible unmasking of the fantasy of autonomy and invulnerability, 'challeng[ing] the very notion of ourselves as autonomous and in control' (2004a: 23). Specifically, it also serves as a reminder of the ways in which we are in her view always already non-autonomous and implicated in lives that are not our own. She claims the possibility of

> undergoing something outside one's control does not dispute the fact of my autonomy, but it does qualify that claim through recourse to the fundamental sociality of embodied life, the ways in which we are, from the start and by virtue of being a bodily being, already given over, beyond ourselves, implicated in lives that are not our own.
>
> (Butler 2004a: 28)

The idea of autonomy as qualified by the sociality of embodied life sounds a chord recurrent in Butler's work – namely, her concern with 'the way in which we are constituted in relationality: implicated, beholden, derived, sustained by a social world that is beyond us and before us' (2005a: 64).

The notion of an embodied political vulnerability in her 'Violence' essay appears against the backdrop of Butler's earlier examination of the necessary discursive vulnerability of the subject to the ambivalent effects of power in *The Psychic Life of Power*. There, Butler argues that 'the vulnerability of the subject to power is unavoidable' (1997b: 20), because all subjects are necessarily constituted within norms, power, and social relations they do not choose. Such power *conditions* – that is, makes possible as well as limits – the agency of subjects. In a recent interview, Butler expressed the point in this way: 'We're not in control, but that does not mean we don't exercise a certain kind of conditioned agency. That's what it means to live in a community. That's what it means to live in society' (2003b). As a consequence of this necessary yet unchosen vulnerability to power, such that the subject 'can never produce itself autonomously' (1997b: 20) but is dependent upon power and norms as well as caregivers, Butler claims that 'vulnerability qualifies the subject as an exploitable kind of being' (1997b: 195). Power, like vulnerability and indeed community itself, is for Butler an ineluctable and constitutive condition, yet one must not forget that it is essentially ambiguous in that it necessarily restricts but also enables, simply by being a condition of possibility. Butler's understanding of vulnerability as a socio-ontological condition of possibility of subjectivity means that the subject 'is implicated in a loss of autonomy that is mandated by linguistic and social life' (1997b: 195) – that is, we are never autonomous, but always already related to and dependent upon others as well as conditioned by power. Though not explicitly thematised as such by Butler (certainly not in *The Psychic Life of Power*, though she comes closer to it recently), there is in her cumulative work the suggestion of a more sombre understanding of community than usually appears in political theory. Sombre because her notion of community constituted via shared and inescapable, yet ambiguous vulnerability entails not only the possibility for attachment, enrichment, and affection but also detachment, loss, and mourning. As such, Butler's community of shared vulnerability, when recognised as such, represents a more realistic, if contingent and uncertain, picture of political community than appears, for instance, in either Hobbes's contractual order of absolute security or communitarianism's traditional order of salutary attachment.

There are two ways in which her more recent account of vulnerability differs slightly from that in *The Psychic Life of Power* – differences of emphasis rather than revision. First, in the post 9/11 essay, Butler subtly shifts the emphasis from the influence of the impersonal power of discursive norms to the personal power of bodies by virtue of their sociality. Butler notes that 'each of us is constituted politically in part by virtue of the social vulnerability of our bodies – as a site of desire and physical vulnerability, as a site of a publicity at once assertive and exposed' (2004a: 20). At its simplest, this bodily vulnerability for Butler means the real possibility of being affected by others in ways we do not choose, whether it is as infants, as adults, or as states: 'We are affected by others. I mean, 9/11 was being affected in a very big way, in a violent way that we radically did not choose' (2003b). This unchosen vulnerability derives from the fact of living in society with and being dependent upon others, that is, not being autonomous or self-sufficient. Most saliently for a post 9/11 politics of security, Butler's view of vulnerability as autonomy qualified by sociality means my security is not fully in my control for it depends on not just what I do or control but on what others do or do not do. In other words, she says that 'my body', insofar as it is 'given over from the start to the world of others' and 'formed within the crucible of social life', both 'is and is not mine' (2004a: 26) because it subject not only to my actions but also to the actions of others.

A second difference of emphasis between her earlier account of vulnerability and the recent return to vulnerability is that in addition to the unchosenness of social vulnerability that qualifies autonomy, Butler in her post-9/11 work bolsters the claim with the idea that this bodily vulnerability, as a condition not just for the inauguration of the subject but for the continued existence of subjects, is inescapable (2005a: 75). It cannot be willed away; it cannot even be argued with (2004a: 19, 23, 29, 31; 2005a: 33, 101). Rather, she conceives vulnerability as an ontological condition of possibility for social, political, and ethical relationships:

> If my fate is not originally or finally separable from yours, then the 'we' is traversed by a relationality that we cannot easily argue against; or, rather, we can argue against it, but we would be denying something fundamental about the social conditions of our very formation.
>
> (Butler 2004a: 22–23)

This understanding conveys Butler's understanding of the always-social individual who because of interdependence is always implicated in the lives of others – indeed, always living in community with others, where community is understood to connote by sharing, not only the good and the bad but also the ambiguous, namely vulnerability.

Finally, though this persistent vulnerability cannot be willed away, it can be exploited, and Butler remarks that 'violence is, always, an exploitation of that primary tie, that primary way in which we are, as bodies, outside ourselves and for one another' (2004a: 27). Butler's invocation of vulnerability in a political context prompts the need to question political theory's traditional opposition between anarchy and order, which Sheldon Wolin summarises in this way: 'In the ontology of political thought, order has been the equivalent of being, anarchy the political synonym for non-being' (2004: 218). The ineliminable condition of vulnerability suggests (*contra* Hobbes) the persistence of the threat of non-being within being at the hands of others – that is, the inescapable threat of death even within political community. In contending that this vulnerability cannot be willed away and is a constitutive aspect of sociality, Butler suggests that there is no perfect security which might be achieved or purchased at the price of civil liberties or any thing else, exploding the familiar post 9/11 political choice. Indeed, she cautions against the impulse to eradicate the vulnerability with which we all live and must live: 'To foreclose that vulnerability, to banish it, to make ourselves secure at the expense of every other human consideration is to eradicate one of the most important resources from which we must take our bearings and find our way' (2004a: 30). In addition to pointing out the ambiguity of vulnerability, this remark suggests politics should involve coming to terms with this inescapable condition. In seeing the inter-subjective or communal dimension of experience as a condition of vulner-ability, Butler reveals a sensibility that is sombre, almost tragic, and thus distinct from the more salutary views of deliberative democrats and com-munitarians.

Constitutive vulnerability in *Mystic River*

The condition of being vulnerable to others – in the sense of being 'impli-cated in lives that are not our own' in ways that are 'irreversible, if not fatal' (2004a: 25) – finds cinematic representation in the very first scene of *Mystic River*, an opening that conditions the rest of the film's narrative. As the haunting initial scene begins, three boys are playing street hockey in a Boston neighbourhood, yet by the end of the scene, one boy, Dave, is seen through the back window of a car, leaving with two male abductors. This scene of Dave's abduction together with the ensuing four-day-long moles-tation marks an initial traumatic event that challenges the audience to identify and come to terms with the terrible facts of vulnerability and loss. This exploitation of childhood vulnerability remains in *Mystic River* like a cursed scar for the rest of the film as the setting jumps twenty-five years ahead to the same neighbourhood where the boys still live as grown men, more or less shaped and haunted by the initial trauma. Through the three adult male characters, the film offers representations of three different con-ditioned responses to later experiences of vulnerability and loss. Whereas Dave (Tim Robbins) finds himself impaired and unable to come to terms with vulnerability,[1] Jimmy (Sean Penn) and Sean (Kevin Bacon) represent two different ways of responding to vulnerability and loss, Jimmy choosing vengeance, Sean choosing non-violence. Before turning to a discussion of how Jimmy and Sean's reactions to later experiences of vulnerability map onto Butler's understanding of the political possibilities that attend vulner-ability, let us consider the ways in which the film's opening scene illuminates some other aspects of Butler's concept of vulnerability.

The lingering force of the initial scene brings into view the sense in which vulnerability entails the ever present possibility for loss that Butler contends is a constitutive feature of social life. More specifically, the scene helps to illustrate the ambivalence Butler attaches to the concept of vulnerability. While the term vulnerability often carries a negative connotation both in her work and in ordinary language, Butler plays on the ambiguity of the term to also suggest the stance of opening oneself up to connection with others, in the sense of emotional availability. 'Loss and vulnerability', she claims, 'seem to follow from our being socially constituted bodies, attached to others, at risk of losing those attachments, exposed to others, at risk of violence by virtue of that exposure' (2004a: 20). Thus, Butler's understanding of vulnerability encompasses an ambivalence consistent with her view of the very social possibility of subjectivity as subjection to power, both attached and exposed to others. On this view, vulnerability is not just a threat but also a chance, and thus vulnerability 'means that we are ... vulnerable to violence; but also vulnerable to another range of touch, a range that includes the eradication of our being at the one end, and the physical support for our lives at the other' (2004a: 31). The initial scene literally sets the stage for the film's consideration of a shared condition of ambiguous vulnerability by showing the enriching connections the boys share through play as well as the damaging connection they share through vulnerability and loss. The very fact of potential violence from our fellow humans dramatises the point that there are some things, some forces that we cannot control and to which we are vulnerable, but also that our lives are made richer and more valuable through our connections with others (when those ties are not exploited). This initial scene establishes a common condition of interdependence among the three boys that persists in the rest of the film in the form of the ties of the grown men later share as well as through the film's attention to the context of the community in which they live and die, flourish and falter. Thus, *Mystic River* conveys a parallel understanding of the inaugural and persistent condition of vulnerability to others.

Juxtaposing Butler's thoughts of vulnerability with the opening scene of *Mystic River* reveals vulnerability to be a constitutive and inescapable, thus universal feature of the human condition, yet one that appears everywhere as a particular. Simply put, vulnerability is an essential feature of what it means to live in society with others. As a universal characterisation, it brings together under one rubric the three 'ontological forces' that Stephen White identifies as constituting Butler's ontology: 'interpellating power, materialization, and the desire to desire' (White 1999: 165). Butler discusses her concept of the 'desire to desire' in *The Psychic Life of Power* (1997a), and in some ways, the concept is similar to the positive potential entailed in that aspect of vulnerability understood as a kind of openness to enriching connection with others. As such, vulnerability must be understood as a foundation for her thinking, but is it a foundation that is in her famous formulation both 'contingent and indispensable'? (Butler 1995b: 133). As presented in 'Violence, Mourning, Politics', Butler's answer is that while vulnerability cannot be willed away, the contingency of vulnerability consists in the question of its recognition: 'A vulnerability must be perceived and recognized in order to come into play in an ethical encounter, and there is no guarantee that this will happen ... But when a vulnerability *is* recognized, that recognition has the power to change the meaning and structure of the vulnerability itself' (2004a: 43).

The crux of Butler's normative political theory as it has come into view since the traumatic events of 9/11 lies in the contingency attending the recognition of vulnerability. Consistent with her view of the operation of power, Butler argues that 'if vulnerability is one precondition for humanization, and humanization takes place differently through variable norms of recognition, then it follows that vulnerability is fundamentally dependent upon existing norms of recognition if it is to be attributed to any human subject' (2004a: 43). Given that we cannot will away this vulnerability, Butler addresses the question of what our political and ethical responses to this condition should be, arguing that 'We must attend to it, even abide by it, as we begin to think about what politics might be implied by staying with the thought of corporeal vulnerability itself, a situation in which we can be vanquished or lose others' (2004a: 29). *Mystic River* offers dramatic personifications of the two main responses Butler identifies to the kind of loss or injury that attends vulnerability: revenge as a denial or non-recognition of vulnerability and grief as a recognition of the inescapability of this condition of vulnerability.

Violent and non-violent responses to losses that expose vulnerability

Loss for Butler produces grief, which exposes our relationality and vulnerability, the sense in which we are tied with others. In contrast to a vengeful response to loss that denies vulnerability, Butler insists we ask 'what, politically, might be made of grief besides a cry for war' (2004a: xii). Butler urges us to forgo 'terrible satisfactions of war' and revenge and instead to learn to live with grief and vulnerability and forge a conception of responsibility appropriate to vulnerability (2003b). Again, Butler's thought suggests not only a re-thinking of responsibility in light of non-autonomy and dependency, but also a re-consideration of our understanding of community and what it means to live amongst others and share with them. Two contrasting characters in Clint Eastwood's *Mystic River* can help in thinking about different responses to loss, responses that not only either deny or recognise vulnerability but also therefore either retard or advance a re-conceptualisation of community and responsibility constituted on a shared, yet ambiguous vulnerability.

In contrast to Clint Eastwood's career-long association with unrepentant violence, vigilantism, and vengeance, *Mystic River* is a thorough-going critique of vengeance, exploring the lingering tragic consequences of each violent act depicted. In other words, there are no gratuitous or enjoyable acts of violence in *Mystic River*, as each one has real consequences and dangerous implications for the characters and the story. Therefore, it is with this film rather than *Unforgiven*[2] that Eastwood signals a real transformation in his approach to violence as he shifts from encouraging his audiences to identify with vigilantism to forcing them to confront vulnerability. Whereas in previous Eastwood films vengeance and vigilantes are portrayed positively insofar as the right person, the 'evildoer' always gets killed, *Mystic River* frustrates audience expectations and upsets audience reactions by culminating in a misplaced act of murderous vengeance as the wrong man is killed in return for something he did not do.

After the opening scene that exposes the common condition of vulnerability, *Mystic River* jumps ahead more than two decades to the same Boston neighbourhood, as the three men once again become implicated in each other's lives – this time because of another terrible loss, the murder of Jimmy Markum's nineteen-year-old daughter, that re-exposes and recalls their common vulnerability. This murder sets in motion two parallel investigations that diverge with tragic consequences: one, a police investigation headed by Sean Devine, now a police detective, and another launched by the ex-con Jimmy and carried out on his behalf by the aptly named Savage brothers. While Sean (Kevin Bacon) pursues a series of leads, Jimmy (Sean Penn) and the Savage brothers home in on Dave, their suspicions aroused by his badly bruised hands.

In the climactic scene of *Mystic River*, as a consequence of his vigilante investigation, Jimmy (Sean Penn) exacts a fatal vengeance upon his scarred childhood friend Dave Boyle (Tim Robbins). He refuses to believe Dave's denials and his explanation that his suspiciously bruised hands are the result of his own vengeful act, killing a child molester, who triggered memories of his own childhood trauma.[3] Displaying only a steely desire for retribution and an utter lack of empathy, Jimmy, full of whisky, suspicion, rage, begs Dave 'Admit what you did, and I will give you your life!' before stabbing him to death. Through his words and actions, Jimmy is repeatedly figured in the film through violence and rage. Through his personification of self-righteous vengeance and the search for clear answers and decisive resolutions, even when they diverge from the truth, Jimmy represents the violent delusion of a sovereign, autonomous subject unable to recognise a constitutive vulnerability that cannot be willed away. Thus, Jimmy's pursuit of revenge reveals the truth of Butler's view that

> Revenge tries to solve the problem of vulnerability. If I strike back, then I am not vulnerable but rather the other person is. I transfer vulnerability from myself to the other. And yet by striking back, I produce a world in which my vulnerability to injury is increased by the likelihood of another strike.
>
> (Butler 2003b)

More indeed than a failure of violent revenge, Jimmy's vengeance also represents a failure of recognition – a failure to recognise the shared and inescapable condition of vulnerability. Repeatedly in the film he is identified not only with violence but also with a lack of communication, imagination, and understanding, an identification that is fully realised in the climactic murder of Dave. After Jimmy's refusal to accept his alibi, Dave seems to see the inevitability of his own death at Jimmy's hands and thus admits to killing Katie, even though he is innocent. Interestingly, however, in submitting to Jimmy's wish, Dave offers Jimmy one last opportunity to identify with Dave's suffering and acknowledge the possibility that it might easily have been Jimmy who was abducted and molested that day while playing street hockey decades earlier. Dave says to Jimmy that seeing his daughter that night at the pub reminded him of a dream – 'a dream of youth – I don't remember having one'. At this grave moment, Jimmy greets Dave's talk of dreams, lost youth, and missed opportunities with utter contempt, saying 'So it was a dream?' In response Dave says, 'You know what I mean, if you'd got in that car instead of me.' In an act that displays the full horror of vengeance as a refusal of empathy, Jimmy then says, 'But I didn't get in that car, Dave. You did', and fatally stabs Dave. This murder, stemming from Jimmy's refusal to abide with his grief, resonates with Butler's description of revenge: 'The quick move to action is a way of foreclosing grief, refusing it, and even as it anaesthetizes one's own pain and sense of loss, it comes, in time, to anaesthetize us to the losses that we inflict upon others' (2003b). Indeed, the full weight of the vengeance problematic is revealed in the following scene when Jimmy (and the audience) discover the next morning that Jimmy killed the wrong man, and that his daughter's murderer is actually the son of a man Jimmy had killed decades earlier. This final revelation deepens not only the film's critique of the futility of the cycle of violence but also the film's understanding of the ineluctable condition of vulnerability.

Jimmy's refusal to identify with suffering in favour of vengeance against what turns out to be the wrong man echoes the notion of the futility of savage vengeance, and reveals the psychological and political force of Butler's view that following an experience of loss it is impossible to 'turn around and foreclose or somehow get rid of the fact that we are affected by others in ways we do not choose. We have to figure out what we can do in light of that very condition of vulnerability' (2003b). The tragic ending of *Mystic River* shows with depth and feeling the senselessness of the self-righteous, yet misplaced violence that humans perpetually prone to error are capable of. The fact that Jimmy's kills the wrong person only strengthens the sense in which vulnerability is not a problem to be solved, but a condition to be recognised and attended to.

In *Giving an Account of Oneself*, Butler poses the question of a non-vengeful response to loss:

> What might it mean to undergo violation, to insist upon not resolving grief and staunching vulnerability too quickly through a turn to violence, and to practice, as an experiment in living otherwise, nonviolence in an emphatically nonreciprocal response?
>
> (Butler 2005a: 100)

Her idea of a 'process by which we develop a point of identification with suffering itself' (2004a: 30) finds expression in the character of Sean. In contrast to Jimmy's illustration of the futility of vengeance, Sean depicts the political virtue of identifying with suffering and 'abiding with' vulnerability (Butler 2003b). Throughout the film, Sean represents not only law and order as opposed to violent vengeance, but also a capacity for identification with others through an empathic understanding of social relationships. He shows this capacity not only in his investigation of Dave as a suspect in Katie's murder, but also in a subplot from his private life, vis-à-vis his wife, who has left him (for reasons unclear to the audience) but who still calls him but does not speak. Rather than hang up in frustration and close the lines of communication, Sean stays on the line, even in silence. Indeed, in one of the final scenes, she calls and Sean initiates a reconciliation by saying 'I'm sorry. I need you to know that. I pushed you away.' Sean's statement reveals not only an understanding of the pain and suffering that his own actions have caused but also an identification with what his wife has suffered. Sean's sincere apology leads her to finally break her silence and apologize too, adding that 'Things have been so messed up. Loving you, hating you.' The differences between them are thus resolved through imaginative identification and communication, through an appreciation of the positive potential of vulnerability.

Sean enacts a similar appreciation of the ambivalence of vulnerability in the film's central plot around Katie's murder where he remains much more reluctant than his police partner to cast suspicion on Dave because of his almost first-hand knowledge about what happened to Dave when they were children playing in the street that fateful day. Sean implicitly identifies with Dave, and shifts suspicion to others, a move that results in the capture of the true killers of Jimmy's daughter Katie. In another dramatic moment, Sean reveals his capacity for abiding vulnerability the morning after Jimmy's murder of Dave, when he returns to the very street where the three boys played hockey decades ago to find Jimmy and tell him the news of the capture. This news causes Jimmy's face to sink as he realises Dave was in fact innocent. Sean asks Jimmy when he last saw Dave, to which Jimmy responds with a statement that betrays the kind of recognition characteristic of classical tragedy: 'That was 25 years ago, going up this street in the back of that car.' Jimmy's statement registers his tardy awareness of not only Dave's suffering and impairment but also the tragic consequences of his own vengeance, and yet it is not the same full recognition Sean has of the constitutive and persistent condition of vulnerability. After Jimmy responds to Sean's question about Dave ('What did you do, Jimmy?') by saying 'Thanks for getting my daughter's killers, Sean. If only you'd been a little faster,' Sean knows that Jimmy has exacted his revenge, but his response stands in direct contrast to Jimmy's act of vengeance and his limited recognition. For Sean extends the condition of vulnerability from Dave to all three boys by saying to Jimmy, 'Sometimes I think all three of us got in that car. And all this is just a dream ... In reality, we're still 11-year-old boys locked in a cellar, imagining what our lives would've been if we'd escaped.' Sean understands not only the randomness and contingency of life and the ways in which the past weighs on the present, but also the very given-ness of the condition of vulnerability as the sense in which our sociality, our connections with others 'tear us from ourselves, bind us to others, transport us, undo us, implicate us in lives that are not [our] own, irreversibly, if not fatally' (Butler 2004a: 25).

In the closing moments of the film's final scene, Sean brings together the two themes of a critique of vengeance (together with an affirmation of rule of law) and a capacity for identifying with suffering in a single gesture that illustrates the ambivalence of vulnerability as well as the possibility for a new understanding of community. A few days after Dave's death, Sean and Jimmy's eyes meet across the street as they watch a parade pass through their neighbourhood. Once again echoing the tragic contrast between vengeance and vulnerability, Sean appears holding his newly born child reunited with his wife, while Jimmy appears flanked by the Savage brothers. As they stare at each other, Sean knowing that Jimmy killed Dave and Jimmy knowing that Sean knows, Sean points his finger in Jimmy's direction and 'mock-shoots' him as if to say, 'I'll get you for what you've done.' But because of who Sean is, because of the slight smirk on his face, and finally because his family reunion evinces his willingness to abide vulnerability, the audience understands that Sean's response will not be executed on the street in cold-blood, but through dedicated detective work carried on in memory of Dave and through identification with the experience of vulnerability learned at too early an age.

Community and politics in light of vulnerability

Beginning from the insight that 'Loss has made a tenuous "we" of us all' and investigating the condition of vulnerability and how we might respond to such loss, Butler in her recent work sets for political theory the ambitious task of 'reimagining the possibility of political community on the basis of vulnerability and loss' (2004a: 20). Indeed, the deep and admirable concern to arrest cycles of violence by resisting the temptations of revenge in response to loss and exposed vulnerability finds inspiration not only in a film like *Mystic River* (or Steven Spielberg's *Munich* (2005)) but also in America's open-ended 'war on terror' and the ongoing Israel–Palestine conflict. For what they reveal are the fatal and inhuman consequences that result from vengeance overwhelming capacities for not only compassion and communication, but also any recognition of the inescapability of vulnerability. Responding to loss with an understanding of ineluctable vulnerability and an identification with suffering – rather than denying vulnerability and violently transferring suffering – represents not an excuse or approval of that suffering, but an improved step in coping with loss, as it harbours the seeds of a wisdom that recognises our fundamental sociality and vulnerability, as well as a different kind of politics. I think an entirely different politics would emerge', Butler says,

'if a community could learn to abide with its losses and its vulnerability. It would know better what its ties to other people are. It would know

> how radically dependent it is on its interrelationship with others ... I
> think we would be able to understand something about the general state
> of fragility and physical vulnerability that people – as humans – live in.
> (Butler 2003b)

The different kind of politics that Butler envisages, based on abiding with
loss and vulnerability, necessitates re-imagining political community in light
of vulnerability. Butler's proposal to re-imagine political community with
attention to the fundamental condition of vulnerability is a wonderfully
suggestive avenue for further political theorising and represents a challenge
to some of the most familiar discourses within political theory, including
both contract theory's binary understanding of anarchy and order, communitarianism's overly optimistic and salutary vision of community, and
deliberative democracy's excessively rational understanding of community.
First, the contrast between contract theory's narrative opposition of
security and insecurity (such as Hobbes's) and Butler's notion of vulnerability could not be sharper, for Hobbes's contract theory allows us to
imagine escaping vulnerability through the institution of a sovereign,
whereas Butler contends that an ambiguous vulnerability entailing promise
and precipice cannot be willed away and must be continually attended to as
the very condition of possibility of power and freedom.[4] Second, communitarianism, in its emphasis on the positive, sustaining aspect of community,
attends to only one aspect of the necessary vulnerability Butler identifies,
refusing a more sombre view of the human condition that understands the
ways in which others can impinge on us. Butler tries to re-think community
on the basis of vulnerability and loss, as well as difference, which traditionally communitarianism has difficulty accounting for. Thus, in contrast to
communitarianism, Butler seeks 'another way of imagining community,
one in which we are alike only in having this condition [vulnerability]
separately and so having in common a condition that cannot be thought
without difference' (2004a: 27). With her theorisation of a constitutive,
inescapable, and ambiguous condition of shared vulnerability, Butler moves
us toward being able to (re)think community again in a post-identity-politics
world.

Extending her thought beyond identity politics and towards something
like a precarious politics, Butler urges us to cultivate a recognition of a
fundamental dependency that is not chosen and cannot be willed away, one
which all individuals and groups as well as communities and states must
reckon with. This extension of her thinking is nevertheless consistent with
the critique of the sovereign, autonomous subject that Butler has pursued
throughout her work. In this respect, Butler's recent political theory of vulnerability and precariousness runs counter to the theory and premises of
deliberative democracy, such as when she echoes Adriana Cavarero's claim
'that it is not because we are reasoning beings that we are connected to one
another, but, rather, because we are *exposed* to one another, requiring a

recognition that does not substitute the recognizer for the recognized' (2004a: 48). Indeed, Butler's recent political theory of vulnerability takes inspiration from Cavarero's vision of politics as 'a field of plural interaction and hence of contingency', such that politics and political theory not only must start from a principled recognition of 'the plurality of human beings insofar as they are unique beings rather than fictitious entities like the individual of modern political doctrine', but also must therefore account most importantly for 'a relational dimension of reciprocal dependency, which exposes as false the autonomy and self-sufficiency on which individualism insists' (Cavarero 2002: 512). While Butler's political theory of vulnerability recalls Cavarero's politicised theory in its attention to difference, plurality, and constitutive sociality, Butler's recent thought departs slightly from Cavarero, as Butler insists on retaining the notion and affirming the possibility of a 'we' – especially in the sense of 'Loss has made a tenuous "we" of us all' (2004a: 20, 48–49). After reiterating her familiar claims about our fundamental dependency/sociality that cannot be willed away, Butler distinguishes her perspective from Cavarero's by asserting the possibility of a kind of community, writing parenthetically '(You can see here that I resort here to the plural *we*, even though Cavarero advises against it, precisely because I am not convinced that we must abandon it)' (2005a: 33). Indeed, Butler returns to the primary individual subject's experience of loss (one might say not only violent losses of others, but also the constitutive loss of autonomy theorised in *The Psychic Life of Power*) to articulate a political vision, writing 'Despite our differences in location and history, my guess is that it is possible to appeal to a "we", for all of us have some notion of what it is to have lost somebody' (2004a: 20).

Finally, however promising her proposed re-imagination of community, it remains politically speaking only a norm and an aspiration, partly because of the difficulty of translating and shifting from the level of the individual subject to the level of collective, political subjects. Butler cautiously suggests that the sociality and vulnerability of the subject applies not just to individuals but also to 'state-centered political cultures' (2004a: 45), though not necessarily in easy or direct ways. For Butler holds that 'when we are speaking about the "subject" we are not always speaking about an individual: we are speaking about a model for agency and intelligibility, one that is very often based on notions of sovereign power' (2004a: 45). Butler wants to challenge the notion of sovereign power at the level of the individual subject by reminding us of a constitutive and ambivalent vulnerability, but it also seems that she wants to argue something similar for states in the realm of the society of states. That is a worthy but complicated goal because the issue of violence is more complex at the level of state interaction as opposed to intra-state action. In the international realm, a key question of political practice to which Butler's normative political theory of vulnerability provides some tenuous guidance, given the variability of circumstances, is exactly how to abide with losses and vulnerability and how to resist the temptations of revenge. Indeed, one could say that Butler's political ethic raises some difficult political questions, such as whether all acts of violence are vengeful, or if not, which ones are and how do we read violence? Though I would not suggest every violent act is vengeful or illegitimate, Butler comes close to this suggestion through a near conflation, at times, of violence and vengeance. While she argues that it is not appropriate to the condition of vulnerability to respond to loss with vengeance, Butler leaves some uncertainty as to the parameters of legitimate response to grievances or offences short of (fatal) loss. In terms of politics, Butler's key terms of loss and vengeance will require interpretation in context. While she may overestimate the power or capacity of abiding with loss and vulnerability as the (contingent) foundation for community, or may draw too sharply the contrast between violent and non-violent responses to loss, Butler nevertheless illuminates the political predicament and offers a particularly significant lesson for our age, an age of terrorism as a sudden address we do not choose: a lesson about our vulnerability, a condition amplified by our recognition of an increasingly global interdependence, that we cannot will away but to which we must attend.

Notes

1 Further exploration would reveal that the character of Dave illustrates other key points of Butler's understanding of subject formation and the limits of subjects' ability to 'give an account of themselves'. First, the scene of Dave's abduction by a man impersonating a policeman echoes Butler's discussion of how the figure of 'the turn' inaugurates the subject as well as her invocation of Althusser's 'infamous example' of interpellation (see Butler 1998: 2–6). Second, the incomplete name Dave writes in the wet-cement sidewalk ('DA') before his abduction together with his struggles as an adult to come to terms with and tell the story of what happened to him suggest a parallel with Butler's account of the necessary partiality of any account of ourselves (see Butler 2005: 77, 78–79). Unfortunately, space limitations do not permit a full exploration of these parallels.
2 The 1992 revisionist western Eastwood starred in and directed, *Unforgiven*, is often hailed as a sharp turning point in Eastwood's career-long association with vengeance, extending from the famed Man-with-No-Name in the spaghetti westerns to the infamous vigilante cop Dirty Harry. In 1994, one critic summarised Eastwood's career screen persona in this way: 'In movie after movie, whether as a cowboy or as a police detective, whether acting within the law or as a vigilante, the Eastwood character used force with no compunction in order to ensure that the innocent were saved and the guilty punished.' As key to his argument that Eastwood had 'gone PC', the same critic cites *Unforgiven* as 'a full-scale act of contrition, a repudiation and dismantling of the whole legendary, masculine character type of which, for this generation, Eastwood himself had become the leading icon'. (See Grenier 1994.) Yet, despite its alleged revision of the Western mythology, in the end *Unforgiven* still delivers the vengeful goods to its audience. Consider that at the end of the film, Eastwood's character, William Munny, dispenses the long-awaited, murderous comeuppance to the menacing, tyrannical sheriff, played by Gene Hackman. However reluctantly Eastwood's character executes this act of vengeance, the audience still revels in the destruction of the villainous sheriff, as the teasing, passive reluctance is finally overcome by the

hero, making the film only a slight revision of the vigilante ethos Eastwood cultivated on screen for decades.

3 Early in the film, the adult Dave draws the suspicion of the audience by returning home from a bar late one night with bruised hands, blood on his clothes, and a wound in his abdomen – suspicious because this occurs the same night as the murder of Jimmy's daughter, Katie. Dave tells his wife that someone tried to mug him and he fought back and may have killed the mugger. Later, in a rare moment of lucidity, Dave says, 'It makes you feel alone – hurting somebody.' Dave's statement reveals the truth of violence as a betrayal of the very vulnerability Butler identified with our social existence. Thus, in contrast to Jimmy's deliberate, self-righteous vengeance, Dave's vengeance is figured as the impulsive response of a damaged man-child and produces a belated recognition of vulnerability.

4 Contrast with Robert Kagan's (2003) near mythical celebration of the US government's hard-headed Hobbesian world view of necessary dominance in contrast to Europe's naïve Kantian view of paradisiacal interdependence. Butler's view resonates more with the Kantian vision of cosmopolitan interdependence not as a symptom of weakness but as a recognition of the reality of a vulnerability that cannot be willed away or dominated.

14 Gender trouble at Abu Ghraib?

Timothy Kaufman-Osborn

'It's not a pretty picture', conceded Defense Secretary Donald Rumsfeld in assessing the photographs taken by US military personnel at Baghdad's Abu Ghraib prison complex during the final three months of 2003 (Highham et al. 2004: 1).[1] Shortly thereafter, en route to Iraq, Rumsfeld contended that 'the real problem is not the photographs – the real problems are the actions taken to harm the detainees' (quoted in Brison 2004: 10). This claim is problematic insofar as it fails to appreciate the transformation of these images into so many free-floating weapons deployed to secure partisan advantage on various cultural and political battlegrounds within the United States. This was perhaps nowhere so evident as in their mobilisation to rehash the struggle over the contemporary import of feminism, especially in light of the equality/difference debate that has vexed feminists and their opponents for decades. The initial purpose of this chapter, accordingly, is to explain how the mass media flap regarding the Abu Ghraib photographs indicates that gender, understood as a set of mobile disciplinary practices, can sometimes become unsettled, thereby provoking efforts to re-stabilise heteronormative understandings of what it is to be masculine or feminine. Giving Rumsfeld his due, however, I employ my discussion of the domestic reception of these photographs as a preface to asking how we might make better sense of the gendered import of the abuses committed at Abu Ghraib. To answer this question, in the second half of this chapter, I argue that much of what appeared so shocking when these photographs were first released can be read as extensions of, but also threats to, the logic of masculinised militarism. The most convenient scapegoat for such 'gender trouble', to appropriate the title of Judith Butler's best-known work (1990), is Lynndie England, a military file clerk who was captured by the camera's eye while restraining an Iraqi prisoner at the far end of a dog leash.

Mistaking Lynndie England

Like all photographic images, those taken at Abu Ghraib do not speak for themselves. Henry Giroux explains:

Photographs such as those that revealed the horrors that took place at Abu Ghraib prison have no guaranteed meaning, but rather exist within a complex of shifting mediations that are material, historical, social, ideological, and psychological in nature. This is not to suggest that photographs do not capture some element of reality as much as to insist that what they capture can only be understood as part of a broader engagement over cultural politics and its intersection with various dynamics of power ... Representations privilege those who have some control over self-representation, and they are largely framed within dominant modes of intelligibility.

(Giroux 2004: 8)

Giroux's point about the framing of photographic meaning in terms of 'dominant modes of intelligibility' is well-illustrated by the contest to determine what to make of the Abu Ghraib images that include Lynndie England. In addition to the photograph mentioned above, another shows England standing next to a naked Hayder Sabbar Abd, a thirty-four-year old Shiite taxi-driver from Nasiriya, as a cigarette dangles from her lips, the thumb of her right hand gestures upwards in triumph, and her left hand, with forefinger cocked, takes aim at Abd's genitalia, as he is forced to simulate masturbation. Still another depicts England, arm in arm with Specialist Officer Charles Graner, as both grin and offer a thumbs-up sign while perched behind a cluster of seven naked Iraqis piled awkwardly atop one another in a human pyramid.

The general tenor of the mainstream press response to these photographs, which altogether displaced documented reports of the abuse of women prisoners at Abu Ghraib (see Harding 2004: 10), is indicated by the subtitle of an article written by *Newsweek*'s Evan Thomas in May 2004: 'How did a wispy tomboy behave like a monster at Abu Ghraib?' (Thomas 2004). It may well be, as Cynthia Enloe has suggested, that the media's horrified representation of England as a sub- or inhuman creature indicates America's visceral response to her violation of conventional norms regarding the conduct becoming to women (Enloe 2004: 91); and, as M.S. Embser-Herbert has suggested, the fixation on these particular photographs may well indicate that Americans today are better prepared to see women come home from Iraq in body bags than to see them return as quasi-sexualised aggressors (Embser-Herbert 2004: 1). There is some truth to both of these readings; and it is equally true that the media's preoccupation with the photographs portraying women involved in 'abnormal' conduct facilitated the Bush administration's interest in representing what transpired at Abu Ghraib as the 'disgraceful conduct by a few American troops who dishonoured our country and disregarded our values', and so as an anomalous departure from established military doctrine (Bush 2004). However, neither of these readings fully captures the ways in which these photographs were mobilised, especially during the months immediately following their release, in the service of larger domestic political and cultural agendas. This proved most strikingly so when the proponents of various right-wing agendas seized on Lynndie England in order to advance a reactionary backlash aimed at reversing whatever advances women have made in the military, under the banner of gender equality, since termination of the all male draft in 1972.

Three examples, all published in May 2004, less than two weeks after the Abu Ghraib photographs initially aired on CBS's *Sixty Minutes II*, suffice to illustrate this appropriation. First, the president of the Center for Military Readiness, Elaine Donnelly, asserted that the photograph of England with leash in hand 'is exactly what feminists have dreamed of for years'. To explain, she represented England's conduct as an articulation of the dispositions displayed by those feminists 'who like to buy man-hating greeting cards and have this kind of attitude that all men abused all women. It's a subculture of the feminist movement, but the driving force in it in many cases, certainly in academia' (quoted in Thibault 2004). On this basis, which figures feminists as so many would-be dominatrixes afflicted by a burning desire to transform men into so many obsequious lap-dogs, Donnelly argued that the US military should abandon its unofficial gender quotas, aimed at enlisting more women, and return to basic training segregated by sex. Arguing on behalf of the same counter-reforms, Peggy Noonan, columnist and contributing editor of the *Wall Street Journal*, claimed that before basic training became co-educational, women

> did not think they had to prove they were men, or men at their worst. I've never seen evidence to suggest the old-time WACs and WAVEs had to delve down into some coarse and vulgar part of their nature to fit in, to show they were one of the guys, as tough as the guys, as ugly at their ugliest.
>
> (Noonan 2004)

On this reading, England is a young woman whose turn to the dark side can be explained by her desire to be embraced by her brutish counterparts, with the implication that she never would have acted as she did had she been excluded from their crass company. Finally, in a screwy twist on much the same narrative, the president of the Center for Equal Opportunity, Linda Chavez, suggested that England's participation in the abuse at Abu Ghraib can be explained by the mounting 'sexual tension' that has accompanied 'the new sex-integrated military'. Because that stress produces hormone-crazed soldiers, which in turn undermines 'discipline and unit cohesion', we should not be unduly surprised when those in uniform occasionally release their pent up passions by sexually abusing their captives (Chavez 2004).

What Donnelly, Noonan, and Chavez share is the conviction, expressly articulated by George Neumayr, columnist for the *American Spectator*, that the conduct of Lynndie England 'is a cultural outgrowth of a feminist culture which encourages female barbarians' (Neumayr 2004). Their concern that women are 'losing their femininity' requires that an unambiguous masculine identity be re-fortified and that it be sharply distinguished from the equally unambiguous gender identity of women (e.g. by re-confining GI Janes to suitably ladylike roles on the sidelines of the military in accordance with their customary roles as civilisers of beastly men). Such claims presuppose an uncritical conception of gender, one which includes a dyadic conception of sexual identity, the naturalness (as well as the apparent irresistibility) of heterosexual desire, and stereotypical, if not essentialised, conceptions of masculine and feminine conduct. Lest there be any doubt on this latter score, also in May 2004, the president of the Eagle Forum, Phyllis Schlafly, asserted that 'the picture of the woman soldier with a noose around the Iraqi man's neck' demonstrates 'that some women have become mighty mean, but feminists can't erase eternal differences' (Schlafly 2004). It is perhaps no surprise that many other right-wing pundits, seeking to appropriate the Abu Ghraib images for partisan ends, also did so by citing the alleged ubiquity of pornography, and especially gay porn, in American culture (see Rich 2004: 1). On this telling, England and her cohorts are marshalled in an effort to combat the excesses of a permissive culture whose primary causes, of course, include the rise of women's and gay liberation movements, both of which celebrate a promiscuous, if not depraved, conception of sexual freedom.

Unhappily, many readings of the Abu Ghraib affair advanced by mainstream liberal feminists have swallowed the bait proffered by the right wing. Embracing the construction of these photographs as a referendum on feminism and its commitment to the equality of women, these readings have demonstrated the stubborn persistence of conceptions of gender, which, although not wedded to the reactionary political agendas advanced by Schlafly and her ilk, are nonetheless quite problematic. This sort of appropriation is best illustrated by Barbara Ehrenreich whose 2004 commencement address at Barnard College, following its publication in the *Los Angeles Times*, became a subject of widespread discussion, especially on the Internet.

'As a feminist', Ehrenreich began, the Abu Ghraib photographs 'broke my heart. I had no illusions about the US mission in Iraq – whatever exactly it is – but it turns out that I did have some illusions about women'. These illusions were based on the belief that women are 'morally superior to men', whether because of 'biology', or 'conditioning', or 'simply the experience of being a woman in a sexist culture'; and it was on this basis that Ehrenreich 'secretly' entertained the 'hope that the presence of women would over time change the military, making it more respectful of other people and cultures, more capable of genuine peacekeeping'. It is these illusions that were shattered when Ehrenreich first saw the image of Lynndie England, her Iraqi prisoner in tow: 'A certain kind of feminism, or perhaps I should say a certain kind of feminist naiveté died in Abu Ghraib. It was a feminism that saw men as the perpetual perpetrators, women as the perpetual victims, and male sexual violence against women as the root of all injustice.' But now, having witnessed 'female sexual sadism in action', Ehrenreich rejects as 'lazy and self-indulgent' any form of feminism that is 'based on an assumption of female moral superiority'. 'A uterus', in sum, 'is not a substitute for a conscience' (Ehrenreich 2004: 1).

In retrospect, Ehrenreich confesses, she should not have been so shocked to learn that 'women can do the unthinkable', for, unlike her right-wing opponents, 'she never believed that women were innately gentler and less aggressive than men'. But the very fact that she was so shocked by England's conduct, as well as the fact that this response was situated at the far edge of comprehensibility ('the unthinkable'), indicates the deep-seated tenacity with which, too often, we cling to a vision of the world that neatly distinguishes between powerful men and powerless women, between those who are guilty of acts of sexual violence and those who are their victims. This vision of the world presupposes the self-evident intelligibility of the category of 'women' as well as their fundamental differences from the equally self-evident category of 'men'; and it presupposes problematic stereotypes about women, including, in Ehrenreich's case, the belief that because they 'do most of the caring work in our culture', they are less inclined 'toward cruelty and violence' (Ehrenreich 2004: 1). As such, and despite their very different political agendas, there are unsettling points of convergence between the conception of gender Ehrenreich embraced before Abu Ghraib and the conception Schlafly and her cohorts continue to promote after Abu Ghraib.

Ehrenreich is to be commended for the intellectual honesty that prompted her to question this conception of gender (although she does not advance any more adequate alternative). It remains true, however, that she accepts her opponents' construction of the Lynndie England affair as a referendum on feminism and its quest for gender equality. That, though, is a misguided enterprise. It is problematic when the revulsion provoked by these photographs is predicated on retrograde gender representations; and it is pernicious when it animates an anti-feminist backlash that seeks to re-situate women in a world where they are compelled to live out those odious stereotypes. Moreover, this construction encourages sterile repetition of unproductive and arguably unanswerable questions (e.g. are women really different from men?); and it plays into the hands of feminism's detractors by inviting them to assert that the ultimate import of the quest for gender equality is revealed in the conduct of Lynndie England. This is not to suggest that we discard the category of gender in thinking about what happened at Abu Ghraib. But it is to suggest that we turn away from the conception that is presupposed whenever someone asks: 'How could women do that?' (Hong 2004). Instead, I urge that we think of gender as something constructed through engagement in a complex set of performative practices, including the abusive techniques deployed at Abu Ghraib, and that we ask how those practices en-gender persons in ways that are not readily reducible to what Ehrenreich or her adversaries mean when they uncritically speak of 'women' and 'men'.

Technologies of emasculation at Abu Ghraib

The official investigative reports issued in the wake of Abu Ghraib do not themselves offer a more nuanced account of its gendered import. Read in light of a more adequate understanding of gender, however, they provide clues toward such an account. The principal documents include the *Taguba* and *Fay-Jones Reports*, both of which were commissioned by Lt. Gen. Ricardo Sanchez, commander of coalition ground forces in Iraq; the *Mikolashek Report*, conducted by the Army's Inspector General; and the *Schlesinger Report*, issued by an independent panel chartered by the secretary of defence. Although conceding certain failures of leadership in higher (but not too high) ranks, all explain what happened at Abu Ghraib in terms of the pathological and/or criminal conduct of a handful of rogue soldiers.[2] The *Schlesinger Report*, for example, concludes: 'The events of October through December 2003 on the night shift of Tier 1 at Abu Ghraib prison were acts of brutality and purposeless sadism' (Schlesinger 2005: 909). In much the same vein, according to the 'psychological assessment' appended to the *Taguba Report*, the events at Abu Ghraib were the work of 'immoral men and women' who engaged in 'sadistic and psychopathic behavior', including 'abuse with sexual themes' (Taguba 2005: 448–49). Finally, the *Fay-Jones Report* determines that 'the primary cause of the most egregious violent and sexual abuses was the individual criminal propensities of the particular perpetrators' (Fay-Jones 2005: 1007).

These readings will not do. They will not do in part because they de-contextualise these deeds, rendering them so many transgressions enacted by a few unruly anomalies. Once Abu Ghraib is defined in these disin-genuous terms, these soldiers, including Lynndie England, can all too easily be assigned the role of patsies whose service to the military now includes distracting attention from the institutional forces that breed and sanction such exploitation. But these readings also will not do because they occlude the ways in which gender is in fact constitutive of what happened at Abu Ghraib. The representation of these events as 'sexual abuse' does not ade-quately specify the particular form of degradation involved here. That degradation is trivialised when James Schlesinger, former Secretary of Defense and lead author of the report bearing his name, refers to Abu Ghraib as 'Animal House on the night shift' ('Abu Ghraib was "Animal House" at Night' 2004). To compare what happened on Tier 1 to so much reprehensible behaviour on the part of intoxicated undergraduates at a fraternity bash is to confound the distinction between sexual abuse, on the one hand, and acts of imperialist and racist violence that mimic sexual exploitation, on the other. It is, moreover, to fail to ask *why* so much of the abuse meted out at Abu Ghraib, as the reports make abundantly clear, trafficked in gendered stereotypes as well as what that might teach us about how gender operates as a complex vector of power within the context of masculinised militarism.

The acts of principal concern to me in this section are a subset of the larger group that exhibited sexualised dimensions. Although the distinction is admittedly problematic, I will primarily confine my attention to those that traded on misogynistic understandings as opposed to those that were patently homophobic as well as arguably homoerotic (e.g. forcing prisoners to masturbate while being photographed; compelling prisoners to engage in simulated fellatio; and sodomising a prisoner with a phosphorous light stick) (see Puar 2004). Instead, my chief concern is with incidents such as the following: compelling otherwise naked men to wear women's underwear, often red and often on their heads; having a servicewoman apply red ink to the face of a prisoner after she placed her hand in her unbuttoned pants and informed him that she was menstruating; forcing men to remove their clothing and then stand before women service personnel; and, lest we forget Lynndie England, placing a leash around a naked prisoner's neck while posing with him for a snapshot.[3]

How are we to make sense of these incidents? Loosely following the lead of Judith Butler (1990, 1993),[4] I propose that we think not about men and women in the unreflective sense in which all of the authors discussed in the previous section employ these terms, but, rather, about complex disciplinary practices that en-gender bodies by regulating, constraining, and constituting their conduct in ways that prove intelligible in light of the never entirely stable or coherent categories of masculine and feminine. 'Men' and 'women', in other words, are constantly being gendered as they participate in practices mandated by cultural norms of masculinity and femininity, which are themselves contingently related to anatomical equipment: 'When the constructed status of gender is theorized as radically independent of sex', Butler argues, 'gender itself becomes a free-floating artifice, with the consequence that *man* and *masculine* might just as easily signify a female body as a male one, and *woman* and *feminine* a male body as easily as female one' (Butler 1993: x). If this is so, then what we should be exploring at Abu Ghraib is the differential production of masculinity and femininity as well as the ways in which specific performances sometimes unsettle foundational illusions about the dependence of gender on sex. This re-direction of inquiry suggests that much, but certainly not all, of what happened at Abu Ghraib can be understood in terms of what I will call the 'logic of emasculation', where the aim of disciplinary techniques is to strip prisoners of their masculine gender identity and turn them into caricatures of terrified and often infantilised femininity. What this implies for our reading of Lynndie England is the question taken up in this chapter's conclusion.

In applying this performative account of gender to Abu Ghraib, it is useful to begin by doing precisely what the *Fay-Jones Report*, which insists that 'no policy, directive or doctrine directly or indirectly caused violent or sexual abuse' (Fay-Jones 2005: 989), discourages us from doing: to relate the exploitation at Abu Ghraib to the US military's approved techniques regarding the treatment of those detained during combat. For present purposes, the directive of principal concern is *Army Field Manual 34–52* (*Intelligence Interrogation* 1992), which officially governed the treatment of those imprisoned at Abu Ghraib. In response to the abuses reported at Abu Ghraib and elsewhere, a proposed new field manual governing 'detainee treatment', including interrogation procedures, was prepared and then posted on the Pentagon's website, only to be withdrawn shortly thereafter. It is my contention that many of the practices commended in this manual, whether employed in the context of formal interrogations or in conjunction with efforts to 'soften up' prisoners as a preface to such interrogations, trade on specific conceptions of masculinity and femininity. One of the principal virtues of the Abu Ghraib photographs, accordingly, is the way they render visible this implicit content.

'Unless this publication states otherwise', *Field Manual 34–52* affirms, 'masculine nouns or pronouns do not refer exclusively to men' (*Intelligence Interrogation* 1992: v). Because *34–52* is formally neutral, revelation of its gendered content must be a matter of plausible inference. An intimation of that content is provided by the Central Intelligence Agency's 1963 manual titled *Counterintelligence Interrogation*, which, according to a correspondent for the *Atlantic Monthly*, 'remains the most comprehensive and detailed explanation in print of coercive methods of questioning' (Bowden 2003: 57–58). Unearthed in 1997 via a Freedom of Information Act request, what came to be known as the *Kubark Manual* is refreshingly candid in specifying the *summum bonum* of disciplinary techniques applied to the incarcerated:

> It is a fundamental hypothesis of this handbook that these techniques ... are in essence methods of inducing regression of the personality to whatever earlier and weaker level is required for the dissolution of resistance and the inculcation of dependence ... [T]he circumstances of detention are arranged to enhance within the subject his feelings of being cut off from the known and the reassuring, and of being plunged into the strange ... Control of the source's environment permits the interrogator to determine his diet, sleep pattern and other fundamentals. Manipulating these into irregularities, so that the subject becomes disorientated, is very likely to create feelings of fear and helplessness.
>
> (*Kubark Counterintelligence Interrogation*, 1963: 41, 86–87)

A 1983 revision of *Kubark*, titled *Human Resource Exploitation Training Manual*, goes on to state: 'Throughout his detention, subject must be convinced

212 Timothy Kaufman-Osborn

that his "questioner" controls his ultimate destiny, and that his absolute cooperation is essential to survival' (*KUBARK Counterintelligence Interrogation* 1983, sec. F20). This can be achieved by radically disrupting

> the familiar emotional and psychological associations of the subject. Once this disruption is achieved, the subject's resistance is seriously impaired. He experiences a kind of psychological shock, which may only last briefly, but during which he is far more open and far likelier to comply ... Frequently the subject will experience a feeling of guilt. If the 'questioner' can intensify these guilt feelings, it will increase the subject's anxiety and his urge to cooperate as a means of escape.
> (*Human Resource Exploitation Training Manual*, 1983, K-1, c-e).

For those familiar with feminist literature on battered women, it is difficult to read these passages without recalling accounts of abusive relationships in which men seek to secure the wholesale subordination of women by isolating and terrifying them either through violence or threats of violence. Such compliance is best secured when a woman, consumed by fear, determines that her situation is helpless, and, still more perfectly, when she concludes that she is ultimately culpable and so guilty for the abuse to which she is subject. In this light, consider the claim, advanced in *Kubark*, that well-designed interrogation techniques strip those undergoing questioning of all vestiges of autonomy, thereby transforming them into creatures who are 'helplessly dependent on their captors for the satisfaction of their many basic needs, and experience the emotional and motivational reactions of intense fear and anxiety' (*KUBARK Counterintelligence Interrogation*, 1963, 83–4). If such techniques harbour tacit gendered baggage, as I believe they do, then arguably the effect of their application is to emasculate subjects by dismantling the qualities conventionally associated with masculinity and replacing them with a hyperbolic incarnation of the qualities stereotypically associated with femininity: obedience, passivity, depression, anxiety, and shame.

Although certain of the harshest techniques prescribed by *Kubark* in 1963 were deleted from its 1983 revision, and are no longer present in either the original 1987 version of *Army Field Manual 34–52* or its 1992 revision, there is little reason to believe that the basic logic of these disciplinary practices has changed in any significant way; and there is every reason to believe that the latent gendered content of that logic announced itself at Abu Ghraib. Consider, for example, the tactics identified as 'futility', which aims to demonstrate that resistance of any sort is hopeless, and 'pride and ego down', which attacks 'the source's sense of personal worth. Any source who shows any real or imagined inferiority or weakness about himself, loyalty to his organization, or captured under embarrassing circumstances, can be easily broken with this approach technique' (*Intelligence Interrogation*, 1992, ch. 3, 18). How the general terms of these tactics were to be translated into practice at Abu Ghraib, as the *Fay-Jones Report* acknowledges, left 'certain issues for interpretation' (Fay-Jones 2005, 1004). How those issues were resolved says much about the conceptions of masculinity and femininity, which, by and large, remain predominant within the US military; and, although I will not deal with this issue with the care it deserves, it also says much about the possibilities of emasculating those who are already effectively infantilised, if not feminised, in virtue of their identity as colonised and racialised others.

Consider, for example, the stripping of male prisoners, who were then forced to stand before American servicewomen. In addition to offending cultural sensitivities, especially those dictated by Islamic law regarding proper attire, this technique emasculates prisoners by exposing them in a way that is familiar from representations of women, including but by no means limited to those conventionally labelled 'pornographic'. What one sees here, in inverted form, is a sort of enforced vulnerability joined to a fantasy of absolute sexualised power. Much the same logic is apparent in the practice of smearing prisoners with red ink said to be menstrual blood; here, emasculation is a function of staining the male body with that which is taken to mark women's bodies as distinctively female and, as such, a source of degradation. And, finally, when some of those imprisoned at Abu Ghraib were required to wear women's underwear on their heads for hours, days, and even weeks, the logic of emasculation achieves its consummation in drag. In each of these cases, misogyny is deployed as a tactic to humiliate prisoners, where the term 'humiliation' can be translated as 'treat like a woman'. That this aim often succeeded is confirmed by Dhia al-Shweiri, who, several months following his release from Abu Ghraib, was quoted as follows:

> They were trying to humiliate us, break our pride. We are men. It's OK if they beat me. Beatings don't hurt us, it's just a blow. But no one would want their manhood to be shattered. They wanted us to feel as though we were women, the way women feel and this is the worst insult, to feel like a woman.
>
> (Quoted in Faramarzi 2004)

This process, whereby the gendered import of formally gender-neutral disciplinary tactics becomes explicit, achieved its official confirmation when, in mid-2005, the US Army released the results of an investigation, conducted by Lt. Gen. Randall Schmidt of the Air Force, into the treatment of those imprisoned at Guantánamo Bay (*Schmidt Report*, 2005). Making clear that many of the abuses now associated with Abu Ghraib were put into play in Cuba and later 'migrated' to Iraq, Schmidt codified these techniques under the rubric of 'gender coercion', which, on his account, includes authorising servicewomen to 'perform acts designed to take advantage of their gender in relation to Muslim males'. Specifically, in late 2002, two 'high-value' but resistant prisoners were subjected to the following actions in accordance with *34–52*'s pride and ego down as well as futility provisions: 'the subject of the first Special Interrogation Plan [Mohamed Qahtani, the alleged twentieth hijacker in the attack of September 11, 2001] was forced to wear a woman's bra and had a thong placed on his head during the course of the interrogation'; had his face marked with alleged menstrual blood; had a leash clasped around his neck, after which he was led around the inter-rogation room 'and forced to perform a series of dog tricks'; and, during a strip search, was 'forced to stand naked for five minutes with females pre-sent'. Concluding his investigation, Schmidt reported that 'the creative, aggressive, and persistent' questioning of this prisoner, especially in light of his solitary confinement for 160 days, as well as his subjection to 18-to-20-hour interrogation periods over 48 out of 54 days, constituted 'degrading and abusive treatment'. However, because 'every technique employed' by the interrogation team at Guantánamo Bay 'was legally per-missible under the existing guidance', Schmidt found no evidence 'of torture or inhumane treatment at JTF-GTMO' (Joint Task Force-Guantánamo Bay). Accordingly, when Schmidt recommended that the commander at Guantánamo Bay, Maj. Gen. Geoffrey D. Miller, be 'admonished' (*Schmidt Report*, 2005: 7, 16, 19–20), he did so not because the specific techniques employed violated policy, but because Miller had failed to supervise the interrogation process adequately. That Miller was not in fact disciplined by Gen. Bantz Craddock, head of the US Southern Command, is telling, as is the fact that Miller was subsequently dispatched by the Pentagon to improve the quality of intelligence extracted from those imprisoned at Abu Ghraib.

The *Schmidt Report* makes clear that interrogation taking the form of sexualised exploitation was conducted prior to the invasion of Iraq, and that the abuse perpetrated at Abu Ghraib was not an aberration. It is not implausible, therefore, to contend that the conduct of Lynndie England and Charles Graner, like that of Miller, was wholly within the parameters of the techniques specified in *Field Manual 34–52*. Indeed, Graner stated that when he ordered England to remove a prisoner from a cell using a leash, he was employing a legitimate cell-extraction technique (Zernike 2005: A1); and England informed military investigators that forcing prisoners to crawl, while attached to dog leashes, was a 'humiliation tactic' intended to facil-itate formal interrogations (Jehl et al. 2004: 7). In this regard, Graner and England were not unusual, for many of the personnel at Abu Ghraib believed that their actions were entirely consistent with established military doctrine. As a warden in Tier 1 stated, 'It was not uncommon to see people without clothing. I only saw males. I was told the "whole nudity thing" was an interrogation procedure used by military intelligence, and never thought much of it' (Zernike and Rohde 2004: 1). In much the same vein, the *Fay–Jones Report* states that 'the use of dogs to "fear up" [another of *34–52*'s authorised approaches] detainees was generally unquestioned and stems in part from the interrogation techniques and counter-resistance policy distributed from CJTF 180 [Combined Joint Task Force], JTF [Joint Task Force] 170 and CJTF' (Fay–Jones 2005: 1084). That these scenes were so often photographed, absent any concerted effort to hide the evidence, may say more about the banality of officially sanctioned evil than it does about the 'sadistic and psychopathic' impulses of England and her cohorts: 'We thought it looked funny', Lynndie stated matter-of-factly, 'so pictures were taken' (Zernike 2004: 16).

Enloe is quite correct to claim that we will not fully grasp what happened at Abu Ghraib until we fully explore the culture of masculinised militarism, and, more particularly, 'the masculinisation of the military interrogators' organizational cultures, the masculinisation of the CIA's field operatives and the workings of ideas about "manliness" shaping the entire political system' (2004: 100). Obviously, it is beyond the scope of this chapter to offer what Enloe rightly calls for. That said, because it offers insight into the specific form assumed by certain of the abuses at Abu Ghraib, I close this section by citing one factor that contributes to the culture of masculinised militarism in the United States.

Some have suggested that the exploitation at Abu Ghraib articulates American servicepersons' knowledge of Muslim culture as well as its alleged taboos and phobias (see e.g. Schneider 2004: 24). With Enloe, though, it seems equally plausible to ask whether

> American military police and their military and CIA intelligence colleagues might have been guided by their own masculinized fears of humiliation when they forced Iraqi men to go naked for days, to wear women's underwear and to masturbate in front of each other and American women guards. That is, belief in an allegedly 'exotic,' frail Iraqi masculinity, fraught with fears of nakedness and homosexuality, might not have been the chief motivator for the American police and intelligence personnel; it may have been their own home-grown American sense of masculinity's fragility ... that prompted them to craft these prison humiliations.
>
> (Enloe 2004: 99)

But where and how might Graner and his cohorts have learned this fear of emasculation that was then arguably incorporated into various techniques aimed at 'softening up' his charges at Abu Ghraib? Although not a complete explanation, this question can be answered in part by pointing to the hazing techniques that remain so prevalent in basic training. Consideration of these techniques requires that, albeit incompletely, I reconnect the misogynistic and homophobic elements of the exploitation at Abu Ghraib, which, to this point, I have separated for analytic purposes, although they are clearly joined in many of the incidents recounted in the investigative reports and depicted in many of the photographs.

In a striking recapitulation of the central premise of *Kubark* (and, by extension, of *Field Manual 34–52*), a former head drill instructor explained that the key purpose of basic training is to

> break [the recruit] down to his fundamental self, take away all that he possesses, and get him started out in a way that you want him to be ... Tell him he doesn't know a damn thing, that he's the sorriest thing you've ever seen, but with my help you're going to be worthwhile again.
>
> (Quoted in Burke 1996: 214)

Techniques employed to achieve this end, explains Carol Burke in a study of Australia's equivalent of West Point, include stripping recent recruits of their clothing; requiring them to run a gauntlet while those in their second and third year slap them with towels, belts, and suspenders; forcing them to sit naked on a block of ice, which is sometimes electrified in order to produce a shock; handcuffing and hooding cadets before their pants are pulled down and a vacuum cleaner hose is applied to their genitals; and the performance of Reverse Vienna Oysters, in which one freshman is required to lie on his back while another, atop him, performs push-ups in a simulation of heterosexual intercourse (Burke 1996: 214–16).

That these are not Australian idiosyncrasies is made evident when Burke, anticipating one of the more infamous Abu Ghraib photographs, explains how, at the US Naval Academy, once a year, a twenty-one foot obelisk is greased with lard, and how all members of the outgoing freshman class, stripped to their underwear, 'scramble to construct a human pyramid secure enough to raise a midshipman to the top more quickly than any preceding first year class'. While the occasional woman cadet sometimes join in this ritual, they 'never get far up the pyramid before her male counterparts toss her off, for no class wants to be the first to send a woman to the top of Herndon' (Burke 1996: 205). Furthermore, in her study of basic training at the Citadel, which erupted into mass-media frenzy when Shannon Faulkner became the first woman to be admitted, Susan Faludi found much the same logic at work. Specifically, one of Faludi's respondents explained how in basic training under same-sex conditions, upperclassmen play the role of men, while 'knobs' play the role of women, 'stripped and humiliated': 'Virtually every taunt', Michael Lake confessed, 'equated him with a woman ... They called you a "pussy" all the time, or a "fucking little girl".' And when Lake showed fear, he was typically asked, 'Are you menstruating?' 'According to the Citadel creed of the cadet', Lake summarises, 'women are objects, they're things that you can do with whatever you want to' (quoted in Faludi 1994: 70).

Obviously, unlike what happened at Abu Ghraib, where the aim was to emasculate in order to subjugate, the aim of hazing techniques employed in basic training is to destroy deficient forms of masculinity, but then to replace these with a construction built on what R. Claire Snyder has aptly

characterised as an 'unstable masculine identity predicated on the denigra-
tion of femininity and homoeroticism' (Snyder 1999: 151). This combination is uneasy because it requires suppression of any 'feminine' impulses
soldiers may have harboured prior to enlistment, but also the very homoeroticism that is cultivated during basic training. Coping with this tension
requires that the well-disciplined serviceman perpetually reiterate what
Snyder calls the ideal of

> *armed masculinity*: He must constantly reestablish his masculinity by
> expressing his opposition to femininity and homoeroticism in himself
> and others. The anger, hostility, and aggressiveness produced in the
> process of constituting *armed masculinity* gets channeled into a desire
> for combat against [or, I would add, abuse of] the enemy.
>
> (Snyder 1999: 151)

In short, perhaps the exploitation at Abu Ghraib is best understood as an
externalised projection of the anxieties bred by a masculine identity that
cannot help but subvert itself.

Conclusion

But what about Pfc. Lynndie England? Is she or is she not a source of
gender trouble? Given my representation of gender as a malleable signifier,
and given my claim that women's bodies can act as vectors of patriarchal
norms, whether as victims, as perpetrators, or as something more vexing
than this binary categorisation suggests, the answer to this question must be
yes and no, depending on the contingencies of the context in which her
deeds were first enacted as well as the contexts into which those deeds subsequently entered via various cultural and media appropriations, domestic
as well as foreign.

Within the context of Abu Ghraib, one might argue that England conducts herself in exemplary accordance with pathologised norms of feminine
submissiveness. Located in the midst of an institutional culture predicated
on the ideal of masculinised militarism, England found herself obliged to
play by the rules of the game, which, in this case, included doing what she
was ordered to do by her superior officers: 'I was instructed by persons in
higher ranks to stand there and hold this leash ... To us, we were doing our
jobs, which meant doing what we were told' (Johnson 2004: 16). This reading is reinforced by the testimony of a psychologist who, during England's
court-marital, argued that her 'overly compliant' personality rendered her
incapable of making an independent judgment about participating in the
exploitation at Abu Ghraib, thereby justifying a defence on the grounds of
'partial mental responsibility' (Cloud 2005a: 28). And, finally, this characterisation would appear to be cemented by the fact that, according to one
of her defence attorneys, her love for Graner, who allegedly has a history of

abusing women, and who is the biological father of the child with whom England became pregnant while at Abu Ghraib, rendered her inordinately susceptible to bad influences: 'She was an individual who was smitten with Corporal Graner, who just did whatever he asked her to do. Compounding all this is her depression, her anxiety, her fear' (Cloud 2005b: 12).

Yet this reading becomes problematic when we recall that England was at the same time participating in abusive conduct aimed at emasculating Iraqi prisoners, who were thereby reduced to something akin to the sort of submissiveness she apparently displayed in her relationship with Graner. If, as Snyder's (1999) analysis implies, Graner must perpetually seek to bolster a troubled conception of masculinity by transforming the targets of his abuse into so many incarnations of a despised conception of femininity, then England's conduct surely complicates this task. That a woman who appears more master than slave is the means of propping up that identity, in other words, would appear to spell gender trouble for Graner (which, although this is entirely speculative, may partly explain why he ultimately left England in favour of another, but less calumniated, of the women of Abu Ghraib). Graner's conundrum, moreover, may be ours as well. As Zillah Eisenstein suggests, England and the other women pictured in the Abu Ghraib photographs are in effect 'gender decoys' who 'create confusion by participating in the very sexual humiliation that their gender is usually victim to' (Eisenstein: 2004).

I do not intend to choose between these rival readings of Lynndie England. Instead, I want to suggest that the apparent tension between them will begin to dissipate only when we abandon the conception of gender discussed in the first section of this chapter and embrace that commended in its second section. On the latter account, what is significant about the Abu Ghraib photographs is not whether the perpetrators of such abuse are anatomically male or female, nor whether Lynndie England is a woman or some sort of gender-bending monster. Rather, what is significant are the multiple ways in which specifically gendered practices are deployed as elements within a more comprehensive network of technologies aimed at disciplining prisoners or, more bluntly, at confirming their status as abject subjects of US military power. In the photographs of principal concern here, gender as a complex structure of asymmetrical power relations has been detached from human bodies, and, once detached, deployed as something akin to so many weapons, weapons that may be employed by and against anyone, male or female. What we see here, in sum, are so many scripted practices of subordination that achieve their ends through the manipulation of gendered stereotypes, all of which work precisely because degradation, weakness, and humiliation remain very much identified with matters feminine. If Ehrenreich is shocked by Lynndie England, I would maintain, it is not because she is not a 'true' woman, but because her conduct reveals the artificiality of normative constructions of gender as well as the untenability of any essentialised account that insists on its rootedness in anatomical equipment. Whether Phyllis Schlafly and her kin can recapture England in a way that deflects her revelation of the way in which gender performances can sometimes simultaneously reinforce and trouble hetero-normative strictures remains to be seen.

What I have offered in this chapter is, I think, a decent first step towards making better sense of certain of the Abu Ghraib photographs, but it is also quite inadequate. This reading does not capture the complexity of the gendered permutations at work in the Abu Ghraib photographs. Specifically, this chapter does no more than touch on the virulent homophobia among US military personnel, although my analysis does imply that when these assaults appear to assume the character of homosexual acts, what is salient is not the imputed sexual orientation of any of the participants, but, rather, the fact that the abused are once again forced, at least in the minds of the perpetrators, to assume the position of those on the receiving end of sexualised violence. Nor does my reading grasp adequately the complex interplay of race and gender in these photographs and the incidents they depict. We must not forget that the three US women who appear in the Abu Ghraib photographs, Megan Ambuhl, Sabrina Harman, and Lynndie England, are all white women, and that those they abuse are all brown men. Nor, finally, does my reading adequately explicate the larger political logic, that of neo-colonialism and imperialism, from which these practices derive much of their sense.

Since I cannot do justice to these elements, let me close by noting that Mark Danner was certainly correct when he contended that 'officials of the Bush administration ... counted on the fact that the public, and much of the press, could be persuaded to focus on the photographs – the garish signboards of the scandal and not the scandal itself' (Danner 2004: 47). Saying so, he effectively indicated the strategic foolishness of Rumsfeld's contention that 'the real problem is not the photographs – the real problems are the actions taken to harm the detainees'. From the vantage point of the Bush administration, far better to encourage a single-minded fixation on these photographs since, in a culture too much saturated by obscene (which should be distinguished from pornographic) imagery, that fixation cannot help but de-politicise what happened at Abu Ghraib. To overcome such de-politicisation we ought to ask how these photographs expose the tangled strands of racism, misogyny, homophobia, national arrogance, and hyper-masculinity as well as how these strands inform the US military's adventure in Iraq. What we ought not to ask is whether or how these photographs should be read as a referendum on the feminist quest for gender equality.

Notes

1 This chapter has its origins in a roundtable titled 'Gender Relations in the Age of Neo-Liberalism', which was conducted in conjunction with the 2005 meeting of the Western Political Science Association. I wish to thank the other participations on that roundtable, Jane Bayes, Mary Hawkesworth, and Judith Hicks

Stiehm, as well as Paul Apostolidis, Renee Heberle, Jinee Lokaneeta, Jeannie Morefield, Aaron Perrine, Kari Tupper, and three anonymous reviewers for their comments on earlier drafts.

2 Those who have been prosecuted and convicted in the Abu Ghraib affair are currently serving sentences ranging from demotion to prison time. A court martial for shift supervisor Ivan Frederick concluded in a ten-year sentence, which was reduced to eight by way of a pretrial agreement. Specialist Charles Graner received the harshest sentence to date, ten years in prison; and Pfc. Lynndie England, following a botched plea bargain, was sentenced to three years in prison as well as a dishonourable discharge.

3 With the exception of that involving fake menstrual blood, which is related in Saar and Novak (2005: 225–29), these incidents as well as others like them, are related in the *Taguba Report* and *Fay-Jones Report* (Greenberg and Dratel 2005: 416–17, 466–528, 1073–95[0]).

4 For a more complete account of my reading of Butler on gender, see Kaufman-Osborn 1997: 120–36.

Bibliography

Abu Ghraib was 'Animal House' at Night (2004) http://www.cnn.com/2004/US/08/24/abughraib.report/ (25 Aug 2005).

Agamben, G. (2005) *State of Exception*. Chicago and London: Chicago University Press.

Alarcón, N. (1990) The Theoretical Subject(s) of *This Bridge Called My Back* and Anglo-American Feminism. In *Making Face/Making Soul*, ed. G. Anzaldúa, 356–66. San Francisco: Aunt Lute.

Althusser, L. (1971) Ideology and Ideological State Apparatuses. In *Lenin and Philosophy and Other Essays*, 127–88. New York: Monthly Review Press.

Arendt, H. (1989) *The Human Condition*. Chicago: University of Chicago Press.

—— (1994) 'What Remains? The Language Remains': A Conversation with Günter Grass. In *Essays in Understanding 1930–1954*, ed. J. Kohn, 1–23. New York: Harcourt Brace.

Austin, J.L. (1975) *How to Do Things with Words*. Cambridge, MA: Harvard University Press.

Badgett, M.V.L. (1997) Beyond Biased Samples: Challenging the Myths on the Economic Status of Lesbians and Gay Men. In *Homoeconomics: Capitalism, Community, and Lesbian and Gay Life*, ed. A. Gluckman and B. Reed, 65–72. New York: Routledge.

Barad, K. (2003) Posthumanist Performativity: Toward an Understanding of How Matter Comes to Matter. *Signs* 28: 801–31.

Beauvoir, S. de (1956) *The Second Sex*. [1st edn 1949.] Harmondsworth: Penguin.

—— (1989) *The Second Sex*. Trans. H.M. Parshley. [1st edn 1949.] New York: Alfred Knopf.

Bender, B. (2006) Cost of Iraq War Nearly $2b a Week, *Boston Globe*, 26 September. [Online] Available: http://www.netscape.com/viewstory/2006/09/28/the-cost-of-the-iraq-war-has-reached-2-billion-per-week/?url = http%3A%2F%2Fwww.boston.com%2Fnews%2Fworld%2Fmiddleeast%2Farticles%2F2006%2F09%2F28%2Fcost_of_iraq_war_nearly_2b_a_week%2F&frame = true [8 Jan. 2007].

Benjamin, W. (2004) Critique of Violence. In *Walter Benjamin: Selected Writings Volume 1, 1913–1926*, ed. M. Bullock and W.M. Jennings, 236–52. Cambridge, MA, and London: Harvard University Press.

Black, D., Gates, G., Sanders, S. and Taylor, L. (2000) Demographics of the Gay and Lesbian Population in the United States: Evidence from Available Systematic Data Sources. *Demography* 37 (May): 139–54.

Bowden, M. (2003) The Dark Art of Interrogation. *The Atlantic Monthly*, October.

Braidotti, R. (2000) *Metamorphoses. Towards a Materialist Theory of Becoming*. Cambridge: Polity.

Brison, S. (2004) Torture, or 'Good Old American Pornography'? *The Chronicle of Higher Education* 50 (39) 4 June, sec. B.

Brown, W. (1995) *States of Injury: Power and Freedom in Late Modernity*. Princeton, NJ: Princeton University Press.

Brown, W. and Hartley, J. (2002) Introduction. In *Left Legalism/Left Critique*, ed. W. Brown and J. Hartley. Durham, NC: Duke University Press.

Burke, C. (1996) Pernicious Cohesion. In *It's Our Military, Too!*, ed. J.H. Stiehm, 205–19. Philadelphia: Temple University Press.

Burnham, G., Doocy, S. et al. (2006) *The Human Cost of the War in Iraq: A Mortality Study, 2002–6*. Bloomberg School of Public Health, Johns Hopkins University/School of Medicine, Al Mustansiriya University. [Online] Available:http://www.jhsph.edu/refugee/research/iraq/Human_Cost_of_WarFORMATTED.pdf [9 Jan. 2007].

Bush, G.W. (2001) *Address to a Joint Session of Congress and the American People*, 20 September. [Online] Available: http://www.whitehouse.gov/news/releases/2001/09/20010920–28.html# [14 Aug, 2006].

—— (2004) *President Outlines Steps to Help Iraq Achieve Democracy and Freedom*. http://www.whitehouse.gov/news/releases/2004/05/20040524–10.html (24 May 2005).

Butler, J. (1987a) *Subjects of Desire*. [1st edn.] New York: Columbia University Press.

—— (1987b) Variations on Sex and Gender: Beauvoir, Wittig, Foucault. In *Feminism as Critique*, ed. S. Benhabib and D. Cornell, 128–42. Minneapolis: University of Minnesota Press.

—— (1988) Performative Acts and Gender Constitution. An Essay in Phenomenology and Feminist Theory. *Theatre Journal* 40 (4): 519–31.

—— (1989a) Gendering the Body: Beauvoir's Philosophical Contribution. In *Women, Knowledge, and Reality: Explorations in Feminist Philosophy*, ed. A. Garry and M. Pearsall, 253–62. Boston: Unwin Hyman.

—— (1989b) Foucault and the Paradox of Bodily Inscriptions. *Journal of Philosophy* 86: 601–7.

—— (1989c) The Body Politics of Julia Kristeva. *Hypatia* 3: 104–18.

—— (1989d) Sexual Ideology and Phenomenological Description. A Feminist Critique of Merleau-Ponty's *Phenomenology of Perception*. In *The Thinking Muse*, ed. J. Allen and I.M. Young, 83–100. [1st edn 1981] Bloomington, IN: Indiana University Press.

—— (1990) *Gender Trouble. Feminism and the Subversion of Identity*. [1st edn.] London and New York: Routledge.

—— (1992) *Contingent Foundations*. In *Feminists Theorize the Political*, ed. J. Butler and J.W. Scott, 3–21. New York: Routledge.

—— (1993) *Bodies that Matter: On the Discursive Limits of 'Sex'*. New York: Routledge.

—— (1994) Gender as Performance: An Interview with Judith Butler. *Radical Philosophy* 67: 32–9.

—— (1995a) Contingent Foundations: Feminism and the Question of 'Postmodernism'. In *Feminist Contentions: A Philosophical Exchange*, 35–58. New York and London: Routledge.

—— (1995b) For a Careful Reading. In *Feminist Contentions: A Philosophical Exchange*, 127–43. New York and London: Routledge.

—— (1996a) Foucaultian Inversions. In *Feminist Interpretations of Michel Foucault*, ed. S.J. Hekman, 59–76. University Park, PA: The Pennsylvania State University Press.

—— (1996b) Gender as Performance. In *A Critical Sense. Interviews with Intellectuals*, ed. P. Osbourne, 109–26. London and New York: Routledge.

—— (1997a) *Excitable Speech: A Politics of the Performative*. New York and London: Routledge.

—— (1997b) *The Psychic Life of Power: Theories in Subjection*. Stanford, CA: Stanford University Press.

—— (1997c) Merely Cultural. *Social Text* (fall/winter): 265–77.

—— (1998) Merely Cultural. *New Left Review* 227: 33–44.

—— (1999a) *Gender Trouble: Feminism and the Subversion of Identity*. [2nd edn] London and New York: Routledge.

—— (1999b) *Subjects of Desire. Hegelian Reflections in Twentieth-Century France*. [1st edn 1987a.] New York: Columbia University Press.

—— (2000a) *Antigone's Claim: Kinship Between Life and Death*. New York: Columbia University Press.

—— (2000b) Politics, Power and Ethics: A Discussion Between Judith Butler and William Connolly. *Theory & Event* 4 (2).

—— (2000c) Interview. In *Politics, Power and Ethics: A Discussion between Judith Butler and William Connolly*, ed. W. Connolly. *Theory & Event* 4 (2). [Online] Available: http://muse.jhu.edu/journals/theory_and_event/toc/archive.html [20 Feb. 2006].

—— (2000d) Competing Universalities. In *Contingency, Hegemony, Universality: Contemporary Dialogues on the Left*, ed. J. Butler, S. Zizek and E. Laclau, 136–81. London and New York: Verso.

—— (2000e) Restaging the Universal: Hegemony and the Limits of Formalism. In *Contingency, Hegemony, Universality: Contemporary Dialogues on the Left*, 11–43. London: Verso.

—— (2003a) Interview. In 'Judith Butler: Philosopher', ed. J. Stauffer. *The Believer* 1, (2) [Online] Available: http://www.believermag.com/issues/200305/?read = interview_butler [10 Mar 2006].

—— (2003b) Peace is a Resistance to the Terrible Satisfactions of War, an Interview with Judith Butler. *The Believer* (May).

—— (2003c) *Giving an Account of Oneself*. [1st edn] Assen: Van Gorcum.

—— (2004a) *Precarious Life: The Powers of Mourning and Violence*. New York and London: Verso.

—— (2004b) *Undoing Gender*. New York and London: Routledge.

—— (2004c) *The Judith Butler Reader*, ed. S. Salih. Oxford: Blackwell.

—— (2004d) Public Lecture, Tate Modern Art Gallery, 1 November.

—— (2004e) Public Lecture, Birkbeck College, University of London, 30 October.

—— (2005a) *Giving an Account of Oneself*. New York: Fordham University Press.

—— (2005b) Merleau-Ponty and the Touch of Malebranche. In *The Cambridge Companion to Merleau-Ponty*, ed. T. Carman and M. Hansen, 181–205. Cambridge: Cambridge University Press.

—— (2005c) *Trouble dans le Genre: Pour un féminisme de la subversion*. Trans. C. Kraus. Paris: Éditions de la Découverte.

Butler, J., Laclau, E. and Zizek S. (2000) *Contingency, Hegemony, Universality: Contemporary Dialogues on the Left*. London: Verso.

Campbell, K. (2002) Politics of Kinship: Review Essay. *Economy and Society* 31: 642–50.

Capsuto, S. (2000) *Alternate Channels: The Uncensored Story of Gay and Lesbian Images on Radio and Television.* New York: Balantine.

Castoriadis, C. (1989) *The Imaginary Institution of Society.* Trans. K. Blamey. Cambridge, MA: MIT Press.

Cavarero, A. (2002) Politicizing Theory. *Political Theory* 30: 506–32.

Cavell, S. (1976) *Must We Mean What We Say? A Book of Essays.* Cambridge: Cambridge University Press.

—— (1979) *The Claim of Reason: Wittgenstein, Skepticism, Morality, and Tragedy.* Oxford: Clarendon Press.

Chambers, S.A. (2003) *Untimely Politics.* Edinburgh: Edinburgh University Press.

—— (2004) Giving Up (on) Rights? The Future of Rights and the Project of Radical Democracy. *American Journal of Political Science* 48: 185–200.

—— (2007) Normative Violence after 9/11: Rereading the Politics of *Gender Trouble.* *New Political Science* 29: 43–60.

Chavez, L. (2004) *Sexual Tension in the Military.* http://www.lindachavez.org (4 June 2005).

Cheney, D. (2002) *Vice President Speaks at VFW 103rd National Convention.* 26 August. [Online] Available: http://www.whitehouse.gov/news/releases/2002/08/20020826.html [14 Aug 2006].

Christian, B. (1987) The Race for Theory. *Cultural Critique* 6: 51–63.

Cloud, D. (2005a) Psychologist Calls Private in Abu Ghraib Photographs 'Overly Compliant'. *New York Times*, 24 September, sec. A.

—— (2005b) Private Found Guilty in Abu Ghraib Abuse. *New York Times*, 27 September, sec. A.

Cohen, C.J. (1999) What Is This Movement Doing to My Politics? *Social Text* 61 (winter): 111–18.

Coole, D. (2000) *Negativity and Politics. Dionysus and Dialectics from Kant to Post-structuralism.* London and New York: Routledge.

—— (2005) Rethinking Agency: A Phenomenological Approach to Embodiment and Agentic Capacities. *Political Studies* 53: 124–42.

Cusset, F. (2003) *French Theory: Foucault, Derrida, Deleuze & Cie et les mutations de la vie intellecutelle aux États-Unis.* Paris: Éditions de la Découverte.

Danner, M. (2004) *Torture and Truth: America, Abu Ghraib, and the War on Terror.* New York: New York Review of Books.

Danto, A. (1981) *The Transfiguration of the Commonplace: A Philosophy of Art.* Cambridge, MA: Harvard University Press.

de Lauretis, T. (1986) *Feminist Studies/Critical Studies.* Bloomington, IN: Indiana University Press.

—— (2005) When Lesbians Were Not Women. In *On Monique Wittig: Theoretical, Political, and Literary Essays*, ed. N. Shaktini, 51–62. Urbana: University of Illinois Press.

Dean, J. (2006) *Žižek's Politics.* New York: Routledge.

Delphy, C. (1993) Rethinking Sex and Gender. [1st edn 1991] *Women's Studies International Forum* 16: 1–9.

—— (1995) The Invention of French Feminism: An Essential Move. *Yale French Studies* 87: 190–221.

—— (2001) *L'ennemi principal: Tome 2, Penser le Genre.* Paris: Nouvelles Questions Féministes.

Derrida, J. (1981) *Positions.* London: Athlone.

—— (1988) *Limited* INC. Trans. S. Weber. Evanston, IL: Northwestern University Press.

Disch, L. (1999) Judith Butler and the Politics of the Performative. *Political Theory* 27: 545–99.

Duchen, C. (1984) What's the French for Political Lesbian? *Trouble and Strife* 2: 24–34.

Ehrenreich, B. (2004) Feminism's Assumptions Upended. *Los Angeles Times*, 4 June, sec. M.

Eisenstein, Z. (2004) *Sexual Humiliation, Gender Confusion and the Horrors at Abu Ghraib.* http://www.peacewomen.org/news/Iraq/June04/abughraib.html (4 June 2005).

Embser-Herbert, M.S. (2004) When Women Abuse Power, Too. *Washington Post*, 16 May, sec. B.

Enloe, C. (2004) Wielding Masculinity inside Abu Ghraib: Making Feminist Sense of an American Military Scandal. *Asian Journal of Women's Studies*, 10 (3): 89–102.

Faludi, S. (1994) The Naked Citadel. *New Yorker*, 5 September.

Faramarzi, S. (2004) *Former Iraqi Prisoner Says U.S. Jailers Humiliated Him.* Associated Press Online. http://web.lexis-nexis.com/universe/document?_m = aaf09e-c4a80bcaafb1317e379d2840c5&_docnum = 3&wchp = dGLbVzz-zSkVb&_md5 = e0a565778a0e145773860ae847210304 (2 May 2005).

Fassin, E. (2005) Trouble-genre. Preface to *Trouble dans le Genre: Pour un féminisme de la subversion* by J. Butler. Paris: Éditions de la Découverte.

Fauré, C. 1981. The Twilight of the Goddesses, or The Intellectual Crisis of French Feminism. Trans. L.S. Robinson. *Signs* 7: 81–6.

Fay–Jones Report [2004] (2005). *Investigation of Intelligence Activities at Abu Ghraib.* In *The Torture Papers: The Road to Abu Ghraib*, ed. K.J. Greenberg and J.L. Dratel. New York: Cambridge University Press.

Foucault, M. (1977) Nietzsche, Genealogy, History. In *Language, Counter-Memory, Practice. Selected Essays by Michel Foucault*, ed. D. Bouchard, 139–64. Ithaca NY: Cornell University Press.

—— (1978) *The History of Sexuality*, vol. 1. New York: Vintage Books.

—— (1986) Of Other Spaces. *Diacritics,* 16: 22–7.

—— (1990) *The History of Sexuality*, vol. 1. [1st edn 1978] London: Penguin Books.

—— (1991) Governmentality. In *The Foucault Effect: Studies in Governmentality*, ed. G. Burchell, C. Gordon and P. Miller, 87–104. Chicago: University of Chicago Press.

—— (1991a) *Discipline and Punish: The Birth of the Prison*. London: Penguin Books.

—— (1991b) *Madness and Civilization: A History of Insanity in the Age of Reason*. London and New York: Tavistock/Routledge.

—— (2002a) Governmentality. In *Power: Essential Works of Foucault 1954–1984*, vol. 3, ed. D.J. Faubion, 201–22. London: Penguin Books.

—— (2002b) About the Concept of the 'Dangerous Individual' in Nineteenth Century Legal Psychiatry. In *Power: Essential Works of Foucault 1954–1984,* vol. 3, ed. D.J. Faubion, 176–200. London: Penguin Books.

—— (2003) *Society Must Be Defended*. London and New York: Allen Lane.

Fraser, N. (1992) Introduction: Revaluing French Feminism. In *Revaluing French Feminism*, ed. N. Fraser and S.L. Bartky, 1–24. Bloomington, IN: Indiana University Press.

—— (1997a) Heterosexism, Misrecognition, and Capital. *Social Text* (fall/winter): 279–89.

—— (1997b) *Justice Interruptus: Critical Reflections on the 'Postsocialist' Condition.* New York: Routledge.

—— (1998a) Heterosexism, Misrecognition and Capitalism: A Response to Judith Butler. *New Left Review* 228: 140–50.

—— (1998b) *Social Justice in the Age of Identity Politics: Redistribution, Recognition, and Participation, The Tanner Lectures on Human Values*, ed. G. Peterson, 6–67. Salt Lake City, UT: University of Utah Press.

Fraser, Nancy (2000) Rethinking Recognition. *New Left Review* NLR3 (May/June): 107–120.

Fraser, N. and Nicholson, L. (1990) Social Criticism without Philosophy: An Encounter between Feminism and Postmodernism. In *Feminism/Postmodernism*, ed. L. Nicholson, 19–39. New York: Routledge, Chapman, and Hall.

Fuss, D. (1995) *Identification Papers*. London: Routledge.

Gallop, J. (1992) *Around 1981: Academic Feminist Literary Theory*. New York: Routledge.

Garrett, D. (1995) Baruch Spinoza. In *The Cambridge Dictionary of Philosophy*, ed. R. Audi, 870–4. Cambridge: Cambridge University Press.

Giddens, A. (1977) Functionalism: Après la lutte. In *Studies in Social and Political Theory*, 96–134. New York: Basic Books.

Giroux, H. (2004) What Might Education Mean After Abu Ghraib? *Comparative Studies of South Asia, Africa and the Middle East* 24: 3–22.

Gitlin, T. (1995) *The Twilight of Common Dreams: Why America Is Wracked by Culture Wars*. New York: Henry Holt and Co.

Grant, J. (1993) *Fundamental Feminism*. New York: Routledge.

Greenberg, K.J., and Dratel, J.L. eds (2005) *The Torture Papers: The Road to Abu Ghraib*. New York: Cambridge University Press.

Grenier, Richard (1994) Clint Eastwood Goes PC. *Commentary* 97 (March).

Guillaumin, C. (1988) Race and Nature: The System of Marks, the Idea of a Natural Group and Social Relationships. [1st pub. 1977] *Feminist Issues* 8: 25–44.

Hall, S. (1980) Race, Articulation and Societies Structured in Dominance. In *Sociological Theories: Race and Colonialism*, ed. UNESCO, 306–27. Paris: UNESCO.

Harding, L. (2004) The Other Prisoners. *Guardian*, 20 May.

Hegel, G.W.F. (1977) *Phenomenology of Spirit*. Trans. A.V. Miller. Oxford: Oxford University Press.

Higham, S., White, J. and Davenport, C (2004) A Prison on the Brink. *Washington Post*, 9 May, sec. A.

Hirsch, M. and Keller, E.F. 1990) *Conflicts in Feminism*. New York: Routledge.

Hobsbawm, E. (1996) Identity Politics and the Left. *New Left Review* 217 (May/June 1996): 38–47.

Hong, C. (2004) *How Could Women Do That?* http://www.salon.com/mwt/feature/2004/05/07/abuse_gender/index.html?x (9 Nov 2005).

Human Resource Exploitation Training Manual (1983) Central Intelligence Agency. http://www.gwu.edu/~nsarchiv/NSAEBB/NSAEBB122/#kubark (28 Oct 2005).

Intelligence Interrogation (1987) *Field Manual 34–52*. Department of the Army. http://www.globalsecurity.org/intell/library/policy/army/fm/fm34–52/index.html (28 Oct 2005).

—— (1992) *Field Manual 34–52*. Department of the Army. http://www.fas.org/irp/doddir/army/fm34–52.pdf (28 Oct 2005).

Irigaray, L. (1985a) *Speculum of the Other Woman*. Trans. G.C. Gill. Ithaca, NY: Cornell University Press.

Irigaray, L. (1985b) *This Sex which is not One*. Trans. C. Porter with C. Burke. Ithaca, NY: Cornell University Press.

Jackson, S. (1995) Récents débats sur l'hétérosexualité: une approche féministe matérialiste. *Nouvelles Questions Féministes* 17: 5–26.

Jay, M. (2005) *Songs of Experience. Modern American and European Variations on a Universal Theme*. Berkeley, Los Angeles, CA, and London: University of California Press.

Jehl, D. and Schmitt, E. (2004) Prison Interrogations in Iraq Seen as Yielding Little Data on Rebels. *New York Times*, 27 May, sec. A.

Jehl, D., Schmitt, E. and Zernike, K. (2004) U.S. Rules on Prisoners Seen as a Back and Forth of Mixed Messages to G.I.s. *New York Times*, 22 June, sec. A.

Jessop, B. (1990) *State Theory: Putting the Capitalist State in Its Place*. University Park, PA: Pennsylvania State University Press.

Johnson, K. (2004) Guard Featured in Abuse Photos Says She Was Following Orders. *New York Times*, 11 May, sec. A.

Joint Doctrine for Detainee Operations (2005) *Joint Publication 3–63*. Joint Chiefs of Staff. http://hrw.org/campaigns/torture/jointdoctrine/jointdoctrine040705.pdf (23 Mar 2005).

Kagan, R. (2003) *Of Paradise and Power: America and Europe in the New World Order*. New York: Knopf.

Kaufman-McCall, D. (1983) Politics of Difference: The Women's Movement in France from May 1968 to Mitterand. *Signs* 9: 282–93.

Kaufman-Osborn, T. (1997) *Creatures of Prometheus: Gender and the Politics of Technology*. Lanham, MD: Rowman & Littlefield.

King, Jr, M.L. (1986) A Time to Break Silence. A Testament of Hope: In *The Essential Writings of Martin Luther King, Jr.*, ed. J.M. Washington. San Francisco: HarperCollins.

Kraus, C. (2005) *Anglo American Feminism made in France*: crise et critique de la représentation. *Cahiers du Genre* 38: 163–89.

Kruks, S. (2001) *Retrieving Experience. Subjectivity and Recognition in Feminist Politics*. Ithaca and London: Cornell University Press.

KUBARK Counterintelligence Interrogation (1963) Central Intelligence Agency. http://www.gwu.edu/~nsarchiv/NSAEBB/NSAEBB122/#kubark (28 Oct 2005).

Laclau, E. (2000). Structure, History and the Political. In *Contingency, Hegemony, Universality*, 182–212. London: Verso.

Laclau, E. and Mouffe, C. (1985) *Hegemony and Socialist Strategy*. London: Verso.

Law, J.D. (1988) Uncertain Grounds: Wittgenstein's *On Certainty* and the New Literary Pragmatism. *New Literary History* 19 (2): 319–36.

Lehr, V. (1999) *Queer Family Values: Debunking the Myth of the Nuclear Family*. Philadelphia, PA: Temple University Press.

Leonard, D. and Adkins, L., eds (1996) *Sex in Question: French Materialist Feminism*. London: Taylor & Francis.

Lilla, M. (1994) The Legitimacy of the Liberal Age. In *New French Thought: Political Philosophy*, ed. M. Lilla, 3–34. Princeton: Princeton University Press.

Lloyd, M. (1999a) Performativity, Parody, Politics. *Theory, Culture and Society* 16: 195–213.

—— (1999b) The Body. In *Contemporary Social and Political Theory*, ed. F. Ashe et al., 111–12. Buckingham and Philadelphia: Open University Press.

—— (2007a) Radical Democratic Activism and the Politics of Resignification. *Constellations* 14: 129–46.

—— (2007b) *Judith Butler: From Norms to Politics*. Cambridge: Polity.

Loizidou, E. (2007) *Judith Butler: Ethics, Law, Politics*. London: Routledge/Cavendish.

McNay, L. (2000) *Gender and Agency*. Cambridge: Polity.

McRobbie, A. (2006) Vulnerability, Violence and (Cosmopolitan) Ethics: Butler's *Precarious Life*. *British Journal of Sociology* 57: 69–86.

Mazzetti, M. (2006) *Spy Agencies Say Iraq War Worsens Terrorism Threat. New York Times, 23 September*. [Online] Available: http://www.nytimes.com/2006/09/24/world/middleeast/24terror.html?ex = 1316750400&en = da252be85d1b39fa&ei = 5088&partner = rssnyt&emc = rss [8 Jan. 2007].

Meijer Costera, I. and Prins, B. (1998) How Bodies Come to Matter: An Interview with Judith Butler. *Signs*, 23: 275–86.

Merleau-Ponty, M. (1962) *Phenomenology of Perception*. London: Routledge.

Mikolashek Report [2004] (2005) The Inspector General, Department of the Army. *Detainee Operations Inspection*. In *The Torture Papers: The Road to Abu Ghraib*, ed. K.J. Greenberg and J.L. Dratel. New York: Cambridge University Press.

Mink, G. (1998) *Welfare's End*. Ithaca, NY: Cornell University Press.

Mohanty, C.T. (1991) Under Western Eyes: Feminist Scholarship and Colonial Discourses. In *Third World Women and the Politics of Feminism*, ed. C.T. Mohanty, A. Russo, L. Torres, 51–80. Bloomington, IN: Indiana University Press.

Motha, S. (2005) Guantánamo Bay, 'Abandoned Being', and the Constitution of Jurisdiction. In *Jurisprudence of Jurisdiction*, ed. S. McVeigh. London: UCL Press.

Mowitt, J. (2002) *Percussion: Drumming, Beating, Striking*. Durham, NC: Duke University Press.

Nealon, J. (1996) Between Emergence and Possibility: Foucault, Derrida and Judith Butler on Performative Identity. *Philosophy Today* 40: 430–39.

Neumayr, G. (2004) Thelma and Louise in Iraq. *The American Spectator*. http://www.spectator.org/dsp_article.asp?art_id = 6522 (5 May 2005).

Nicholson, L. and Fraser, N., eds (1990) *Feminism/Postmodernism*. New York: Routledge.

Noonan, P. (2004) *A Humiliation for America*. http://www.opinionjournal.com/columnists/pnoonan/?id = 10005043/ (6 May 2005).

Nussbaum, M. (1999) The Professor of Parody. *The New Republic* 220 (8): 37–45.

Oakeshott, M. (1991) Introduction to *Leviathan*. In *Rationalism in Politics and Other Essays*. Expanded edn, 221–94. Indianapolis, IN: Liberty Fund.

Olkowski, D. (1999) *Gilles Deleuze and the Ruin of Representation*. Berkeley CA: University of California Press.

Passavant, P.A. (2002) *No Escape: Freedom of Speech and the Paradox of Rights*. New York: New York University Press.

—— (2005) The Strong Neoliberal State: Crime, Consumption, Governance. *Theory Event* 8 (3). Available through Project Muse at http://muse.jhu.edu.

Passavant, P.A. and Dean, J. (2001) Laws and Societies. *Constellations* 8 (3): 376–89.

Pears, D. (1988) *The False Prison: A Study of the Development of Wittgenstein's Philosophy*, vol. 2. Oxford: Clarendon Press.

Piven, F.F. and Cloward, R. (1979) *Poor People's Movements: Why They Succeed, How They Fail*. New York: Vintage Books, 1979.

Plato (1952) *Gorgias*. Trans. C.W. Hembold. Upper Saddle River, NJ: Prentice-Hall.

Poulantzas, N. (1973) *Political Power and Social Classes*. London: New Left Books.

Puar, J.K. (2004) Abu Ghraib: Arguing against Exceptionalism. *Feminist Studies* 30: 322–54.

Raissiguier, C. (2002) Bodily Metaphors, Maternal Exclusions: The Sexual and Racial Politics of Domestic Partnerships in France. In *Violence and the Body: Race, Gender and the* State, ed. A. Aldamam, 94–112. Bloomington, IN: Indiana University Press.

Rejali, D. (2004) *Torture's Dark Allure. Salon.com, 18 June.* [Online] Available: www.salon.com/opinion/feature/2004/06/18/torture_1/print.html [3 Mar. 2006].

Rich, F. (2004) It Was the Porn that Made Them Do It. *New York Times*, 30 May, sec. 2.

Rorty, R. (1998) *Achieving Our Country: Leftist Thought in Twentieth-Century America.* Cambridge, MA: Harvard University Press.

Saar, E., and Novak, V. (2005) *Inside the Wire.* New York: Penguin.

Salih, S. (2004) with Butler, J., eds, *The Judith Butler Reader.* Oxford: Blackwell.

Santner, E. (2006) Miracles Happen: Benjamin, Rosenzweig, Freud, and the Matter of the Neighbor. In *The Neighbor: Three Inquiries in Political Theology* by S., Žižek, E.L. Santner and K. Reinhard, 76–133. Chicago: University of Chicago Press.

Sassen, S. (1996) *Losing Control.* New York: Columbia University Press.

Scarry, E. (1985) *The Body in Pain: The Making and Unmaking of the World.* New York: Oxford University Press.

Schlafly, P. (2004) *Feminist Dream Becomes Nightmare.* http://www.townhall.com/columnists/phyllisschlafly/ps20040517.shtml (18 May 2005).

Schlesinger Report [2004] (2005) *The Final Report of the Independent Panel to Review DoD Detention Operations.* In *The Torture Papers: The Road to Abu Ghraib*, ed. K.J. Greenberg and J.L. Dratel. New York: Cambridge University Press.

Schmidt Report. 1 April, 2005 (amended 9 June 2005). *Investigation into FBI Allegations of Detainee Abuse at Guantánamo Bay, Cuba Detention Facility.* http://balkin.blogspot.com/Schmidt%20Furlow%20report.pdf (28 Oct 2005).

Schneider, H. (2004) In Breaking Taboos, Photos Add Insult to Injury. *Washington Post*, 7 May, sec. A.

Schulman, S. (1998) *Stagestruck: Theater, AIDS, and the Marketing of Gay America.* Durham, NC: Duke University Press.

Scott, J. (1988a) Deconstructing Equality-versus-Difference: Or, the Uses of Post-structuralist Theory for Feminism. *Feminist Studies* 14: 33–50.

—— (1988b) *Gender and the Politics of History.* New York: Columbia University.

Seery, J. (1999) Castles in the Air: An Essay on Political Foundations. *Political Theory* 27: 460–90.

Serrano, R.A. (2004) 'Prison Interrogators' Gloves Came off before Abu Ghraib'. *Los Angeles Times*, 9 June.

Shklar, J.N. (1984) *Ordinary Vices.* Cambridge, MA: Harvard University Press.

Skocpol, T. (1995) *Protecting Soldiers and Mothers: The Political Origins of Social Policy in the United States.* Cambridge, MA: Harvard University Press.

Smith, A.M. (2004) Homophobia, In *Poverty and Social Welfare in America: An Encyclopedia.* ed. Gwendolyn Mink and Alice O'Connor. Santa Barbara, CA: ABC-CLIO, 2004, 362–64, 373–75, 657–59.

—— (2007) *Welfare Reform and Sexual Regulation.* New York: Cambridge University Press.

Snyder, R.C. (1999) *Citizen-Soldiers and Manly Warriors.* Lanham, MD: Rowman & Littlefield.

Spinoza, B. de (1955) *On the Improvement of the Understanding, The Ethics, Correspondence* [1st edn 1677] Trans. R.H.M. Elwes. New York: Dover.

Spivak, G.C. (2003) *A Critique of Postcolonial Reason: Toward a History of the Vanishing Present.* Cambridge, MA: Harvard University Press.

Steiner, G. (1984) *Antigones.* Oxford: Clarendon Press.

Stone, A. (2005) Towards a Genealogical Feminism: A Rereading of Judith Butler's Political Thought. *Contemporary Political Theory* 4: 4–24.

Stone, M. (2000) Wittgenstein on Deconstruction. In *The New Wittgenstein*, ed. A. Crary and R. Read, 83–117. London: Routledge.

Taguba Report [2004] (2005) *Article 15–6 Investigation of the 800th Military Police Brigade.* In *The Torture Papers: The Road to Abu Ghraib*, ed. K.J. Greenberg and J.L. Dratel. New York: Cambridge University Press.

Thibault, D. (2004) *Abu Ghraib is a Feminist's Dream, Says Military Expert.* http:// www.cnsnews.com/ViewNation.asp?Page = %5CNation%5CarchiveE%5C200405% 5CNAT20040510b.html (10 May 2005).

Thomas, E. (2004) *Explaining Lynndie England: How did a wispy tomboy behave like a monster at Abu Ghraib?* http://msnbc.msn.com/id/4987304/ (15 May 2005).

Tully, J. (2003) Wittgenstein and Political Philosophy: Understanding Practices of Reflection. In *The Grammar of Politics: Wittgenstein and Political Philosophy*, ed. C. Hayes, 17–42. Ithaca, NY: Cornell University Press.

Turcotte, L. (1992) Changing the Point of View. Foreword to *The Straight Mind* by M. Wittig, vii–xii. New York: Harvester/Wheatsheaf.

United States Department of Labor, Office of Policy Planning and Research (1965) *The Negro Family: The Case for National Action* ['Moynihan Report']. Washington, DC: Government Printing Office.

Varikas, E. (1993) *Féminisme, modernité, post-modernisme. Pour un dialogue des deux côtés de l'océan.* Futur Antérieur: Paris.

Warner, M. (1999) *The Trouble with Normal: Sex, Politics, and the Ethics of Queer Life.* New York: Free Press.

Weber, M. (1949) *The Methodology of the Social Sciences.* Glencoe, IL: Free Press.

—— (1978) *Economy and Society: An Outline of Interpretive Sociology*, 2 vols, ed. G. Roth and C. Wittich. Berkeley, CA: University of California Press.

Webster (2002) *Webster's Third International Dictionary*, unabridged. *s.v.* 'trill'.

Weed, E. (1989) *Coming to Terms: Feminism, Theory, Politics.* New York: Routledge.

Weeks, J. (1981) *Sex, Politics, and Society: The Regulation of Sexuality since 1800.* New York: Longman.

—— (1995) *Invented Moralities: Sexual Values in an Age of Uncertainty.* New York: Columbia University Press.

White, S.K. (1999) As the World Turns: Ontology and Politics in Judith Butler. *Polity* 32: 155–77.

Wittgenstein, L. (1958) *Philosophical Investigations.* [1st edn] Oxford: Basil Blackwell.

—— (1964) *The Blue and Brown Books.* Oxford: Blackwell.

—— (1967) *Zettel*, ed. G.E.M. Anscombe and G.H. von Wright. Trans. G.E.M. Anscombe. Oxford: Blackwell.

—— (1968) *Philosophical Investigations* [3rd edn]. Trans. G.E.M. Anscombe. New York: Macmillan.

—— (1969) *On Certainty*, ed. G.E.M. Anscombe and G.H. von Wright. Trans. D. Paul and G.E.M. Anscombe. New York: Harper & Row.

—— (1980) *Remarks on the Philosophy of Psychology*, vol. 1., ed. G.E.M. Anscombe and G.H. von Wright. Trans. G.E.M. Anscombe. Oxford: Blackwell.

Wittig, M. (1971) *Les Guérillères.* Trans. D. Le Vay. New York: Avon Books.

—— (1992) *The Straight Mind.* New York: Harvester/Wheatsheaf.

Wolin, S. (2004) *Politics and Vision.* Expanded edn. Princeton, NJ: Princeton University Press.

Young, I.M. (2004) *On Female Body Experience.* Oxford: Oxford University Press.

Zerilli, L.M.G. (1998) Doing Without Knowing: Feminism's Politics of the Ordinary. *Political Theory* 26 (4): 435–58.

—— (2005) *Feminism and the Abyss of Freedom.* Chicago: University of Chicago Press.

Zernike, K. (2004) Prison Guard Calls Abuse Routine and Sometimes Amusing. *New York Times,* 16 May, sec. A.

—— (2005) Behind Failed Abu Ghraib Plea, A Tale of Breakups and Betrayal. *New York Times,* 10 May, sec. A.

Zernike, K. and Rohde, D. (2004) Forced Nudity is seen as a Pervasive Pattern, Not Isolated Incidents. *New York Times,* 8 June, sec. A.

Žižek, S. (1999) *The Ticklish Subject.* London: Verso.

—— (2000) *The Fragile Absolute* London: Verso.

—— (2005) Neighbors and Other Monsters. In *The Neighbor: Three Inquiries in Political Theology,* by S, Žižek, E.L. Santner and K. Reinhard, 134–90. Chicago: University of Chicago Press.

—— (2006) *The Parallax View.* Cambridge, MA: The MIT Press.

Index